SAINTLY COMPANIONS

SAINTLY
COMPANIONS

A Cross-reference of sainted Relationships

Vincent J. O'Malley, CM

A·LBA·HOUSE   NEW·YORK

SOCIETY OF ST. PAUL, 2187 VICTORY BLVD., STATEN ISLAND, NEW YORK 10314

Library of Congress Cataloging-in-Publication Data

O'Malley, Vincent J.
    Saintly Companions: a cross-reference of sainted relationships /
    Vincent J. O'Malley.
        p.   cm.
    Includes bibliographical references.
    ISBN 0-8189-0693-6
    1. Christian saints — Biography.   I. Title.
    BX4655.2.O395   1995
    282'.092'2 — dc20   95-3115
    [B]   CIP

Produced and designed in the United States of America by the
Fathers and Brothers of the Society of St. Paul,
2187 Victory Boulevard, Staten Island, New York 10314,
as part of their communications apostolate.

ISBN: 0-8189-0693-6

Printing Information:

Current Printing - first digit   1   2   3   4   5   6   7   8   9   10

Year of Current Printing - first year shown

1995   1996   1997   1998   1999   2000

DEDICATION

To young people: children, grandchildren,
sisters and brothers, nieces and nephews,
cousins, classmates and friends; may this book
be for you informative and inspirational.

ACKNOWLEDGMENTS

Certain published works were of great assistance in this project. I single out especially John Delaney's *Dictionary of the Saints*, published by Doubleday; *The Book of Saints*, by the Monks of Ramsgate Benedictine Abbey, published by Morehouse; and the most recent edition of *Butler's Lives of the Saints*, published by Christian Classics.

To do this research required the assistance of the librarians at Mary Immaculate Seminary in Northampton, Pennsylvania, Cait Kokolus and Mary Ellen Cser; and Fr. Bonaventure Hayes, O.F.M., at Christ the King Seminary in East Aurora, New York.

Secretaries were of immense assistance: Colleen Kleintop, Audrey Morris, and Ann Vitovitch at Northampton, Pennsylvania; Sandy Moody and Christine Schwartz at Niagara University, New York. Regina Kernin rendered much needed and much valued advice and assistance regarding the use of the computer.

Gratitude is expressed to members of religious communities who provided me with the primary source material which was used within this book. Appreciation is extended to priests of the Eastern rites and the Orthodox Church for material on the lives of the saints whom they honor.

My colleague, Sr. Mary Minella, S.T.D., and my confrere, Fr. Francis Prior, C.M., served as readers for this project and offered invaluable criticism.

I would like to thank my family members, religious community members and close friends for their constant encouragement.

Biblical Abbreviations

OLD TESTAMENT

Genesis	Gn	Nehemiah	Ne	Baruch	Ba
Exodus	Ex	Tobit	Tb	Ezekiel	Ezk
Leviticus	Lv	Judith	Jdt	Daniel	Dn
Numbers	Nb	Esther	Est	Hosea	Ho
Deuteronomy	Dt	1 Maccabees	1 M	Joel	Jl
Joshua	Jos	2 Maccabees	2 M	Amos	Am
Judges	Jg	Job	Jb	Obadiah	Ob
Ruth	Rt	Psalms	Ps	Jonah	Jon
1 Samuel	1 S	Proverbs	Pr	Micah	Mi
2 Samuel	2 S	Ecclesiastes	Ec	Nahum	Na
1 Kings	1 K	Song of Songs	Sg	Habakkuk	Hab
2 Kings	2 K	Wisdom	Ws	Zephaniah	Zp
1 Chronicles	1 Ch	Sirach	Si	Haggai	Hg
2 Chronicles	2 Ch	Isaiah	Is	Malachi	Ml
Ezra	Ezr	Jeremiah	Jr	Zechariah	Zc
		Lamentations	Lm		

NEW TESTAMENT

Matthew	Mt	Ephesians	Eph	Hebrews	Heb
Mark	Mk	Philippians	Ph	James	Jm
Luke	Lk	Colossians	Col	1 Peter	1 P
John	Jn	1 Thessalonians	1 Th	2 Peter	2 P
Acts	Ac	2 Thessalonians	2 Th	1 John	1 Jn
Romans	Rm	1 Timothy	1 Tm	2 John	2 Jn
1 Corinthians	1 Cor	2 Timothy	2 Tm	3 John	3 Jn
2 Corinthians	2 Cor	Titus	Tt	Jude	Jude
Galatians	Gal	Philemon	Phm	Revelation	Rv

TABLE OF CONTENTS

Acknowledgments vii

Biblical Abbreviations viii

Preface xi

Introduction xiii

Chapter 1: The Benefit of Saintly Companions 1

Chapter 2: Husband and Wife Saints 19

Chapter 3: Parent(s) and Child(ren) Saints 41

Chapter 4: Sibling Saints 71

Chapter 5: Saintly Relatives 103

Chapter 6: Saintly Friends 131

Chapter 7: Teacher-Student Saints 163

Chapter 8: Master and Disciple Saints 191

Chapter 9: Saintly Co-Founders 227

Chapter 10: Saintly Co-Workers 247

Chapter 11: Saintly Co-Martyrs 275

Epilogue: The Images of Saints 311

Bibliography 317

Saints Listing 329

PREFACE

Religious statuary and stained glass windows almost always portray the saints as solitary figures. In reality, however, the opposite was true. The saints surrounded themselves with people.

They took seriously the Gospel mandate to live Christian community. They shared their prayer and material goods. They went forth two by two to seek out and serve other people. The saints loved people. They expressed their love for God by their love of people. After all, they were only doing what the Lord himself had done and had commanded that they do: "love one another as I have loved you" (Jn 15:12).

Religious art has generally presented the saints alone. Even the Holy Family is usually presented in our churches with the Blessed Mother and child Jesus on one side shrine of the church and Joseph with a carpenter tool on the other side. Would it not be appropriate to present them as a single family? Those times when the saints are presented with other people, the saints are usually in caring roles rather than mutually supportive relationships. Would it not be appropriate to present the saints with their saintly companions with whom they enjoyed supportive life-goals, lifestyle, friendship with each other as well as with the Lord?

Jesus is the model for all Christians. Jesus enjoyed numerous holy relationships. He enlightened and empowered his companions; he was for them the way, the truth and the life. He regarded the Church as his spouse. He grew up with his parents, without siblings but then regarded as his brothers and sisters all persons who wished to do God's will. He had numerous kinfolk. He was blessed with numerous friends. He called himself "teacher" more than any other title; he perceived himself in relation to those who wished to hear the word of God. He was the master to whom thousands flocked. He founded the Church to develop the kingdom of God here on earth; he entrusted its development to his apostles and disciples. He worked hard, with and for his Father and his disciples. He gave up his life and knew that the servants of the master would be asked to do the same. The single life which Jesus lived was hardly a solitary life. He lived with and for other people.

The saints reflect the life of Jesus. They are spouses, parents, children, brothers and sisters, relatives, friends, teachers and students, masters and disciples, co-founders, co-workers, co-martyrs. What good they did, they did with and for other people.

INTRODUCTION

"Show me your friends and I'll tell you who you are." This anonymous adage remains as true today as it has been for all times. It was true for the saints as well.[1] Many hundreds of saints were blessed with saintly companions.

The purpose of this book is to identify, exemplify and provide observations regarding saintly companions. Saints shared with one another a common vision and common way to live out that vision, appropriate for their time and place. These Christian heroes and heroines mutually helped each other to live religiously heroic lives. The role of the saints in heaven is to provide for persons on earth an example for life on earth, intercession in heaven, and revelation of God's grace.

Relationships are central to the meaning of life, from the life of the Trinity itself to each individual who has been created in the image of our Trinitarian God. Relationships give profound meaning to life. Relationships bind people together. Relationships affect people, sometimes marginally, sometimes profoundly. Relationships help to make people who they are. Saintly relationships can help to make people saints.

The audience anticipated for this book are persons who value relationships. This book is intended for family members, friends and all who share Christian ministry. Especially, this book is intended for youth and the adults who accompany them: parents, relatives, preachers and teachers.

Kinds of Companions

The relationships among the saints whom we will discuss fall into ten categories: husband and wife, parent and child, siblings, relatives, friends, teacher and student, master and disciple, co-founders, co-workers and co-martyrs. Many saints fit into multiple categories. Some saintly couples had saintly children. Some saintly brothers and sisters had saintly uncles and aunts. Some saintly co-founders were also close friends.

Each kind of relationship is treated in a separate chapter. These chapters follow the same format; there is a text, a list of companions and an appendix with biographical information. The text consists of an introduction to the human and sacred reality of the relationship, four particular examples supported usually by primary sources, and general observations of similarities abstracted from the saints in the category. The fourth example is a 20th-century or near 20th-century relationship in which not all the persons may be officially declared saints. The lists provide a summary view of the saints included in the category. The appendices describe briefly the saints who are listed. Some saints may be mentioned very briefly in one appendix because they are described more fully in the appendix or text of another chapter.

At the end of the book is included an extensive cross-reference which indicates graphically the kinds of relationships that the saints enjoyed. This work focuses on the influences that these saints had on one another. The phenomenon of the kinds and quality of these relationships is extraordinary. The author does not intend to demonstrate why these persons have been designated as saints. There will be no lists of good deeds achieved, miracles performed or books written.

Virtually all persons named in this text are officially declared saints, with a few exceptions. Some persons are identified by the Church, and therefore in this text, as Venerable (Ven.) or Blessed (Bl.), which are intermediary steps in the process of being advanced to sainthood. Some persons were acclaimed saints popularly but not officially. Some political figures are named in order to provide historical context. Some 20th-century persons are included who enjoyed a relationship with a contemporary saint.

Accuracy of Sources

Historical accuracy is a main concern in this book. Doubtful or insufficient historical information about a saint's life generally has been excluded from the text. In those few instances when questionable information is included, it is clearly identified as doubtful.

For example, Patrick's sister Darerca, who is considered a saint in some texts, has not been included because of the serious doubt about the authenticity of her fame and the fact of their relationship. Patrick's nephew Mel, however, is included but with the usual caution that surrounds much of Patrick's life.

The Roman Emperor Constantine and his mother, Helen, are both included. No question surrounds Helen's inclusion. Constantine's inclusion, however, remains doubtful. The most authoritative sources are divided on the question. The Bollandists include Constantine in the *Acta Sanctorum* and even devote ten pages to describing him and five more pages to describing icons which honor him. The *Bibliotheca Sanctorum* includes Constantine but literally places a question mark next to the word *santo*. *Butler's Lives of the Saints* excludes Constantine. The four volume work of *Orthodox Saints* not only includes him but describes him in the most laudatory manner; the Eastern Church regards Constantine as the thirteenth apostle.

Both primary and secondary source material are used

in this work. The primary sources are the writings of the saints. The secondary sources are the biographical information about the saints. The main secondary sources used in this book are various dictionaries of saints.

1. The Bollandists' *Acta Sanctorum* provides approximately 19,500 entries in its herculean sixty-seven volumes. The first volume was published in 1643; the most recent volume was published in 1931.

2. The *Bibliotheca Sanctorum* intends to include all saints from all countries among its 12,900 named entries and 8,200 anonymous martyrs.[2] This twelve-volume work was published in 1961. Its scholarship is universally acclaimed as second only to that of the Bollandists.[3]

3. The classical four-volume set of *Butler's Lives of the Saints*, which was edited, revised and supplemented by Herbert Thurston, S.J. and Donald Attwater, was published in 1956 and reprinted in 1990 in a paperback edition. It lists 2,565 saints. This represents a substantial development over the original 1756-59 edition with its 1,486 entries.

4. The *Roman Martyrology* originated before the seventh century and received additions and corrections from the time of its first publication in 1584 until its augmentation in 1749. It contains over 4,500 names.

5. John J. Delaney's *Dictionary of Saints*, published in 1980, describes over 5,000 saints.

6. *The Book of Saints* compiled by the Benedictine monks of St. Augustine's Abbey at Ramsgate, in its 1989 sixth edition, contains names and biographical information of over 10,000 saints.

7. The thirty-year research of Mary Ryan D'Arcy resulted in the comprehensive 1974 publication of

The Saints of Ireland. This collection contains over 200 entries of Irish saints.

8. D.H. Farmer's *Oxford Dictionary of Saints* concentrates on saints of England and the British Isles. It includes in its 1987 second edition the Eastern saints of Greece and Russia. This renowned work describes almost 1,100 saints.

9. George Poulos compiled a four-volume work of *Orthodox Saints*. The 1991 second edition presents 491 celebrated saints.

10. Books that treat the saints and *beati* of particular men's and women's religious communities have also been incorporated into this study; the communities include the Barnabites, Benedictines, Daughters of Charity, Daughters of Our Lady Help of Christians, Daughters of Wisdom, Dominicans, Franciscans, Jesuits, Sisters of Mercy and Vincentians.

No complete list and definitive number of saints exists. This surprises many who view the Catholic Church as definitive about many other matters. Only since 1170 has the pope reserved to himself the authority to declare persons saints. Before that time local churches named saints by the process of popular proclamation. Many saints, therefore, may be recognized in one diocese, region, nation, or rite and not in another. The Church does provide a universal calendar which specifies principal feasts and saints' days, but this represents a small number of saints. The total number of saints remains elusive. "While no official list of saints exists, researchers have found mention of 9,000 saints in Latin texts, 1,500 in Greek manuscripts, and another 1,300 in the Church's Eastern archives — and that's not all."[4] The total number of saints is estimated to be between 12,000 and 14,000. Not even the Vatican has a definitive list of saints from the earliest times. The precise Vatican list does identify the 679 saints canonized since the process was formalized in 1588.

Significant efforts have been made to include in this study the saints of the Orthodox Church and the Eastern rites, particularly, the Armenian, Byzantine, Ethiopian, Maronite and Ukrainian rites.

The author does not intend this book to be an exhaustive study. Except for the three chapters pertaining to the relationships of husband-wife, parent-child and co-founders, dozens of additional saints could have been included in each chapter. The author simply presents the evidence that hundreds of saints were blessed with saintly companions.

Historical Process of Naming Saints

The reason for the unspecified number lies in the past process of naming saints. In the earliest centuries the martyrs and confessors were proclaimed saints by popular acclamation. These martyrs and confessors proclaimed their faith in Jesus, and expressed their willingness to die for Jesus and his Church. Their stories were told in imitation of Jesus' story. Martyrs were killed for the faith. Confessors were tortured for witnessing to the faith. The fame of martyrs and confessors spread. The Christian community of one town would communicate to the Christians in a neighboring town the practice of honoring a certain saint. The cult of the saint spread. Adherents publicized the names and life stories of the saints. Followers preserved the saints' relics and writings. Christian communities named new churches in honor of these saints. Local communities developed feast days to give recognition to them and to their heroic deeds. The process of gathering and handing on information about these martyrs and confessors was oftentimes inconsistent. Many saints became recognized in one diocese, region, nation, or rite but not in another. Thus began the discrepancy in the counting of the saints.

In the post-persecution period of the Church, faith-filled men and women were still willing to die for the name of Jesus but no government persecuted them. As a matter of fact an increasing number of Christians in the less tense post-persecution era eventually lived their religious lives less intensely. Those who wished to give their whole minds, hearts and bodies to Jesus decided to flee from the cities to the deserts. They wished to renounce the world and its pleasures and to sacrifice their lives to Jesus through the slow death of life-long mortification. These ascetics became recognized as the new saints.

"By extending the idea of sanctity to the living, the Church gradually came to venerate persons for the exemplarity of their lives as well as of their deaths."[5] Similar to the martyrs and confessors, the fame of the ascetics was hailed locally and passed on inconsistently. Bishops requested that relics and writings be gathered, churches be built and feast days be named in honor of the saintly ascetics. The counting of saints continued with much variance.

The kinds of spirituality changed as the centuries changed. Successive periods of martyrs, confessors and ascetics gave way to new waves of itinerant monks, preachers, teachers and apostolic servants of society. Many new saints came from the ranks of founders and early members of these new religious communities. As political organization and Christianization developed simultaneously in Western civilization, saints came from the echelons of political and ecclesiastical leaders. When the great missionary movements of the 16th and 19th centuries occurred, the ranks of saints became filled by missionaries and native martyrs. Always saints responded to the spiritual and material needs of their times. Saints captured the holiest yearnings of the human spirit. They embodied in exemplary ways the contemporary Christian spirit. Every age in history has its saints.

The first canonization of a saint by a pope took place in 993. This action, however, represented more of a confirmation than canonization. The local bishops were still the ordinary canonizing agents. The bishop of Augsburg asked the visiting pope, who happened to be presiding over a local synod, to hear and give assent to the local bishop's proposal of canonization for his predecessor. The citation of fame for holiness was read. The pope gave his assent. The first time a pope reserved the authority to himself to name saints took place in 1170. Pope Alexander III wished to defend clearly the religious rights of the Church against the encroaching power of the secularistic and unsaintly Holy Roman Emperor Frederick Barbarossa and King Henry II of England. Alexander wished to defend, too, the nature of sanctity because a Swedish bishop had just approved the cult of a popular monk who had been killed in a drunken brawl. "Brawling monks were not the sort of examples of holiness, Alexander observed, that the Church wanted the people to imitate."[6]

The process of naming and proclaiming saints became increasingly bureaucratic during the Church's second millennium. In 1234 Pope Gregory IX promulgated his *Decretals*, which restricted to the bishop of Rome the authority for selecting saints. He reasoned that saints were to be honored by the universal Church and not local churches only. Unofficial publications of stories about miracles or reputed holiness were prohibited, as were statues with haloes about the heads of alleged but unapproved saints. While canonization in the early Church had been a liturgical action, now canonization became a legal undertaking. A juridical process was instituted between a petitioner of a candidate's cause and the Defender of the Faith who became popularly known as the Devil's Advocate. The Defenders of the Faith succeeded in purifying the process of exaggerated hagiographical testimony. They succeeded, too, in strictly limiting the number of canonized saints, only twenty-six between 1200 and 1334. Popularly, however, the proliferation of alleged saints continued unabated.

The pope then instituted the distinction between *beati* (blessed) and *sancti* (saints). The *beati* were accepted as local cults of holy persons whereas *sancti* were approved for the universal Church. Eventually beatification became a prior step in the total process of canonization.

Martin Luther and the Protestants reacted against many aspects of the Church's cult of the saints. Luther rejected the practice of the cult as being idolatrous, ineffectual, unnecessary and replete with legend rather than fact. He argued that the exaggerated reverence paid to the saints distracted from the worship due to Jesus. He contended that Jesus alone had saved us and intercedes for us. Luther meanwhile valued the lives of the saints as examples to Christians in their appropriate relation to Jesus. He wrote:

> Next to Holy Scripture there certainly is no more useful book for Christians than that of the lives of the saints, especially when unadulterated and authentic. For in these stories, one is greatly pleased to find how they sincerely believed in God's Word, confessed it with their lips, praised it by their living, and honored and confirmed it by their suffering and dying. All this immeasurably comforts and strengthens those weak in the faith and increases the courage and confidence of those already strong far more than the teachings of Scripture alone, without any examples and stories of the saints. Although the Spirit performs His work abundantly within, it nonetheless helps very much to see or to hear the example of others without. Otherwise a weak heart always thinks: See, you are the only one who so believes and confesses, acts, and suffers.[7]

To the Reformers' criticisms, Rome responded in 1588 when Pope Sixtus V established the office of the Congregation of Rites. This Church board was charged with the responsibility of preparing and presenting causes for canonization. "But it was only during the pontificate of Urban VIII (1623-44) that the papacy finally gained complete control over the making of saints."[8] The distinction between *beati* and *sancti* was reiterated, as was the prohibition against publishing any work or promoting the cult of anyone not yet declared a saint by the Church. Later centuries witnessed further refinements.

Contemporary Process of Naming Saints

A major breakthrough in the policy and procedure of naming saints occurred in 1983 under Pope John Paul II. He removed the process from the control of Vatican lawyers and returned it to local bishops. He wanted the fundamental criterion to be not law but history. The adversarial position of the Devil's Advocate was eliminated. The number of miracles required was reduced from two to one for the beatification of a non-martyr and from two to one for the canonization of a martyr and a non-martyr. The petition was to be conducted not in a courtroom style but in the context of academia in which an historically accurate document of the candidate's life would be presented for study and review. The change in underlying thinking was revolutionary. The process reversed a thousand-year practice. Now local churches under the authority of the bishop have the responsibility for initiating a canonization. Local churches are to gather accurate information about a candidate's sanctity of life and verification of miracles. Pope John Paul II has canonized more saints than any other pope.[9]

Some persons may suggest that an apparently disproportionate number of priests and religious are declared saints in relation to the laity, married or single. For those who are interested, Leonard Foley presents in his two-volume *Saint of the Day* a composite according to gender and ecclesiastical status of the 173 saints commemorated by name in the current Roman Missal. Donald Weinstein and Rudolph M. Bell provide in *Saints and Society* a comprehensive study of 864 saints who lived between 1000 and 1700 according to their age, sex, place, social class and cleric, religious or lay vocation. In *Making Saints*, Kenneth Woodward writes:

> But the one group that is clearly under-represented is the laity. Between the year 1000 and the end of 1987, popes held 303 canonizations, including group causes. Of these saints, only 56 were laymen and 20 were laywomen. Moreover, of the 63 lay saints whose state of life is known for certain, more than half never married. And most of these lay saints were martyred, either individually or as members of a group.[10]

Clearly more lay saints, married or single, would provide example and inspiration to the state in life which the huge majority of Christians live. Perhaps the ratio between religious and lay saints may not be disproportionate, since religious commit themselves publicly and institutionally to live the vowed life of the evangelical counsels. Priests and religious dedicate the whole of their lives to preaching the Gospel in word and deed. It is hoped that many of them would lead exemplary lives in fulfilling their commitments.

Another explanation for the very high number of canonized priests and religious is found in the modern process of canonization. Much time, expense, and evidence-gathering are required. These cross-generational resources are more likely to be available through religious communities than lay situations or even dioceses.[11] For example, the canonization of Mother Elizabeth Ann Seton in 1975 was completed 154 years after her death and forty-six years after an intense effort for her canonization was begun. The documentation of virtuous living according to the theological and cardinal virtues required ten volumes of evidence. The process' cost of $250,000 was provided by the proceeds of the forty-year-old Mother Seton Guild and the five women's communities who claim her as their foundress. The project was directed by a religious community's Postulator for the Cause, which position changed hands four times over a period of four and a half decades.[12] Would this holy woman be known officially as a saint today if only her natural family, relatives and their descendants had pursued the declaration of sainthood?

Holy persons not included:
Solo Saints, Non-Catholics and Non-Christians

Many saints lived and labored with good people who have not been canonized by the Church. Neither these saints nor their good companions have been included in this study. This work is restricted to saints who enjoyed the companionship of other saints.

For that reason no mention is made of St. Frances of Rome who with her sister-in-law, Vannozza, heroically served the urban poor. St. Thérèse of Lisieux's blood and Carmelite sisters greatly assisted her in pursuing her vocation but none of the sisters is a saint. The Venerable Catherine McAuley and Frances Ward made excellent contributions to the Church. Catherine founded in Ireland the Sisters of Mercy, who now number more members among themselves than any other English-speaking community of women. Frances, best friend and confidante of Catherine, founded the Sisters of Mercy in the United States. Frances Ward, in the service of the Lord, traveled more miles than Paul of Tarsus and opened more convents than Teresa of Avila. Of these two outstanding women, only one so far is named venerable; therefore, they are not included in this work. Bl. Kateri Tekakwitha, the famed Lily of the Mohawks, was born in Auriesville, New York just ten years after Saints Isaac Jogues and Jean de Lalande had been martyred in her village. Undoubtedly she heard stories and bore the spirit of the Jesuit Martyrs of North America, but unfortunately no living saint accompanied her. Elizabeth Ann Seton, who was born and raised in New York City and ministered in Baltimore and Emmitsburg, was greatly influenced in her conversion to Catholicism by her Roman friends, Antonio Felicchi and his wife. The ever-solicitous Antonio accompanied the young widow Elizabeth on her return voyage to the USA, and the pair continued to exchange endearing and supportive letters. Elizabeth is canonized. Antonio is not. Neither, therefore, is included in this volume. These holy persons and the saints with whom they had associated and hundreds more who enjoyed relationships like theirs are not included because both persons are not yet officially declared saints. Their lives are saintly but their official status is not yet saint or blessed or venerable.

The cross-reference at the end of the book includes over 800 saints. Many thousands of saints, not to mention *beati* or *venerati*, do not appear. Some saints had no saintly companion. Some companions of saints have not yet advanced sufficiently along the process of canonization. Some relationships may not have been discovered by the author. So many relationships exist that not all could be included here.

Another group of holy persons not included in this work are those of non-Catholic Christian denominations and non-Christian religions. All religious groups lay claim to holy persons who epitomize the group's religious values. The Hindus have their avatars and gurus. Theravada

Buddhists propose their arahats while the Mahayana Buddhists present their bodhisattvas. Confucianists offer their sages. Islam puts forward its sufis and walis. Judaism points to outstanding rabbis. Non-Catholic Christians uphold as heroes and heroines their religious founders, missionaries and martyrs.[13] All these persons are upheld as models for imitation. They achieved fame for either their asceticism, wisdom, care for others, miracle-working or martyrdom. They embody the best of the religion's ideals. These persons are not called saints in the technical sense since that term pertains particularly to Catholics, but they are saints in the broad sense of being renowned for holiness. "To say that the term 'saint' has some meaning in each tradition is not to say it has the same meaning in each tradition."[14] The measure of holiness differs according to different religious traditions and value systems.

While Catholic Christian saints are the focus of this book, their ultimate focus is Jesus Christ. By definition the saints lived their lives in imitation of Jesus, the unique model of the Christian life. Jesus is the model for all the kinds of relationships presented in this book. Jesus had no spouse, but St. Paul presents the profound analogy that the Church is the bride of Christ. Paul exhorts Christian spouses: "Husbands, love your wives as Christ loved the Church"(Eph 5:25). Regarding the parental relationship, the Gospels relate that the incarnate Son of God and Son of Man repeatedly calls God his Father.[15] The Gospels provide no record of the conversation between Jesus and his foster father Joseph, but we do have record of conversation between Jesus and his mother Mary.[16] Jesus had no sibling but he welcomes into that kind of intimacy "all those who do the will of God" (Mk 3:35). His townsfolk in Galilee clearly knew his relatives (Mk 6:3). He speaks of himself as friend (Lk 5:20), teacher (Jn 13:13) and master (Mk 11:3). He was the founder of the Christian Church (Mt 16:18). He worked in ministry with the twelve apostles and countless women and men disciples. He shed his blood on the cross in fulfillment of the Father's will (Jn 19:30). Historically and/or spiritually, Jesus has entered into all ten kinds of relationships presented in this book.

Notes for Introduction

[1] The title "saint" is regarded herein in the technical, rather than the Scriptural sense. The title is applied to those whom the Church, either by tradition or formal canonization, recognizes as being in heaven and worthy of honor.

[2] Over half of the anonymous martyrs came from the Vandal- and Arian-led persecution (c. 484 A.D.) against the bishops Felix and Cyprian and 4,975 other North African Christians. *Bibliotheca Sanctorum*, vol. V, col. 555-61, October 12. Cf. also *Butler's Lives of the Saints*, vol. IV, pp. 93-94.

[3] James Patrick McCabe, *Critical Guide to Catholic Reference Books*, p. 52. "While this work is not on the level of the *Acta Sanctorum* in size and thoroughness, it may well be the next best thing."

[4] Paul Galloway, "Heaven Can Wait," p. 10.

[5] Kenneth L. Woodward, *Making Saints*, p. 54.

[6] Ibid., p. 67.

[7] Quoted in *Sainthood: Its Manifestations in World Religions*, p. 7.

[8] Woodward, p. 75.

[9] Between October 1978, when Pope John Paul II began his tenure, and December 1993, at the time of this writing, the current pope has beatified 596 persons, of whom 451 were martyrs; and he has canonized as saints 267 persons, of whom 240 were martyrs. *The Tablet*, Vol. 86, No. 34; November 20, 1993; p. 2.

[10] Woodward, p. 336.

[11] "For every lay person who is canonized there are 20 priests or sisters. And for every diocesan saint, you'll have 10 who are members of religious orders." Lawrence Cunningham, theology professor at University of Notre Dame, as quoted by Paul Galloway, p. 10.

12 Private conversation on March 15, 1991 with Rev. William W. Sheldon, C.M., who served from 1975 until 1990 as the Postulator General at the Vatican for the Vincentian Community and the Daughters of Charity.

13 *Fox's Book of Martyrs* is a classic, if rather partisan, example of this.

14 *Sainthood*, p. 246.

15 Mk 14:16, in the Garden of Gethsemane; oftentimes in Luke, especially in the account of the passion, death and resurrection, cc. 22-24; repeatedly in Matthew, especially in the Sermon on the Mount, cc. 5-7; and more than 100 times in John.

16 At the finding in the Temple, Lk 2:48; at the wedding feast of Cana, Jn 2:1-11; and at the foot of the cross, Jn 19:25-27.

CHAPTER 1

THE BENEFIT OF SAINTLY COMPANIONS

Many hundreds of saints enjoyed relationships with other saints. These saints supported one another along the path of sanctity. Two, three or four dozen pairs of saints can be identified in almost all of the ten categories which we will discuss. In these relationships a common theme emerges: these saintly companions shared a common vision and a common way of living out that vision that drew them close to each other and to God.

Common Vision

Saintly companions, like all saints, shared a vision based in Jesus Christ. They perceived in Jesus' life a sense of purpose for their own lives. Some saints possessed this vision from their youngest years. Others grew into it later in life. Ultimately these saints shared and grew in a vision that few others could see. An example of companions who shared the same Christian vision were John Chrysostom (c. 347-407) and the deaconess, Olympias (c. 361- c. 408). Both were well-born. John was the son of an imperial military officer and Olympias came from a wealthy noble family. Both possessed deep Christian commitments. John was baptized about age twenty as was customary in his time and place, spent six years as a monk and hermit,

1

became ordained a priest and developed fame as an eloquent preacher—some would say "the greatest preacher who ever lived."[1] His earned surname, Chrysostom, means "golden-mouthed." Olympias married the prefect of the Empire but was widowed after only a few years. She then repeatedly refused the marital offers of many men, including the emperor's cousin. The emperor retaliated by taking out of her hands and placing in a trust her great wealth until she reached the age of thirty. Upon receiving her trust, Olympias became a consecrated deaconess and formed a community of Christian ladies. She founded a hospital, orphanage and shelter for refugees. She so lavishly distributed her wealth to the poor that even Chrysostom advised her to practice more moderation in her charity.

In 398 John was appointed Patriarch of Constantinople. He set out to reform the Church. He preached and practiced generous charity to the poor. He simplified his lifestyle and the liturgy, and called upon all bishops and priests to follow his example. He railed against the insufficient charity and extravagant entertainment pursued by the imperial court; with a very thin veil he directed most of his verbal attacks against the empress. She knew it and decided to get rid of Chrysostom. After five years of John's leadership many bishops too were tired of the patriarch's criticisms, no matter how eloquent they were. They called a synod and recommended to the emperor that John be deposed. The emperor concurred. The implementation was delayed, however, by a huge public outcry and an earthquake that was interpreted to be an act of God. Two months later John again insulted the empress. This time he was secretly removed far from the city. He barely survived a forced march of seventy days which signaled the beginning of the continuing terrible treatment he would receive in exile. Chrysostom and Olympias had become best friends. She corresponded with him the entire time; seven-

teen of his letters to her are extant. Four years later he died.
She followed him by a few months.

> To the most worthy deaconess, beloved of God,
> Olympias, John the Bishop sends greetings in the
> Lord.

> Come now, I am going to ease the soreness of your
> despondency and scatter the thoughts which have
> given rise to this sombre cloud. What bewilders your
> mind, why do you grieve and torment yourself?
> Because the storm that has rushed upon the Churches
> is fierce and threatening, because it has shrouded all
> in moonless darkness and is working up to a crisis,
> day after day bringing cruel shipwreck while the
> whole world is toppling over into ruin? I am aware of
> this too; there is no one to deny it. Whenever you hear
> that one of the Churches has been submerged, an-
> other tossed in dire distress, this one drowned by the
> angry flood, that mortally injured in some way, that
> a certain Church has received a wolf instead of a
> shepherd, a second a pirate instead of a helmsman, a
> third an executioner instead of a physician, be sad-
> dened by all means, for one ought not to endure such
> things without pain. But since grieve you must, at the
> same time set a limit to your sorrow. If you like, I will
> sketch the present position for you to depict the
> tragedy in even clearer lines.

> We see the ocean upheaved from its very bed, we see
> the dead bodies of sailors floating on the surface,
> others overwhelmed by the waves, ships' decks split
> asunder, sails rent, masts broken in pieces, the oars
> slipped out of the hands of the rowers, the helmsmen
> sitting idle on the decks opposite their tillers, hands
> folded on knees. Before the hopelessness of the situ-
> ation they can only groan aloud, utter piercing shrieks,
> wail, lament. No sky visible, no sea: everything lies in
> deep obscure and gloomy darkness; no man can
> descry his neighbour. The roaring waves swell and
> thunder, sea beasts rise on every side to threaten the

voyagers. Why try to find words for what cannot be expressed? For whatever simile I choose for present-day evils, words elude and fail me altogether.

I am conscious of these disasters, yet for all that I do not relinquish a most firm hope. I keep my mind fixed on the Pilot of all things; He does not ride the storm by steersmanship, but by a mere nod He breaks the surging of the sea, and if not immediately, if not at once, that precisely is His way. He does not cut calamities short at the outset, but averts them only as they approach their climax when almost all have abandoned hope. Only then does He show forth wonders and miracles and display that power which is His alone, while he schools the sufferers in patience. Do not lose heart then. There is only one thing to be feared, Olympias, only one trial, and that is sin. I have told you this over and over again. All the rest is beside the point, whether you talk of plots, feuds, betrayals, slanders, abuses, accusations, confiscation of property, exile, sharpened swords, open sea or universal war. Whatever they may be, they are all fugitive and perishable. They touch the mortal body but wreak no harm on the watchful soul. Hence when blessed Paul wanted to stress the insignificance of earthly weal and woe, he summed it up in a single phrase: 'The things that are seen are temporal" (2 Cor 4:18). Why then fear the things that are temporal which will roll on in an ever-flowing stream? Whether pleasant or painful, the present does not last forever.

Do not be perturbed therefore, by all that is going on. Give up crying for help to this person or that and chasing shadows — for such is all human endeavour. Rather should you incessantly invoke Jesus whom you adore, that He may but turn His face towards you. Then, in one decisive moment, all your trouble is ended.[2]

Common Way

Vision needs embodiment. Insight needs implementation. The saintly companions who shared a common vision
oftentimes shared their way of living out that vision.
Together they prayed, studied, served the poor, evangelized, began new communities, or suffered martyrdom. An
example of saints who shared a way of living out their
vision is Basil the Elder (d. 370) and his wife, Emmelia (d.
370).

This couple and their family stand out as extraordinary even among the most exceptional saints. Basil the
Elder's mother, Macrina the Elder (c. 270-340), was a
saint. During the persecution of Diocletian she had to flee
into exile to preserve her life and faith. A generation later,
during the persecution of Galerius Maximinus, Basil the
Elder and Emmelia similarly had to flee for the sake of
their lives and faith. This couple raised ten children, four
of whom became saints. The parents performed their
responsibilities so well that the sainted children surpassed
even the parents in renown for holiness. The parents loved
their family and their faith, and made great sacrifices for
both.

Basil the Elder and Emmelia's four children were Basil
the Great (329-79), Gregory of Nyssa (c. 330- c. 395),
Peter of Sebastea (c. 340-91) and their sister Macrina the
Younger (c. 330-79). The three sons became monks and
then bishops. They gained fame for their pastoral and
doctrinal heroism. In the face of famine, they organized
effective responses. In the face of Arianism, they elo-
quently and convincingly explained their adherence to the
teaching of the Council of Nicea. They suffered exile for the
faith, like their parents and paternal grandparents. The
daughter Macrina was as well educated as her brothers. As
a matter of fact, she taught Gregory and Peter. She is
credited also with deflating Basil the Great's exaggerated

ego. After he returned home from being away at school for twelve years, this very able student was "puffed up" with himself. As only a sibling could, Macrina let him know it and made it clear that she was not going to tolerate his obnoxious manner. His oldest sister put in his place her oldest brother.

Basil the Great and Gregory Nazianzen were students together for about twelve years, in Constantinople and Athens. After both of Basil's parents died in the same year, Gregory wrote a panegyric in which he lauded Basil the Elder and Emmelia and their ancestors for their worldly achievements and their practice of the faith:

> How many details could I have gathered from his ancestors to redound to his glory! Nor would I have had to yield any advantage to history in this respect, possessing this advantage above all, that my subject is embellished not by fictions and fable, but by facts themselves to which there are many witnesses . . . Hence, we can match his mother's family with that of his father. As for military commands, high civil offices, and power in imperial courts, and again, as to wealth and lofty thrones and public honors, and splendors of eloquence, what family has been more often or more highly distinguished?

> The union of his parents in a common esteem of virtue no less than in body was evidenced in many ways, notably in their care of the poor, their hospitality toward strangers, their purity of soul, achieved through austerity, the dedication of a portion of their goods to God — a practice not yet pursued by many at that time, though today quite widespread and honored, thanks to such previous examples, and in many other noble actions, shared alike by Pontus and Cappadocia, which have been a source of satisfaction to all who have heard of them. But their greatest and most distinguishing feature, in my opinion, is the excellence of their children. Legend does, perhaps, record men whose children were many and beautiful. But

these parents are known to us through actual acquaintance, and their character was such as to suffice for their own glory, even if they never had such children. Yet they brought forth children of such a character that, even if they themselves had not been so zealous for virtue, they would have surpassed all by the excellence of their children. That one or two of their children should merit praise may be ascribed to nature, but when eminence is found in all, the honor is clearly due to those who reared them. This is evidenced by the enviable number of priests and virgins, and of those who in marriage did not in any way allow their union to be an obstacle to an equal repute for virtue, making the distinction between them consist in a choice of career rather than in conduct.

Who has not known Basil, our Basil's father, a great name among all, who attained a father's prayer as very few have ever done? Though he surpassed all in virtue, he was prevented from gaining the first place only by his son. Who has not known Emmelia, whose name was a presage of what she became or whose life exemplified her name. She truly bore the name of Emmelia, which means harmony, for, to speak briefly, she was regarded among women as he was among men. And so, if he whose eulogy we are now undertaking was to be given to men to serve the bondage of nature, like any one of the men of old who were given by God for the public benefit, it was neither fitting that he be born of any other parents, nor that they be called the parents of any other than him.[3]

Common Bond Between Saints

Persons who shared a common vision and common way oftentimes developed a common bond with each other. They drew close together. They operated on the same wavelength. They spoke honestly, understood each other, loved and encouraged each other. They appreciated the humanness and holiness of each other. Examples of this bondedness are the best friends and confidants, Bl. Raymond of Capua (1330-99) and Catherine of Siena (1347-80).

Raymond and Catherine lived at the same time in Siena for only six years. He met her in 1374. Two years later this Dominican priest became spiritual director for this Dominican tertiary. She had gained renown for holiness and attracted numerous priests and lay followers. She attracted Raymond too. She had prayed continuously for him one day, when he was deathly ill. When he recovered the very next day, he believed that the grace of God truly worked through her. Although she was sixteen years younger than he, he let her take the lead in their service to the Church and society. He cooperated with her in her attempts to end division in the Church, promote another crusade, serve the victims of the plague and assist in the conversion of sinners. Side by side they worked to restore unity to the Church and to provide for the poor. Sometimes she would send to him sinners whose confessions he would hear then all day long.

After Catherine's death Raymond so successfully served as the twenty-third Master General of the Order of Preachers that he is generally regarded as the community's second founder. He is remembered for promoting holiness among the members of the community and for encouraging the expansion of the third order.

Raymond and Catherine shared a vision of Church unity at a time when the Church was experiencing disintegration. For seventy years French popes chose to live not in Rome but in Avignon, and not in imitation of the Lord, "who had no place to lay his head," but in the style of lords of the manor. Finally, in 1377 the pope returned to Rome, where he died one year later. His successor attempted reforms but in a way that alienated many Churchmen.

Opponents named another pope. This began the Great Western Schism in which two and sometimes three rivals feuded as popes and anti-popes for the next forty years.

Raymond and Catherine, in consultation with the duly elected pope in Rome, agreed in 1378 upon a plan for achieving papal unity. Raymond was to cross from friendly Italy into hostile France to seek the assistance of King Charles V to help to heal the separation. Raymond learned that soldiers of the anti-pope might be waiting to capture and kill him. He, nevertheless, willingly undertook his ambassadorial journey. Reaching the French border, though, he became fearful for his life and decided instead to turn around and head home without completing his mission. He wrote to Catherine that she must be very disappointed in him, and undoubtedly would love him less on account of his cowardice. Catherine responded to his letter:

Dearest father in Christ gentle Jesus,

I, Catherine, servant and slave of the servants of Jesus Christ, write to you in his precious blood, desiring to see in you the light of most holy faith that illuminates for us the way of truth.

I beg you dearest father to pray earnestly that you and I together may drown ourselves in the blood of the humble Lamb. This will make us strong and faithful. We shall then feel the fire of divine love, and we shall, through its grace, become doers instead of undoers and spoilers. In this way we shall express our fidelity to God and our trust in his help, rather than in our own or others' expertise.

With this same faith we shall love creatures, for just as love of neighbor results from love of God, so does faith, in general and in particular. In other words, just as our love for all people in general corresponds to a general faith, so a particular faith operates between those who love each other more closely, as you and I do. For, beyond a general love, there is between us a very close and special love which expresses itself in faith. And it expresses itself in such a way that it can neither believe nor imagine that the other could want anything except our good. It believes that the other constantly seeks that good with great urgency in the sight of God and creatures, and is always trying to bring about the glory of God's name and the soul's good. It believes also that the other is always begging for divine help, so that when our burdens increase, our courage and perseverance may increase too. This faith carries the one who loves and it never decreases for any reason whatsoever, no matter what people say or how the devil tries to deceive, and no matter how great a distance separates the two. If it were otherwise, it would be a sign that their love of God and neighbor was imperfect.

It seems, from what I have gathered from your letter, that you are experiencing many different struggles and diverse thoughts, caused by the devil's deceit and by your own extreme sensitivity. You felt that your burden was too heavy for you to bear, and that you were not strong enough to be measured by my standards. Accordingly, you began to doubt whether my love and concern for you had decreased. But you did not realize, though you yourself showed this to be the case, that my love had increased while yours had diminished. I love you with the love with which I love myself and with a lively faith that what is lacking on your part will be made up for by God in his goodness . . . So my love for you is greater than before, not less. . . .

I beg you to forgive anything I have said that is not to God's honor or is lacking in respect toward you. My love is my excuse. There is no more to be said. Remain in the gentle, holy love of God. Gentle Jesus, Jesus love.[4]

Common Bond With God

Saints who enjoyed close bonds with one another became bonded simultaneously in the Lord. Saint Paul writes about "friendship in the Lord" which he enjoyed with his followers and companions on his missionary journeys. Paul writes that "the life I live now is not my own; Christ is living in me" (Gal 2:20). By the same token, not merely human relationship but relationship in the Lord binds the saints together. The bond of friendship is so profound between two good persons that they perceive the divine goodness in each other. Through friends "the face of God" is seen. Aelred of Rievaulx observes in his 12th-century book *Spiritual Friendship* that "in friendship eternity blossoms, truth shines forth, and charity grows sweet."[5] Just as John the evangelist summed up God's identity in love, Aelred suggests that "God is friendship."[6] An example of a common bond between saints that is simultaneously a bond with God is found in the experience of Paul Miki (1562-97) and his companions.

The native Japanese Jesuit priest Paul Miki and his twenty-five companions died in 1597 at Nagasaki during the first of three great waves of government-initiated anti-Christian and anti-foreigner persecution. The emperor attempted to justify the persecution on the grounds that a Spanish sea captain had boasted that the foreigners intended to conquer Japan. The emperor decided to take the offensive by eliminating the foreigners and their religion. Foreign influence was significant. In the nearly fifty years since Francis Xavier had arrived in Japan in 1549, the Christian religion had mushroomed to over 200,000 baptized members. Paul Miki, the son of a military leader, became a religious leader whose preaching attracted many disciples. His companions included two more Japanese Jesuits, six foreign-born Franciscans, and seventeen native Japanese Franciscan lay tertiaries. All the victims were tortured before being crucified on a hill overlooking the city. All but two had their left ears cut off. All were paraded through various towns on the way to Nagasaki. A crowd of sympathetic Christians joined them. Arriving at the destination, the martyrs' arms and legs were bound to crosses with ropes and chains. Their necks were restrained with an iron collar. The base of each of the crosses, which were separated by four feet, were set into holes which would double as gravesites. An executioner with lance in arm stood ready for duty at the side of each of the Christians. Each one refused to recant the faith. At a signal, all the martyrs were simultaneously slain. The following account was written by an eyewitness:

> The crosses were set in place. Father Pasio and Father Rodriguez took turns encouraging the victims. Their steadfast behavior was wonderful to see. The Father Bursar stood motionless, his eyes turned heavenward. Brother Martin gave thanks to God's goodness by singing psalms. Again and again he repeated: "Into your hands, Lord, I entrust my life." Brother Francis Branco also thanked God in a loud voice. Brother Gonsalvo in a very loud voice kept saying the Our Father and Hail Mary.
>
> Our brother, Paul Miki, saw himself standing now in the noblest pulpit he had ever filled. To his "congregation" he began by proclaiming himself a Japanese and a Jesuit. He was dying for the Gospel he preached. He gave thanks to God for this wonderful blessing and he ended his "sermon" with these words: "As I come to this supreme moment of my life, I am sure none of you would suppose I want to deceive you. And so I tell you plainly: there is no way to be saved except the Christian way. My religion teaches me to pardon my enemies and all who have offended me. I do gladly pardon the Emperor and all who have sought my death. I beg them to seek baptism and be Christians themselves."

Then he looked at his comrades and began to encourage them in their final struggle. Joy glowed in all their faces, and in Louis' most of all. When a Christian in the crowd cried out to him that he would soon be in heaven, his hands, his whole body strained upward with such joy that every eye was fixed on him.

Anthony, hanging at Louis' side, looked toward heaven and called upon the holy names — "Jesus, Mary!" He began to sing a psalm: "Praise the Lord, you children!" (He learned it in catechism class in Nagasaki. They take care there to teach the children some psalms to help them learn their catechism.)

Others kept repeating "Jesus, Mary!" Their faces were serene. Some of them even took to urging the people standing by to live worthy Christian lives. In these and other ways they showed their readiness to die.

Then, according to Japanese custom, the four executioners began to unsheathe their spears. At this dreadful sight, all the Christians cried out, "Jesus, Mary!" And the storm of anguished weeping then rose to batter the very skies. The executioners killed them one by one. One thrust of the spear, then a second blow. It was over in a very short time.[7]

Applications For Today

Many hundreds of saints were blessed with saintly companions. These saints successfully called forth and sustained other saints in living heroically the Christian life. In our day, with our companions, we too are called to be saints. Some reflections on the lives of the saints pertinent to our lives follow.

1. Choose wisely those companions whom we can choose. As Francis de Sales says: "Sanctity does not consist in being odd, but it does consist in being rare."[8] Would

Olympias have been a saint if Chrysostom had not initially inspired her and later moderated her charity? Would he have been such a staunch proponent of the faith if she had not supported him by her spoken and written words, and deeds of charity? Would Basil the Great have been so great if he had not been blessed with saintly parents, siblings and grandmother? Would Basil the Elder be known if it had not been for his son Basil the Younger? Bl. Raymond of Capua and Catherine of Siena made plans together for the restoration of the Church. What would or could either one have done alone? Paul Miki and his companions supported each other and their faith in God when it most needed support. Without mutual support, would the faith of one or some have waned?

We must choose our companions wisely. They affect our happiness for life on earth and in eternity. Companions can either clarify or cloud our vision. Companions can either facilitate or complicate our way. The adage, "Show me your friends and I'll tell you who are," remains as valid today as ever.

2. All kinds of relationships matter, whether at home, school, church or work. Basil the Elder's mother was a saint. He then chose a wife who with him became a saint. They raised their children to be saints. The grandmother, Macrina the Elder, taught Basil the Great. The sister, Macrina the Younger, taught her brothers, Gregory of Nyssa and Peter of Sebastea. Catherine of Siena was the youngest of twenty-five children. None of her siblings was a saint but she developed sanctity with her confidant Raymond of Capua. Olympias and Chrysostom discovered sanctity away from their homes; they found it in church. They found sanctity in preaching, hearing and implementing the word of God. Paul Miki and companions became holy through their work and witness for the Lord.

Openness to the possibility of new and emerging relationships is of critical importance. Relationships involve both a universality and a uniqueness. Since we already possess a common origin and end with all persons by virtue of creation, we discover oftentimes that we already share a common vision and common way by virtue of faith. We can be quite surprised with whom we discover the "elusive more." We can neither foretell nor force when and with whom a relationship might "click."

3. Each person is called to holiness. Vatican Council II teaches that "the Lord Jesus Christ, the Teacher and Model of all perfection, preached holiness of life to each and everyone of his disciples, regardless of their station."[9] All states of life and all relationships are affected. "By this holiness a more human way of life is promoted even in this earthly society."[10]

Various states of life and relationships are exemplified in this chapter. A husband and wife couple is Basil the Elder and Emmelia. The parent and child relationship is manifested in Basil the Elder, who was not only the son of Macrina the Elder but also, with Emmelia, parent of ten children, of whom four are counted as saints. Siblings include the brothers Basil the Great, Gregory of Nyssa and Peter of Sebastea along with their sister Macrina the Younger. These four saints were grandchildren to Macrina the Elder. Friends are represented by Basil the Great and Gregory Nazianzen, Chrysostom and Olympias, plus Catherine of Siena and Bl. Raymond of Capua. Macrina the Elder taught Basil the Great. Her granddaughter and namesake, Macrina the Younger, taught Gregory of Nyssa and Peter of Sebastea. Olympias began as a disciple of Chrysostom and became his friend. Raymond began as a disciple of Catherine and became her friend. Co-martyrs are Paul Miki and his twenty-five companions. None of the saints mentioned in this chapter are identified explicitly as co-workers but all these saints certainly worked together.

4. The four benefits of saintly companions, that is, common vision, common way, bondedness with others,

and bondedness with God, form a whole. They do not represent successive steps or progressive stages. One benefit is not possessed without the others. Saints cannot possess a vision and not act on it. Saints cannot love another person and not love God who is his or her first love. These benefits are four expressions of one saint-making process.

Some saints possessed a vision of life and then found a way to express it. Other saints joined an established way of life and subsequently grew into its sustaining vision. Some saints fell in love with God and then gave themselves in love to others. Other saints were attracted to a flesh and blood person and through love of him or her were drawn closer to God. The lives of the saints support the integration of all of these aspects of life.

5. Faith, hope and love form the foundation of the Christian life. These three theological virtues, which are to be lived absolutely and not moderately like the moral virtues, are the theological equivalent of the saints' vision, way, and bondedness with others and God. Faith provides a vision that gives values and direction to life. Hope enables believers to trust that their way of earthly life leads to eternal life. Love impassions persons to draw close to God and others whom they encounter along the way. All the saints' lives are rooted in faith, hope and love.

Conclusion

Holiness is our individual and universal vocation. We live not in isolation but relation. We are not independent but interdependent. Yahweh adopted the Israelites not as individuals but as a nation: "I shall take you as my own people, and you shall have me as your God" (Ex 6:7). Jesus declares that the criterion of the last judgment consists not in isolated behavior, but in interaction: "Whatever you do to the least of my brothers and sisters, that you do unto me" (Mt 25:45). Simultaneously we draw close to God and each other, and through each other to God. We become saints together. We share our visions and our ways to holiness. Home, church, school and work are the pathways along which we draw close to God and to one another. We are all called to be saints and to invite our companions to be saintly with us.

Notes for Chapter 1

1   *Butler's Lives of the Saints*, vol. I, p. 180.

2   *Letters from the Saints* (1964), pp. 22-24.

3   Gregory Nazianzen on Basil the Great's parents, *Funeral Orations*, pp. 29, 33-34.

4   *Catherine of Siena: Selected Spiritual Writings*, pp. 48-49.

5   Aelred of Rievaulx, *Spiritual Friendship*, p. 65.

6   Ibid.

7   From the Office of Readings, for February 6, in *The Liturgy of the Hours*, vol. III, pp. 1367-68.

8   *The Wisdom of the Saints: An Anthology*, p. 5.

9   "Dogmatic Constitution on the Church", ch. V, para. #40; as in *The Documents of Vatican II*, p. 66.

10 Ibid., p. 67.

CHAPTER 2

HUSBAND AND WIFE SAINTS

Married until natural death

1. Mary and Joseph
2. Zechariah and Elizabeth
3. Cleophas and Mary Cleophas
4. Priscilla and Aquila
5. Anne and Joachim
6. Basil the Elder and Emmelia
7. Gregory Nazianzen the Elder and Nonna
8. Emperor Justinian and Empress Theodora
9. Stephen of Hungary and Bl. Gisella
10. Isidore of Madrid and Maria de la Cabeza
11. Bl. Louis of Thuringia and Elizabeth of Hungary
12. Bl. Luchesio of Pongibossi and Bl. Bonnadonna
13. Elzear and Bl. Delphine
14. Louis and Zelie Martin*

Married until death by martyrdom

15. Philemon and Apphia
16. Getulius and Symphorosa

---

* Louis and Zelie Martin are not canonized saints. Their causes for canonization, however, have been introduced; hers in 1959 and his in 1960.

17. Cecilia and Valerian
18. Chrysanthos and Daria
19. Timothy and Maura
20. Melasippus and Carina
21. Bl. Dominic Xamada and Bl. Clare
22. Bl. John Naisen and Bl. Monica
23. Bl. Frances Bizzocca and Bl. Leo

Married, then separated to enter religious life

24. Melania the Younger and Pinian
25. Amator and Martha
26. Gundleus and Gwladys
27. Walbert and Bertilia
28. Waldetrudis and Vincent Madelgarius
29. Hidulphus and Agia
30. Bl. Nicholas Giustiniani and Bl. Anna Michela

Married, widowed, then entered religious life

31. Ethelburga of Kent and King Edwin of Northumbria
32. Bl. Pepin of Landen and Bl. Itta
33. Adalbald and Rictrudis
34. Holy Roman Emperor Henry II and Cunegund

The Two Shall Be As One: Husband and Wife Saints

Marriage is a universal human reality. Every culture, from the most primitive to the most developed, possesses some form of married life. History demonstrates nature's way whereby men and women care for each other and continue the species.

Marriage is not only a human reality but also a sacred

institution. The Old Testament tells us: "The Lord God said, 'It is not good for man to be alone. I will make a suitable partner for him.' . . . That is why a man leaves his father and mother and clings to his wife, and the two of them become one body" (Gn 2:18, 24). The New Testament esteems marriage so much that the husband-wife relationship is used to describe analogously the relationship between Christ and the Church: "As the Church submits to Christ, so wives should submit to their husbands in everything . . . And husbands, love your wives, as Christ loved the Church" (Eph 5:24-25).

Many married couples grace the annals of the Church's saints. These husbands and wives shared a common vision and common way of living out that vision. Their lives were based in Christian faith, hope and love. They prayed often privately and publicly. They served God and their neighbors, especially the most needy. They drew out the best in each other and then shared that goodness with others.

Particular examples

1. MELANIA AND PINIAN

Melania the Younger (383-439) married Pinian (d. 432) against her wishes. She had wanted to dedicate her whole life to God as a virgin. Her father, however, who was a distinguished Roman senator, wanted an heir to receive and protect the family's great wealth. Melania married Pinian when she was fourteen and he was seventeen. The groom did not agree to the bride's request for a celibate relationship. Two pregnancies occurred: a girl and a boy. Both infants died shortly after childbirth. The young mother's life too was threatened. "Melania lay between life and death, and Pinian, who was sincerely and devotedly attached to her, swore that if she were spared she would be free to serve God as she wished. Melania recovered and

Pinian kept his vow."[1] Her father, however, still resisted. He insisted that the young couple conform at least exteriorly to the forms of married life. Five years later on his deathbed the father experienced a change of heart and repented of his insistence.

Her mother Albina and Pinian became more and more reconciled to Melania's new way of life; they adopted it themselves and the three left Rome for a villa in the country. Pinian was gradually won over, but long insisted on wearing the rich dress affected by those of his rank. The biographer gives a touching and convincing account of how his wife persuaded him to lay aside his expensive clothes, and to be content with plain garments made by herself. They took with them many slaves and set an example by their treatment of them. Soon many young girls, widows and over thirty families had joined them. The villa became a center of hospitality, of charity and of religious life. But St. Melania was fabulously wealthy — estates belonging to the Valerii were to be found all over the Empire — and she was burdened by all these possessions. She knew that the surplus of the rich belongs to their hungry and naked neighbors and that, as St. Ambrose says, the rich person who gives to the poor does not bestow an alms but pays a debt. She therefore asked, and received, the consent of Pinian to the sale of some of her properties for the benefit of the needy. This plan angered and frustrated other family members, who had hoped for huge inheritances. Eventually, Melania and Pinian needed the intervention of the emperor to protect them and ensure that the proceeds from the estates would benefit the poor. These proceeds were as far-flung as the lands themselves: the poor, the sick, captives, bankrupts, pilgrims, churches, and monasteries were relieved and endowed in large numbers all over the Empire, and in two years Melania gave freedom to some eight thousand slaves.[2]

Melania, Pinian and her mother oftentimes traveled

from their villa to the monasteries founded by them near Rome and in North Africa. The threesome journeyed to Jerusalem, where they put down permanent roots. Melania's mother died in Jerusalem in 431 and Pinian died there the following year.

Melania built a convent near the tombs of her husband and mother. Many women ascetics flocked there. Melania presided over this convent for seven years. She is remembered for her commitment to the monastic life, solicitude for its members, and generosity to the poor.

2. GREGORY NAZIANZEN THE ELDER AND NONNA

Gregory Nazianzen the Elder (c. 276-374), an adherent of the monotheistic Hypsistarian sect and magistrate of Nazianzos in today's Turkey, married Nonna (d. 374), a young woman who had been raised in the Christian religion. His wife soon influenced him to become a convert, and within a period of three years, he became a Christian, priest and bishop. He served as bishop for forty-five years.

Gregory and Nonna had three children. The eldest received the father's name and became one of the greatest theologians of the Christian Church. He followed in his father's footsteps as priest and bishop. He helped his mother to guide his father away from the heretical teaching to which he had been leaning. The second child, the daughter Gorgonia, married and raised three children. The youngest child, Caesarius, became a physician. The whole family was extraordinary, "one of the most famous and brilliant saintly families of Christian history."[3] Gregory Nazianzen the Younger wrote about his father and mother and their love for God and each other:

He was the son of undistinguished stock, and one not naturally disposed toward piety. I am not ashamed of his beginnings, because of my confidence in the final issue of his life. It was a stock not planted in the house of God, but a most strange and unusual one, compounded of two extremes — pagan error and legal absurdity. . . . Indeed, I do not know which to praise more: the grace which called him, or his own good will and purpose.

Even before he entered our fold he was one of us. Just as many of our own are not with us because their lives alienate them from the common body of the faithful, in like manner many of those outside are with us, insofar as by their way of life they anticipate the faith and only lack in name what they possess in attitude. . . . What better or more striking proof of his uprightness can be advanced than the fact that he held the highest offices in the State, yet did not enrich himself by a single penny, although he saw others reaching with the hands of a Briareus into the public funds and swollen with their ill-gotten gains? . . . As a reward for his conduct, I think, he received the faith. Let us show how this came about, for so important a matter should not be passed over in silence.

I have heard sacred Scripture saying: "Who shall find a valiant woman?" and also that she is a gift of God, and that a good marriage is arranged by the Lord. Those outside, too, have the same thought — if indeed the saying is theirs: "There is no greater boon for a man than a good wife, no worse, than the opposite." It is impossible to mention anyone who was more fortunate than my father in this respect. For I believe that, if anyone, from the ends of the earth and from all human stocks, had endeavored to arrange the best possible marriage, a better or more harmonious union than this could not be found. For the best in men and women was so united that their marriage was more a union of virtue than of bodies. Although they surpassed all others, they themselves were so evenly matched in virtue that they could not surpass each other. . . . But she who was given by God to my father became not only a helper — for this would be less wonderful — but also a leader, personally guiding him by deed and word to what was most excellent. Although she deemed it best, in accordance with the law of marriage, to be overruled by her husband in other respects, she was not ashamed to show herself his master in piety. While she is deserving of admiration for this, he is to be admired all the more for willingly yielding to her. While beauty, natural as well as artificial, is wont to be a source of pride and glory to other women, she is one who has ever recognized only one beauty, that of the soul, and the preservation and, to the best of her power, the purification of the divine image in her soul.[4]

3. Holy Roman Emperor Henry II and Cunegund

Henry the Good (972-1024) and Cunegund (d. 1033) achieved fame by the sanctity demonstrated in their public and private lives. Henry "worked his hardest to promote the peace and happiness of his realm."[5] He expanded and unified the Empire and the Church. He crossed into Italy with his army to assert his authority against minor kings, and he continued on to Rome where he asked the pope to crown him king of the Holy Roman Empire. Henry's strategy of centralizing political and religious authority gained for him the opposition of many local political and ecclesiastical leaders.

Henry assisted the Church by founding many new dioceses and building many churches, cathedrals, convents and monasteries. He cared for the practical needs of the poor and established services for their benefit. To support the Cluniac reform, he took great care about the appointment of bishops. "He refused his support to ecclesiastical aggrandizement in temporal concerns, while maintaining the Church's proper authority."[6]

The story is told that Henry wished to spend the last years of his life as a monk. He applied to the monastery of Saint-Vanne at Verdun. The abbot received his royal candidate and then cleverly ordered him under obedience to continue functioning as emperor. "This and similar accounts of his ascetic practices do not entirely accord with what is known of his character and life; Henry was one of the great rulers of the Holy Roman Empire, and triumphed precisely as a Christian statesman and soldier, whose ways were, in the nature of things, not those of the cloister."[7]

Cunegund persuaded Henry to build many cathedrals, monasteries and convents. She promoted the good of the Church as her husband promoted the good of the Empire. On an anniversary of her husband's death the widow invited numerous prelates to a dedication of a church. After the proclamation of the Gospel the empress stepped forward. Before all present she laid aside her imperial robes and put on the simple habit and veil of a cloistered nun.

> Once she had been consecrated to God in religion, she seemed entirely to forget that she had ever been an empress and behaved as the lowest in the house, being convinced that she was so before God. She feared nothing more than anything that could recall her former dignity. She prayed and read much and especially made it her business to visit and comfort the sick.[8]

4. LOUIS AND ZELIE MARTIN

The causes for canonization of Thérèse of Lisieux's parents, Louis (1823-94) and Zelie Martin (1831-77), have been submitted to the Congregation for Sainthood Causes; hers in 1959 and his in 1960. Together they were declared Servants of God in 1994. It is expected that they will be canonized together, or not at all.

Some questions remain about the relevancy of the model of married life that the Martins present to the contemporary world. Marriage was their second choice;

religious life had been their first. Both, however, had been rejected from that vocation: she apparently because of poor health, and he for a poor background in Latin. Just three months after they had met, the thirty-five-year-old watchmaker and twenty-seven-year-old lace maker married. On their wedding morning, however, Zelie "went to the iron gate outside the convent cloister and wept that she still wanted to be a nun."[9] The couple had no sexual relations for ten months after their wedding day, and Louis was preparing to model their relationship after that of Joseph and the Virgin Mary, since a life without sex would represent "more perfectly the chaste and wholly spiritual union between Jesus and his Church."[10] Zelie later wrote about that experience to her second daughter:

> You, Pauline, who love your father so much will think, perhaps, that I was making him unhappy, that I had spoilt our Wedding Day for him. But no, he understood me and consoled me as well as he could; I even think our mutual affection was increased. We always thought alike and he was always my comfort and support.[11]

Their parish priest convinced them to live married life as God had intended it. They then bore nine children: four died in childhood, and the five surviving daughters entered the religious life.

Theirs was a faith-filled home. The parents went to morning Mass daily and received communion more often than the current practice of receiving it once a week. They kept the Church fasts, which had ceased being the common practice. Family prayers and readings of the lives of the saints were shared daily. Both parents were known locally for their generous practical service of the sick and poor.[12] Thérèse of Lisieux writes: "God gave me a mother and father more worthy of heaven than of earth."[13]

Imagine the sorrow of the parents when they lost three children in infancy and a fourth child as a five-year-old.

Recognize the parents' faith, which transcended their sorrow. Zelie writes about the deaths of her children:

> When I closed the eyes of my dear little children and prepared them for burial, I was indeed grief-stricken; but thanks to God's graces, I have always been resigned to His will. People say to me: "It would have been much better if you had not given birth to those whom you lost so soon after their coming." I cannot bear to endure such sentiments! I do not find that the pains and sufferings can at all compare with the eternal happiness of my little ones, eternal happiness which, of course, would never have been theirs, had they never been born. Moreover, I have not lost them for always. Life is short. Soon I shall find my little ones in Heaven.[14]

General Observations

Husband and wife saints are found from the New Testament era up to the 17th century and span countries from the Holy Land to Western Europe and Japan. Every reader of the New Testament recognizes the names of Mary and Joseph, Zechariah and Elizabeth, Cleophas and Mary Cleophas, Priscilla and Aquila. Tradition from the post-New Testament era provides us the names of Mary's parents Joachim and Anne. Turkey, part of which was once called Cappadocia, lays claim to the couples Basil the Elder and Emmelia, and Gregory Nazianzen the Elder and Nonna. Italy, then a composite of city-states, can claim the martyrs Getulius and Symphorosa, the philanthropists Melania and Pinian, and the monastics Nicholas Giustiniani and Anna Michela. France, formerly called Gaul, proudly claims Amator and Martha, Bl. Pepin of Landen and Bl. Itta, Adalbald and Rictrudis, and Elzear and Bl. Delphine. Wales points to Gundleus and Gwladys. England rejoices in Ethelburga of Kent and Edwin of Northumbria. Flanders boasts of Walbert and Bertilia, and their daughter Waltrudis, who married Vincent Madelgarius. Germany claims the Holy Roman Emperor Henry II and Cunegund. Spain boasts of Isidore of Madrid and Maria de la Cabeza. At the end of the historical and geographical spectrum, we meet eight Japanese couples who suffered death during their nation's 17th-century anti-Christian persecutions.

These couples represent a cross section of classes and careers. Joseph worked as a carpenter. Priscilla and Aquila earned their living as tentmakers. Zechariah served as an Old Testament priest. Gregory Nazianzen the Elder served as a New Testament priest and later bishop. Gundleus and his spouse Gwladys, before their conversion, lived by their banditry. Edwin reigned as a local king with Ethelburga as his queen. Pepin gained fame as mayor of the palace. Adalbald was a French courtier. Walbert was a Flemish courtier. Elzear served as French ambassador to Naples. Henry II ruled as the Holy Roman Emperor and Cunegund as his empress. Isidore and Maria worked as farmers. Nicholas Giustiniani lived the consecrated monk's life before and after marriage with Anna Michela.

These couples practiced ordinary Christian virtues to extraordinary degrees. Wealthy couples like Melania and Pinian, as well as Elzear and Delphine practiced philanthropy. Poor couples like Isidore of Madrid and Maria shared all, as little as that was. Politically powerful couples assisted evangelization by establishing peace and promoting the faith. We think of Edwin and Ethelburga, Pepin and Itta, Henry II and Cunegund. Many other couples forsook the world and devoted themselves to the monastic life. Some entered the monastery or convent after the death of their spouses, e.g., Melania, Ethelburga of Kent, Bl. Itta, Rictrudis, and Cunegund. Other couples, by mutual agreement, entered separate houses in religious life *before* the death of their spouses, namely, Gundleus and Gwladys, Walbert and Bertilia, Waldetrudis and Vincent Madelgarius.

Nicholas Giustiniani was granted dispensation from religious life for the purpose of raising progeny for his heirless family. He accomplished his mission well, begetting nine children, and then he returned to his monastery. His wife Anna also then joined a separate monastery. Some couples lived virginal lives from the beginning of their marriages, namely, Mary and Joseph, and Elzear and Delphine. Melania and Pinias lived as virgins after the birth of two children.

Conversion to Christianity, when it occurred among these couples, was initiated by Christian wives. Nonna converted Gregory Nazianzen the Elder from the mixed Jewish-pagan Hypsistarian sect. Ethelburga of Kent converted Edwin from pagan practices.

Many saints were married, but not as many saints were blessed with a saintly married partner. This is understandable in that it is difficult enough for one person, let alone two, to be recognized as saints. Married saints not included in this chapter are the apostles, Monica, Paulinus of Nola, Queen Radegund, Bathildis the wife of Clovis II, Bl. Hildegard the wife of Charlemagne, Hedwig, Elizabeth of Portugal, King Louis IX of France, Ferdinand III king of Castile, Bl. James of Lodi, Frances of Rome, John of Capistrano, Catherine of Genoa, Cecilia of Ferrara, Thomas More, Francis Borgia, Bl. James Fenn, Alphonsus Rodriguez, Bl. Marie Acarie, Jane Frances de Chantal, Louise de Marillac, Marguerite d'Youville, Elizabeth Anne Seton, Bl. Anna Maria Taigi, Joaquina de Vedruna, numerous blesseds and four saintly grandmothers: Adele, Clotilde, Ludmilla and Olga.

Application Of The Theme

Common Vision: These husbands and wives were sacraments of God's love. They saw God's love in each other. They signified God's love for the other. They revealed the image of God and the goodness of God. Their spousal love was simultaneously trinitarian love. God's love was made present through them to each other.

Common Way: These spouses not only symbolized but also realized God's love. God, who is spiritual, needs flesh and blood people to make his love visible, audible and tangible. These couples supported themselves in good times and bad, in sickness and health. They walked side by side on the path of righteousness.

Common Bond With Each Other: These husbands and wives enriched each other. They communicated to each other, in words and in deeds, their mutual faith, hope and love. They grew together as they grew in goodness. Day by day, the process was virtually imperceptible. Year by year, the process was undeniable.

Common Bond With God: The quality of their faith, hope and love for each other was correlative to the quality of their faith, hope and love for God. Their mutual love had its origin and end in God. Their union with each other was simultaneously a union in the Lord. They brought each other to God.

APPENDIX: HUSBAND AND WIFE SAINTS

MARRIED UNTIL NATURAL DEATH

Mary (1st century) and **Joseph** (1st century), the mother and foster father of Jesus, were betrothed when she was probably fifteen years old and he no more than nineteen. The infancy narratives of Matthew and Luke relate the story. Joseph discovered that Mary was already pregnant. An angel appeared to Joseph on three occasions: once to instruct him not to divorce Mary, once to flee to Egypt for safety's sake, and a third time to return again to Israel. Joseph is described as a righteous man and a carpenter by trade. He and Mary both resided in Nazareth before the birth of Jesus, and were well known to the citizens there. We read no more of Joseph in the Scriptures after the finding in the Temple of the adolescent Jesus. Mary appears at the beginning of Jesus' public ministry at Cana, travels to Capernaum with her son, and according to John's Gospel stands at the foot of the cross. No scriptural or extra-biblical source gives information about the remainder of her life or occasion of her death.

Zechariah (1st century) and **Elizabeth** (1st century), the elderly parents of John the Baptist "were just in the eyes of God, blamelessly following all the commandments and ordinances of the Lord" (Lk 1:6). When Zechariah doubted the message of an angel that his wife would conceive, he was struck speechless. His speech was restored when he indicated that the child was to be named John. Elizabeth was visited by her cousin, Mary. When the two pregnant women met, the babe in Elizabeth's womb leapt for joy. Elizabeth then spoke the often repeated words: "Blest are you among women and blest is the fruit of your womb" (Lk 1:42). Elizabeth's neighbors asked the question posed about every new-born since then: "What will this child be?" (Lk 1:66). No more mention of this husband and wife is to be found following the first chapter of Luke.

Cleophas (1st century) and **Mary Cleophas** (1st century) are thought to have been either best friends or relatives of the Holy Family. Some believe her to be a sister to Mary, the mother of Jesus (cf. Jn19:25). Scholars dispute the relationship, however. He was one of two disciples to whom the risen Jesus appeared on the road to Emmaus. She was present at the Crucifixion and the empty tomb.

Priscilla (1st century) and **Aquila** (1st century) fled from Rome when the emperor forbade Jews to live there. This couple moved to Corinth, where Paul converted them and lived with them. All three moved to Ephesus and then back to Rome, where the couple's home was used as an early church. Like Paul, they made their living as tentmakers. Paul's letter to the Romans concludes with a salutation to this couple.

Joachim (1st century) and **Anne** (1st century) are believed traditionally to be the parents of Mary, the mother of Jesus. They are not mentioned in the Scriptures. Joachim has been honored in the East since time immemorial and in the West since the 16th century. The cult of Anne originated in the 6th century in the East and in the 8th century in the West.

Basil the Elder (d. 370) and **Emmelia** (d. c. 370) were parents to ten children, four of whom are recognized as saints. The parents suffered exile during the persecution of Galerius Maximinus. They later were permitted to return to Caesarea in Cappadocia.

Gregory Nazianzen the Elder (c. 276-374) and **Nonna** (d. 374) are described in this chapter.

Emperor Justinian (482-565) and the **Empress Theodora** (6th century) are considered saints in the Orthodox Church.[15] Not only did they establish political, economic and legal policies that endured for hundreds of years but also they singularly propagated the faith. They spearheaded the construction of dozens of churches, including the magnificent Hagia Sophia in Constantinople. They also involved themselves in the theological questions of the day, although at times they were particularly repressive towards non-Christians and theological non-conformists. Justinian convened the Second Council of Constantinople. He appointed and deposed Church leaders, legislated and enforced Church discipline, and surrounded himself with ecclesiastical advisors in the administration of the Empire. Justinian and Theodora privately practiced a simplicity of lifestyle and religious devotion.

Stephen of Hungary (975-1038) and **Bl. Gisella** (11th century) became the first king and queen of Hungary. The pope sent the crown which the king wore. Stephen fought many wars of consolidation and pursued policies of Christian evangelization which assisted the unification of the country. Stephen organized a hierarchical political system and a reformed legal code which helped him to establish and maintain order. He began a building program of churches and monasteries which helped to spread the faith. Gisella was the sister of the duke of Bavaria, who became emperor of the Holy Roman Empire.

Isidore of Madrid (1070-1130) and **Maria de la Cabeza** (12th century) were farmers, who worked for their entire lives for one wealthy landowner, who lived on an estate just outside the city. This couple became famous for their devotion and charity. "He (Isidore) married a girl as poor and as good as himself."[16] Despite their poverty they shared what goods they had with all in need. The royal family initiated their cause for canonization. Isidore was canonized along with Ignatius of Loyola, Francis Xavier, Teresa of Avila and Philip Neri. In Spain this illustrious quintet are esteemed as "The Five Saints."

When **Bl. Louis of Thuringia** (1200-27) was twenty-one years of age, he married **Elizabeth of Hungary** (1207-31), who was then fourteen years old. They had known each other from their youngest years, since she had been raised from age four in the castle of his father. Louis and Elizabeth were married for only six years and were raising four children when Louis died. They were regarded as an ideal married couple. He ruled justly, imposing fair penalties on those who committed crimes. She sponsored the construction of two hospitals and personally cared for the sick, the aged and the poor.

Bl. Luchesio of Pongibossi (d. 1260) and **Bl. Bonnadonna** (d. 1260) had involved themselves in the worldly pursuits of politics, making and lending money. After their children died, they decided to devote themselves to the care of the sick and poor. They sold their property and became Franciscan tertiaries, perhaps the first couple to be invested by Francis of Assisi himself.

Elzear (1285-1323) and **Bl. Delphine** (1283-1360) were engaged as children and married at sixteen years of age. Both were educated in separate abbeys; he, by an uncle who was abbot; and she, by an aunt who was abbess. Seven years after they married, Elzear inherited his father's estates in

Naples. They traveled from their native France to take charge of their inheritance. At Naples Elzear served as tutor to the local prince, eventually becoming ambassador and regent for the principality. He managed his estates with firmness and prudence. The couple prayed daily, received communion frequently, and were generous to the poor and sick. When they were first married, "it is said that the girl, encouraged by a Franciscan friar asked her husband to agree to a virginal union, but it was sometime before he would do so."[17] She survived her husband by thirty-seven years and was present at his canonization the year before she died. In 1309 Elzear had stood as godfather for an infant who fifty-three years later became pope. In 1369 the godson presided at the canonization of his godfather.[18]

Louis (1823-94) and **Zelie Martin** (1831-77) are described in this chapter.

MARRIED UNTIL DEATH BY MARTYRDOM

Philemon (1st century) received a letter from Paul requesting that he receive back his runaway slave Onesimus, and regard him "no longer as a slave but as more than a slave, a beloved brother, especially dear to me" (Phm 16). Tradition holds that Philemon and his wife, **Apphia** (1st century), were martyred at Colossae.

The Roman couple **Getulius** (d. c. 120) and **Symphorosa** (d. c. 135) suffered martyrdom during the reign of emperor Hadrian. When Getulius, who was an officer in the army, converted to Christianity, he retired to his country estate at Tivoli near Rome. The legate Cerealis was sent to arrest him. The legate instead was converted by this couple. The emperor then ordered that Getulius, Cerealis and Getulius' brother Amantius, who was a tribune in the army and a Christian, be arrested and executed. Symphorosa was later drowned in the Anio River by order of the same emperor.

Cecilia (dates unknown) reportedly converted her husband **Valerian** (dates unknown), and his brother

Tiburtius (dates unknown). All three devoted themselves to burying the bodies of martyred Christians. Probably during the reign of Emperor Alexander (222-35) the three were martyred. First the two men were arrested and beheaded, then after Cecilia had buried their bodies, she too was arrested and challenged to deny the faith or die. She chose death. Suffocation was attempted but failed. Beheading was likewise tried but was botched. For three days she lay dying from her wounds. Her name is mentioned in the First Eucharistic Prayer. Much of her story is legend, "so that even the date of her death is uncertain and is estimated as having occurred anywhere from 177 to the fourth century."[19]

Chrysanthos (d. 283), an Egyptian patrician and Christian, married **Daria** (d. 283), a Greek priestess of the goddess Minerva. Apparently he converted her and they set out to convert others. They were martyred during the reign of the Roman emperor Numerian.

In Upper Egypt the lector **Timothy** (d. 286) was arrested during the persecution of Diocletian. He was ordered to hand over the Church's sacred texts, but refused. His wife **Maura** (d. 286), to whom he had been married for only twenty days, was called in to persuade him to cooperate with the imperial authorities. Instead she encouraged him to be faithful to Jesus and his Church. The young couple suffered terrible tortures before being nailed alive to a wall where they lingered for nine days before expiring.

Melasippus (d. 360) and **Carina** (d. 360) and their child were martyred together at Ancyra during the reign of Julian the Apostate. The couple was tortured to death; their child was beheaded.

During the Japanese persecutions of 1597 and 1617-32, at least nine couples were martyred. The practice was that the whole family was executed if the head of the household was condemned to death; "comprehensive punishment had long been counted one of the administrator's most effective weapons."[20] In 1622 **Bl. Dominic Xamada** and his wife **Bl. Clare**; four women named Mary, viz.,

Tanaca, Tocuan, Xum and Sanga with their husbands; and a Korean, Bl. Antony, with his wife were slain.[21] In 1624 at Simabura, the elderly Bl. Louisa and her husband were burnt to death. In 1626 in Nagasaki, **Bl. John Naisen** and his wife **Bl. Monica** were beheaded, and **Bl. Frances Bizzocca** and her husband **Bl. Leo** were burnt alive for having given shelter to missionaries.

MARRIED THEN SEPARATED TO ENTER RELIGIOUS LIFE

Melania the Younger (383-439) and her husband **Pinian** (d. 432) are described in this chapter.

Amator (d. 418) and **Martha** (5th century) stretch our credulity in hagiography. Amator's biography seems to be "for the most part an audacious fiction."[22] On good historical evidence, however, Amator married Martha, soon separated, was ordained priest and bishop, and ordained the priests, Germanus of Auxerre and Patrick of Ireland. An incident from the couple's wedding day illustrates the general criticism of this biography.

> Accidentally or providentially (the elderly bishop) Valerian, instead of reading the nuptial blessing, recited the form which was used in the ordination of deacons — a mistake which was noticed only by the bride and bridegroom. When the service was over the young couple agreed to live a life of virginity, and Martha within a short time retired to a convent. Amator, after having labored for some years as a priest, was elected bishop of Auxerre.[23]

Gundleus (6th century) and **Gwladys** (6th century) lived a raucously violent life of banditry until their son, Cadoc, persuaded them to change their ways. The marriage began ominously: when Gundleus asked Gwladys' father for the hand of his daughter and the request was rejected, Gundleus returned with an army of three hundred men and kidnaped Gwladys.

The nobleman **Walbert** (d. c. 678), duke of Lorraine and count of Hainault, and **Bertilia** (7th century) raised two girls before agreeing to separate for spiritual reasons. He entered a monastery. She became a recluse near a church which she had founded at Maroeuil in Flanders.

Waldetrudis (d. c. 688) married **Vincent Madelgarius** (c. 615-77) and raised four children. In 643 he entered the Benedictine monastery which he had founded at Hautmont. Later he established another abbey at Soignies, which he led and where he died. For two years Waltrudis lived as a recluse before she founded and entered a convent at Chateaulieu.

Hidulphus (d. c. 707), count of Hainault, married **Agia** (d. c. 714). He served as a courtier in the palace of Austrasia. After they agreed to separate to enter religious life, he entered the monastery at Lobbes and she entered the convent at Mons.

Bl. Nicholas Giustiniani (d. c. 1180) received an unusual dispensation from Rome to temporarily leave his monastery of San Niccolo del Lido to raise up progeny for his family, whose other sons had died without issue in wars at Constantinople. The doge of Venice, the city's leading political figure, had sought the dispensation. Interestingly, Nicholas then married the doge's daughter, **Bl. Anna Michela** (12th century). "He accordingly married and had six sons and three daughters."[24] Having provided heirs for his family, Nicholas returned in 1160 to his monastery where he remained until his death twenty years later.[25] Anna, too, exchanged her marriage vows for monastic vows. She entered a woman's monastery which the couple had established on the island of Aniano.

MARRIED, WIDOWED THEN ENTERED RELIGIOUS LIFE

Ethelburga of Kent (d. c. 647) married the pagan widower **Edwin, King of Northumbria** (c. 585-633). She was his second wife. Her entourage included her confessor, Paulinus, who later converted her husband. Although Edwin had been favorably disposed to Christianity, he delayed his actual baptism. The pope wrote to Ethelburga and urged her to do all she could to bring about her husband's conversion. With the king's eventual conversion and the royal couple's encouragement, the Christian faith was developed in Northumbria for the first time. Edwin ruled ably. He became the most powerful king in England. When he died while fighting the pagan Mercians, he was hailed as a martyr. Ethelburga returned to Kent and founded the convent of Lyminge, where she became a nun and later the abbess.

Bl. Pepin of Landen (d. c. 639) and **Bl. Itta** (7th century) were ancestors of the Carolingian dynasty of French kings; they were grandparents to Pepin of Herstal and great-grandparents to Charles Martel. Pepin, who was mayor of the palace under three kings, was regarded as "the wisest statesman of his time."[26] He promoted the faith by protecting the Christians from Slavic invasions and by selecting only virtuous men as bishops. After Pepin's death Itta entered the Benedictine convent at Nivelles, where their famous daughter became abbess.

Adalbald (d. 652) and **Rictrudis** (c. 612-88) met when he had gone as a soldier to Gascony to quell an insurgency among the townspeople. They married, although some of her relatives disapproved of the union. "Both husband and wife spent much time in visiting the sick, relieving the poor and even in trying to convert criminals."[27] After sixteen years of happily married life in Flanders Adalbald visited his wife's relatives in Gascony, who ambushed and murdered him. After several years of widowhood the king insisted that Rictrudis remarry. She refused, with the support of her spiritual director, Amandus, and retired to a male-female monastery, which she had founded in Flanders, where a relative was already abbess. Rictrudis later succeeded her as abbess. Three of her four children eventually joined her there.

Henry II, the Holy Roman Emperor, (972-1024) and **Cunegund** (d. 1033) are described in this chapter.

Notes for Chapter 2

[1]   *Butler's Lives of the Saints*, vol. IV, p. 646.

[2]   Ibid., pp. 646-47.

[3]   Butler, vol. III, p. 268.

[4]   *Funeral Orations*, pp. 122-25.

[5]   Butler, vol. III, p. 105.

[6]   Ibid., p. 105.

[7]   Ibid. p. 106.

[8]   Butler, vol. I, p. 471.

[9]   *Catholic Standard & Times*, June 11, 1992; p. 30.

[10]   Ibid., p. 30.

[11]   Letter from Zelie to daughter Pauline, March 4, 1877; as quoted in Louis and Marjorie Wust, *Louis Martin*, p. 41.

[12]   Albert H. Dolan, *The Little Flower's Mother*, pp. 20-22.

[13]   Barbara Foley, *Zelie Martin*, p. 28.

[14]   Letter of Zelie Martin, October 17, 1870; as found in Wust, p. 55.

[15]   Poulos, *Orthodox Saints*, vol. IV, pp. 117-18.

[16]   Butler, vol. II, p. 323.

[17]   Butler, vol. III, p. 662.

[18]   Ibid.

[19]   Delaney, *Dictionary of Saints*, pp. 140-41.

[20]   Butler, vol. I, p. 260.

[21]   Butler, vol. III, pp. 533-35.

[22]   Butler, vol. II, p. 207.

[23]   Ibid.

[24]   *The Book of Saints*, p. 415.

[25]   *Bibliotheca Sanctorum*, vol. VII, column 5.

[26]   Butler, vol. I, p. 384.

[27]   Ibid., p. 236.

CHAPTER 3

PARENT(S) AND CHILD(REN) SAINTS

Mother and Father and Child(ren)

1. Mary, Joseph and Jesus
2. Zechariah, Elizabeth and John the Baptist
3. Cleophas, Mary Cleophas and James the Younger
4. Basil the Elder, Emmelia and their children Basil the Great, Gregory of Nyssa, Peter of Sebastea and Macrina the Younger
5. Gregory Nazianzen the Elder, Nonna and their children Gregory Nazianzen, Caesarius and Gorgonia
6. Gundleus, Gwladys and Cadoc
7. Bl. Pepin of Landen, Itta and their daughters Begga and Gertrude of Nivelles
8. Adalbald and Rictrudis and their children Adalsind, Clotsind, Eusebia and Mauront
9. Walbert, Bertilia and their daughters Aldegundis and Waldetrudis
10. Vincent Madalgarius, Waldetrudis and their children Landericus, Aldetrudis, Madalberta and Dentelinus
11. King Stephen of Hungary, Bl. Gisella and their son Emeric
12. Bl. John Naisen, Bl. Monica and their son Louis
13. Louis and Zelie Martin with Thérèse of Lisieux*

---

* Thérèse of Lisieux was canonized in 1925. Her parents are not yet canonized, although their causes for canonization have been introduced; hers in 1959, and his in 1960.

Mother and Child(ren)

14. Mary and Mark
15. Mary Salome and her sons James the Elder and John the Beloved
16. Priscilla of Rome and her son Pudens
17. Helen and Constantine the Great
18. Macrina the Elder and her son Basil the Elder
19. Monica and Augustine
20. Paula and her daughters Blesilla and Eustochium Julia
21. Celina and her son Remigius
22. Sylvia and Pope Gregory the Great
23. Sexubrga and her daughters Ercongota and Ermenilda
24. Ermenburga and her daughters Milburga, Mildred and Mildgytha
25. Matilda and Bruno of Cologne
26. Queen Wilfrida and Edith of Wilton
27. Queen Margaret of Scotland and David I of Scotland
28. Bl. Joan of Aza and her sons Dominic and Bl. Mannes
29. Elizabeth of Hungary and Bl. Gertrude of Altenberg
30. Bridget of Sweden and Catherine of Sweden

Father and Child(ren)

31. The priest Saturninus and his four children Felix, Saturninus, Mary and Hilarion
32. Nerses I the Great and Isaac the Great
33. Pope Hormisdas and Pope Silverius
34. King Ethelbert and his daughter Ethelburga
35. Authaire and his son Ouen
36. Arnulf of Metz and his son Clodulf of Metz
37. Richard of Lucca and his children Willibald, Winebald and Walburga

38. John the Georgian and his son Euthymius of Mount Olympus
39. Vladimir of Kiev and his sons Boris and Gleb
40. King Canute IV of Denmark and Bl. Charles the Good
41. Duke Theodore and his sons David and Constantine of Yaroslav
42. Bl. Michael Cozaki and his son Bl. Thomas

Show Them the Path to Life: Parent and Child Saints

"The acorn doesn't fall far from the tree." "Children learn what they live." These anonymous sayings emphasize the fundamental role of parents in raising their children. Parents provide for their children the double influences of nature and nurture.

The Scriptures often comment on the mutual respect to be shared between parents and children. The Old Testament teaches: "Whoever reveres his father will live a long life; he obeys the Lord who brings comfort to his mother. He who fears the Lord honors his father, and serves his parents as rulers" (Si 3:6-7). In the New Testament Jesus often cites the interaction between parents and children to prove a point. He teaches the parable of the Prodigal Son to demonstrate the lifelong love of a parent for a child. He miraculously heals the life and limbs of children, relieving the anxiety of the parents. He repeatedly and affectionately addresses God as "Father." St. Paul advises the Christian family: "You children, obey your parents in everything as the acceptable way in the Lord. And fathers, do not nag your children lest they lose heart" (Col 3:20-21).

Many saintly parents raised saintly children. The parents conceived and reared their children in a spirit of faith, hope and love. Not all the children, however, of

saintly parents became saints. Nor have all the parents of
saints been canonized. The Christian family simply provides the opportunity for response-ability to God. The
actual response depends on each individual's cooperation
with the gift of God's grace.

Particular examples

1. MONICA AND HER SON AUGUSTINE

Monica (c. 331-87) prayed for years for the conversion of her son Augustine (354-430). She certainly exemplifies the adage: "Parenting is forever."

Augustine lived a wayward life for many years. He left
home at age sixteen to study at the university at Carthage.
Two years later, he and his mistress, with whom he lived
for the next fifteen years, gave birth to a son. At age twenty-
nine Augustine left Carthage for Rome, and Monica pursued him there. Three years later he moved to Milan. So did
Monica. She indefatigably prayed and worked for his
conversion. Her entreaties succeeded when he was thirty-
three years old.

Augustine writes often and movingly in his *Confessions* about the profound conversations that he and his
mother shared. This excerpt is taken from their conversation during the last week of Monica's life:

> The day was now approaching when my mother
> Monica would depart from this life; you knew that
> day, Lord, though we did not. She and I happened to
> be standing by ourselves at a window that overlooked
> the garden in the courtyard of the house. At the time
> we were in Ostia on the Tiber. We had gone there after
> a long and wearisome journey to get away from the
> noisy crowd, and to rest and prepare for our sea
> voyage. I believe that you, Lord, caused all this to
> happen in your own mysterious ways. And so the two

of us, all alone, were enjoying a very pleasant conversation, "forgetting the past and pushing on to what is ahead." We were asking one another in the presence of the Truth . . . for you are Truth . . . what it would be like to share the eternal life enjoyed by the saints, "which eye has not seen, nor ear heard, which has not even entered into the heart of man." We desired with all our hearts to drink from the streams of your heavenly fountain, the fountain of life.

That was the substance of our talk, though not the exact words. But you know, O Lord, that in the course of our conversation that day, the world and its pleasure lost all their attraction for us. My mother said: "Son, as far as I am concerned, nothing in this life now gives my any pleasure. I do not know why I am still here, since I have no further hopes in this world. I did have one reason for wanting to live a little: to see you become a Catholic Christian before I died. God has lavished his gifts on me in that respect, for I know that you have even renounced earthly happiness to be his servant. So what am I doing here?"

I do not remember how I answered her. Shortly within five days or thereabouts, she fell sick with a fever. Then one day during the course of her illness she became unconscious and for a while she was unaware of her surroundings. My brother and I rushed to her side but she regained consciousness quickly. She looked at us as we stood there and asked in a puzzled voice: "Where was I?"

We were overwhelmed with grief, but she held her gaze steadily upon us and spoke further: "Here you shall bury your mother." I remained silent as I held back my tears. However, my brother haltingly expressed his hope that she might not die in a strange country but in her own land, since her end would be happier there. When she heard this, her face was filled with anxiety, and she reproached him with a glance because he had entertained such earthly thoughts. Then she looked at me and spoke: "Look what he is saying." Thereupon she said to both of us: "Bury my body wherever you will; let not care of it cause you any concern. One thing only I ask you, that you remember me at the altar of the Lord wherever you may be." Once our mother had expressed this desire as best she could, she fell silent as the pain of her illness increased.[1]

2. STEPHEN OF HUNGARY AND HIS SON EMERIC

Stephen of Hungary (975-1038) and his only son Emeric (1007-31) were canonized together in 1083. Stephen's wife and Emeric's mother, Bl. Gisella (d. c. 1095) outlived by over half a century both men in the family. She retired to a convent at Passau and is remembered for her life of charity and prayer.

Stephen, who had inherited the position of ruler of the Magyars, emerged after a series of wars as King of Hungary. He achieved a political reorganization of the government and the Christianization of the populace. He instituted a new legal code, provided for the poor, united the Magyars and made Hungary independent. He appointed an archbishop who established various dioceses, built churches and ordered tithes to be paid for the support of the churches.

Emeric, the heir apparent, was killed in a hunting accident when only fourteen years old. Many miracles were reported at the youth's tomb. The father had earlier instructed the son in a letter about rightly serving God and God's people. The authenticity of the instruction is denied by some.[2]

My dearest son, if you desire to honor the royal crown, I advise, I counsel, I urge you above all things to maintain the Catholic and apostolic faith with such diligence and care that you may be an example for all those placed under you by God and that all the clergy may rightly call you a man of true Christian profession. Failing to do this, you may be sure that you will not be called a Christian or a son of the Church. Indeed, in the royal palace after the faith itself, the Church holds second place, first propagated as she was by our head, Christ; then transplanted, firmly constituted and spread through the whole world by his members, the apostles and holy fathers. And though she always produced fresh offspring, nevertheless in certain places she is regarded as ancient.

However, dearest son, even now in our kingdom the Church is proclaimed as young and newly planted; and for that reason she needs more prudent and trustworthy guardians lest a benefit which the divine mercy bestowed on us undeservedly should be destroyed and annihilated through your idleness, indolence or neglect.

My beloved son, delight of my heart, hope of your posterity, I pray, I command, that at every time and in everything, strengthened by your devotion to me, you may show favor not only to relations and kin, or to the most eminent, be they leaders or rich men or neighbors or fellow-countrymen, but also to foreigners and to all who come to you. By fulfilling your duty in this way you will reach the highest state of happiness. Be merciful to all who are suffering violence, keeping always in your heart the example of the Lord who said: I desire mercy and not sacrifice. Be patient with everyone, not only with the powerful, but also with the weak.

Finally be strong lest prosperity lift you up too much or adversity cast you down. Be humble in this life, that God may raise you up in the next. Be truly moderate and do not punish or condemn anyone immoderately. Be gentle so that you may never oppose justice. Be honorable so that you may never voluntarily bring disgrace upon anyone. Be chaste so that you may avoid all the foulness of lust like the pangs of death.

All these virtues I have noted above make up the royal crown and without them no one is fit to rule here on earth or attain to the heavenly kingdom.[3]

3. Brigid of Sweden and her Daughter Catherine

Bridgid of Sweden (1303-73) at age fourteen became the second wife of her eighteen-year-old husband, a prince and wealthy landowner. She bore him eight children during their twenty-eight years of married life. She had experienced remarkable visions and revelations throughout the whole of her life. After her husband died, she left her court position as lady-in-waiting to the queen and went on various pilgrimages within Sweden, to Rome and to Jerusalem. She confidently and kindly denounced publicly people in high places, namely the pope for not returning from Avignon to Rome, and the king and queen for frivolous living. At Vadstena she founded a monastery and the Order of the Most Holy Savior, later known as the "Bridgettines."

Catherine (c. 1331-81) was the fourth of eight children. She traveled to Rome in 1350 to visit her widowed mother. Later that same year Catherine too was widowed. She remained in Rome as the inseparable companion of her mother for the next twenty-five years. When her mother died, Catherine returned to the monastery at Vadstena. While Bridgid had founded the religious order of the Bridgettines, it was Catherine who developed the community. Shortly before Catherine died the congregation received papal approval. This excerpt indicates clearly how the mother shared with her daughter the Christian vision and its practical implementation:

> Mother took me and my sisters with her to the hospital which she built, and without disgust she bound the wounds and sores with her own hands . . . and when mother was reproached for taking her little girls with her, that we might be infected from the stench of sick people, she answered that she took us while we were still small, so that we might learn at an early age to serve God and His poor and sick . . . and already, while father was still living, and later when mother was a

widow, she did not sit down at the table without having given twelve poor people food to eat, and every Friday she washed their feet herself. Each year mother sent clothes to the poor and alms to the many convents around the country.[4]

4. THÉRÈSE OF LISIEUX AND HER FATHER LOUIS MARTIN

Thérèse of Lisieux and her father got along marvelously. He cared for her as though she were a little flower; he protected her, provided for her, supported her growth. He loved her and made every sacrifice possible to please her. Perhaps he bestowed such attention upon her because her mother had died when she was only four years old. Perhaps this holy man sensed early on how holy his daughter was. In any case, their relationship was extraordinary.

The father had already given two daughters to the Carmelite convent. When this third child asked his support, he aided her wholeheartedly. Even though she was only fourteen years of age, he took her to the local convent. When she was refused entrance there because of her age, he took her to the local bishop. When she was refused accommodation there, he took her to the pope. When the pope encouraged her in her vocation, and in the virtue of patience, the father daily supported his daughter in her desire to be a nun. Thérèse loved her father and writes tenderly of their relationship:

> The moment to speak came in the late afternoon, after Vespers. Daddy was sitting on the edge of the cistern. He sat with folded hands gazing on the loveliness of nature: the sun, its midday heat lost, gilded the treetops and the birds joyously sang their evening hymn. Daddy's face had a heavenly look and I felt that his soul was completely at peace. I went and sat beside him without saying a word. There were tears in my eyes. He looked at me tenderly, pressed my head

against his breast, and said: "What's the matter, my little queen? Tell me." He got up as if to hide his own emotion and began to walk slowly up and down, holding me close to him. Through my tears I told him of my wanting to enter Carmel. His tears mingled with mine, but he said no word to turn me from my vocation. All he said was that I was still very young to make so serious a decision, but I pleaded my cause so well that his simple, upright nature was soon convinced that my desire came from God. His great faith made him exclaim that God honoured him greatly by asking him to surrender his children. We walked up and down for a long time, and I was happy because of the kindness with which my incomparable father had received my avowal. He seemed to feel that tranquil joy which comes from a sacrifice which has been freely accepted.

We went up to a low wall where he showed me some small white flowers looking like miniature lilies. He picked one and gave it me, telling me with what care God had created it and preserved it until that day. As I listened to him I thought I was hearing the story of my own life, so great was the similarity between what Jesus had done for this little flower and for little Thérèse. I took the flower as if it were a relic. I saw that Daddy had picked it without breaking any of its roots, so it seemed as if it were destined to grow on in a more fertile soil than the velvety moss where it had spent its early days. Daddy had just done a similar thing for me in letting me go to the mountain of Carmel and leave the gentle valley of my childhood. I put the little white flower in *The Imitation* at the chapter headed: "Love of Jesus." It is still there, but its stem is broken near the root — by which God seems to tell me that He will soon break the bonds of His little flower and not leave her to wither away down here on earth.[5]

General Observations

In a few families both parents and all the children are considered saints. This is exemplified in the Holy Family and the family of John the Baptist. Gregory Nazianzen the Elder and Nonna raised all three of their children as saints. Adalbald and Rictrudis raised four. Walbert and Bertilia raised two. One of their daughters, Waldetrudis, married Vincent Madelgarius and their four children are all considered saints.

Some holy couples were blessed with many saintly children. Some of these families were mentioned in the preceding paragraph. Other families include Basil the Elder and Emmelia, who raised four saints. Gregory Nazianzen the Elder and Nonna raised three. Bl. Pepin of Landen and Bl. Itta's two daughters are recognized as saints.

In contrast, many saintly couples raised children who were never regarded as saints. Six of the ten children of Basil the Elder and Emmelia are not named among the saints. Bl. Nicholas Giustiniani and his wife Bl. Anna raised six sons and three daughters, none of whom is named a saint.[6] Melania and Pinian gave birth to two children but both died in infancy and neither, of course, was sainted. Nothing noteworthy is known about Monica's other two sons, and Augustine's own son Adeodatus. Paula gave birth to five children, two of whom are regarded as saints, while the other three are not. Bl. Joan of Aza raised four sons of whom two are saints: Dominic and Bl. Mannes. Bridgid parented eight children among whom only Catherine is regarded as a saint. Margaret of Scotland raised eight children, of whom only David is recognized as a saint.

Many saintly couples apparently never had any children. We hear of no children belonging to Priscilla and Aquila, the martyrs Getulius and Symphorosa, Emperor

Henry II and Cunegund, nor the Franciscan tertiaries Eleazar and Delphine.

Many saintly couples bore children who in many ways were more famous than the parents. Mary and Joseph are the mother and foster-father of Jesus. Zechariah and Elizabeth were the parents of John the Baptist. Joachim and Anne are traditionally regarded as the parents of Mary, the mother of Jesus. Basil the Great made his parents, Basil the Elder and Emmelia, famous. Gregory Nazianzen earned a similar recognition for his parents, Gregory Nazianzen the Elder and Nonna. Bl. Pepin and Bl. Itta were parents to the visionary Gertrude of Nivelles and were grandparents to the Christian but unsainted Charlemagne, founder of the Carolingian dynasty in France.

Many saintly children followed in the footsteps of their saintly parents. Nerses the Great and his son Isaac the Great, when widowed, eventually became monks. Nerses became the Katholikos of Armenia and was succeeded by Isaac. Macrina the Elder, and a generation later, Basil the Elder, attempted to reform Cappadocia religiously and socially; for their trouble mother and son suffered exile. Gregory Nazianzen the Elder chose his son Gregory to succeed him as bishop. Pope Hormisdas was succeeded, after an interval of thirteen years and six short-lived popes, by his son Silverius. Arnulf and Clodulf were successive bishops of Metz. Sexburga successively entered two monasteries and was named abbess in both, and her daughter Ermenilda, entered the same monasteries and eventually assumed the same positions. King Canute of Denmark was murdered in a church by political rivals, and forty-one years later, his son Charles the Good was slain in another church by grain merchants whose profits he attempted to regulate during a famine.

Some children did not follow their parents but instead simultaneously walked with their parents. The North African priest Saturninus and four of his children were martyred together. Paula and her daughter Eustochium Julia jointly renounced the secular world of Rome and settled in a monastery in Jerusalem. John and Euthymius co-founded the famous Iviron Monastery at Mt. Olympus. Queen Wilfrida took her infant Edith to Wilton Abbey where the two lived together until the daughter died twenty-three years later. Bridgid of Sweden and her daughter Catherine, after both were widowed, began a religious community in which they lived together for twenty-five years.

Even when saintly parents and children pursued different vocations, they oftentimes shared similar values. Celina and Remigius, who was the bishop of Rheims for seventy years, were both famous for prayer and practical charity. The widow Sylvia and her son Gregory the Great sought the quiet of monastic life, although later he was called from the monastery to immerse himself in ecclesiastical service; as pope, however, he universally renewed and restored monastic life. Richard of Lucca with two of his sons made a pilgrimage to Rome, near which he died and then his sons and daughter decided to enter religious life. Queen Matilda's son Bruno who personally eschewed political life, became a bishop. Mother and son both demanded high moral standards in court and Church alike. Vladimir of Kiev, ruler of Russia, was converted from cruel barbarity to peaceable Christianity. His sons Boris and Gleb by his Christian wife (who was one of six wives) refused to take up the sword. In separate incidents the peaceable sons died defenseless. Theodore, duke of Yaroslav, shared with his sons David and Constantine care for those otherwise uncared for. Queen Elizabeth of Hungary, who had been raised in a castle, chose to raise her daughter Gertrude in a monastery; both became renowned for their charity to the poor.

Some of these relationships between parent and child were particularly intimate. Jesus presents his mother as the model of Christian life: "Those who hear the word of God and act upon it are mother and brother and sister to me" (Lk 8:21). Mary was the first to hear the word of God and act upon it. Augustine's autobiographical accounts of conversations with his mother Monica moves to tears the hearts of his readers. Paula and Eustochium Julia shared a kindred spirit during their nineteen years of shared monastic life. Richard of Lucca and his sons Willibald and Winebald daily prayed together during their pilgrimage from England to Rome. Wilfrida and her suspected "love child" Edith spent their entire lives together praying in the same convent, until the daughter died. Stephen's tender solicitude for Emeric is recorded in the father's letters. Catherine of Sweden's writings immortalize her admiration for her mother Brigid.

Relations between saintly parents and children, however, were not always idyllic. Monica prayed for and pursued Augustine for fifteen years to urge him to adopt the Christian way. Vladimir and his two Christian children were at odds because of his violent pagan ways. He converted but not all his sons did, and internecine conflicts killed his two Christian sons. Matilda and her child Bruno got along fine, but she and her other two sons feuded terribly; she suffered a sense of failure with them. Cadoc struggled to persuade his parents to cease their banditry. Eventually he succeeded. During the ceremony when she was about to take her vows as a nun, Edith's father tempted her with gifts of gold and silver.

Some irregularities occurred in the lives of a few of these saints. Vladimir of Kiev was an illegitimate child, born of his father's mistress. Vladimir himself had five wives before meeting and marrying his Christian wife; her condition for marriage was that he cease his polygamous ways. King Canute of Denmark was born to his royal father's mistress. Edith, child of Queen Wilfrida, was fathered by someone other than the king; immediately after the birth, the mother and infant entered Wilton Abbey, and neither left the premises again.

Numerous New Testament era persons are represented among the parent-child saints. Zechariah and Elizabeth were parents of John the Baptist; Cleophas and Mary Cleophas, of James the Younger. Another Mary was mother to John Mark. Salome was the solicitous mother of the apostles James the Greater and John the Beloved. Priscilla, different from the woman with the same name who is the wife of Aquila, was the mother of the Senator Pudens. Her home served as Peter's headquarters in Rome, and the ground under her home became used as catacombs.

Many relationships in this category involve persons of high political position. Queens include Sexburga, mother of Ercongota and Ermenilda; Matilda, mother of Bruno; Wilfrida, mother of Edith; and Margaret of Scotland, mother of David. Kings include Ethelbert of Kent, whose daughter was Ethelburga; Stephen of Hungary, father of Emeric; David of Scotland, son of Queen Margaret; and Canute, father to Charles the Good. Other politically powerful persons include Pudens, one of the first Christian aristocrats and a Roman Senator; Bl. Pepin the mayor of the Franks; his daughter Begga, who was mother of Charles Martel and grandmother of Charlemagne; Elizabeth of Hungary, the landgrave's wife, and Duke Theodore of Yaroslav.

Some parents bore the immense pain of burying their children. Mary attended Jesus during his crucifixion and burial. Melania twice lost infants at birth. Stephen lost his young son Emeric through a hunting accident. Paula's newlywed daughter Bl. Blesilla died suddenly at age twenty. Wilfrida's daughter Edith died at age twenty-three. Gregory Nazianzen the Elder and Nonna saw all three of their children live to adulthood, but the parents outlived Caesarius and Gorgonia.

Many sainted parents are not mentioned here because none of their children became saints. Paulinus of Nola's only child died a week after birth. Bl. Hildegard raised nine children. Duchess Olga of Kiev raised one son. Adelaide bore one child by her first husband and five children by her second husband. Hedwig had eight children. Elizabeth of Hungary had four children. Elizabeth of Portugal had a son and a daughter. King Louis IX of France had eleven children. Thomas More had four children by his first wife. Nicholas von Flue fathered ten children. Francis Borgia was a widower with eight children before he entered the Jesuits. Louise de Marillac had one son. Jane Frances de Chantal had six children. Elizabeth Seton had two sons and three daughters. Marguerite d'Youville had six children, only two of whom reached adulthood. Joaquina de Vedruna was blessed with eight children. None of these great saints, however, was blessed with saintly children.

Some parents raised particularly difficult children. Elizabeth of Portugal earned the title "Peacemaker" because she succeeded in the difficult task of reconciling her husband with their son who twice led armed rebellions against his father. Louise de Marillac's son gave her headaches and heartaches until he reached his mid-forties. He had entered the seminary but the vocation was more his mother's choice than his. He remained there a couple of trouble-filled years. He never kept a job nor stayed with one woman until he married at mid-life. Elizabeth Ann Seton raised five children and two of them followed her into the convent. One son, however, never learned to manage his own life. He could neither hold a job nor pay his debts. He spent his time sowing wild oats until at mid-life he joined the navy. Monica's son Augustine had a concubine for fifteen years, finally separated from that liaison, and immediately took up with another woman for one more year.

Some sainted children were deprived from their youth of one of their parents. Constantine's father divorced his wife Helen when the son was just a couple of years old. Martin de Porres' father, who was a Spanish conquistador, abandoned his black wife and mulatto son when Martin was twelve years old. Louise de Marillac was born out of wedlock; her father adopted her as a step-child into his family and she never knew her mother. Edith of Wilton was born out of wedlock; mother and child fled to a convent and Edith never knew her father. Thérèse of Lisieux's mother died when Thérèse was four years old; her father and sisters raised her.

Application Of The Theme:

Common Vision: Most of these parents trained their children in the faith. Parents taught by word and deed, by explanation and example. Their homes were schools of faith. Not all the children, however, embraced the faith. As all experienced teachers know: "You can teach students but you cannot learn for them."

Common Way: These parents literally led their children along the path of faith. They led them in prayer at home. They led them to church. They led them hand-in-hand into the homes of the poor, whom the parents and children fed and clothed. These parents not only gave physical life to their children but they nurtured their spiritual life as well.

Common Bond Among Themselves: Most of these parents and children became best friends as adults. These children imbibed and incorporated the values of their parents. Parents, the erstwhile trainers of children, became best friends with their children. A bond of mutual faith, trust and love grew. Parents and children grew together.

Common Bond With God: The common vision and common way had a common object: union with God. Eventually parents and children became peers in relationship with God. They shared their prayer, practical service, revelations and inspirations. As adults, they all saw themselves as children of God, praying to their common Father.

APPENDIX: PARENT AND CHILD SAINTS

MOTHER AND FATHER AND CHILD(REN) SAINTS

The Holy Family of **Joseph** (1st century), **Mary** (1st century) and **Jesus** (4 B.C.-30 A.D.) is described in the early chapters of the Gospels of Matthew and Luke. The couple was engaged "but before they lived together, she was found to be with child through the power of the Holy Spirit" (Mt 1:18). Joseph decided to divorce his fiancée quietly. An angel appeared to Joseph, and assured him that a divine intervention had occurred. "He had no relations with her at any time before she bore a son, whom he named Jesus" (Mt 1:25). The child was circumcised and presented in the Temple in Bethlehem. Shepherds and astrologers visited the young family. An angel advised Joseph during his sleep to flee to Egypt to escape the murderous fury of the jealous Herod, and again appeared to him to tell him it was time to return to Nazareth. In this Galilean town Jesus was known by his kinsfolk as the son of Mary and Joseph the carpenter. "Jesus, for his part, progressed steadily in wisdom, age and grace before God and men" (Lk 2:52).

Zechariah (1st century) and **Elizabeth** (1st century) parented the prophet **John the Baptist** (1st century), who later lived in the desert of Judea and preached along the banks of the Jordan River. He proclaimed to his hearers: "Reform your lives! The reign of God is at hand" (Mt 3:2). He baptized Jesus, protesting: "I should be baptized by you, yet you come to me" (Mt 3:14). John castigated the powerful tetrarch Herod for his adulterous and incestuous marriage to his brother's wife Herodias, who then accomplished through her daughter Salome the beheading of John. Jesus said of John: "History has not known a man born of woman greater than John the Baptizer" (Mt 12:11).

Cleophas (1st century) and **Mary** (1st century) parented **James the Younger** (1st century), who was one of the twelve apostles. Recent scholarship wonders if there might not have been two persons named James: one who was the apostle and a second who was the "brother of the Lord," author of the letter of James and authorative head of the primitive Church in Jerusalem.

Basil the Elder (d. 370) married **Emmelia** (d. c. 370) and among their ten children were four saints: their sons **Basil the Great** (329-79), **Gregory of Nyssa** (c. 330-95), **Peter of Sebastea** (c. 340-91) and their daughter **Macrina the Younger** (c. 330-79). The three brothers were well educated, became bishops and struggled heroically against Arianism, which threatened to destroy the orthodoxy of the Church in the East. The daughter too was well educated. When her fiancé and then her father died, she and her mother withdrew to the family's country estate to live a life of prayer and contemplation in a community which thrived there.

Gregory Nazianzen the Elder (c. 276-374) and **Nonna** (d. 374) bore three children all of whom became saints: **Gregory Nazianzen** (c. 329-89), **Caesarius of Nazianzen** (d. 369) and **Gorgonia** (d. c. 372). The relationship of the parents is described in this chapter. The son Gregory lived as a hermit before being ordained a priest and then bishop by his father, who was a bishop. Caesarius was a doctor and political assistant to three emperors. Gorgonia lived an exemplary married life.

Cadoc (d. c. 575) converted his parents **Gundleus** (d. c. 500) and **Gwladys** (6th century). The Welsh chieftain Gundleus, who had forcefully captured his bride, involved his wife in his livelihood of banditry. This couple tried to bring up their son in the ways of their career. They were unsuccessful. After he was educated by the Irishman Tatheus, he founded a monastery at Lancarfan, Wales and became an itinerant monk, who labored throughout Ireland, Wales, and Scotland. He also made pilgrimages to Rome and Jerusalem. When he returned to the monastery, he was named abbot. The son convinced his parents to give up their banditry. The parents agreed and lived out their days as hermits.

Bl. Pepin of Landen (d. c. 639) and **Itta** (7th century) were blessed with the daughters **Begga** (d. 693) and **Gertrude of Nivelles** (626-59). Pepin, mayor of the palace, propagated the faith, defended the region against Slavic invaders, chose responsible bishops for vacant sees and rebuked the king for licentious living. When Pepin died, Itta built a monastery in which Gertrude became abbess. Begga married the son of bishop Arnulf of Metz. Begga's son founded the Carolingian dynasty.

Adalbald (d. 652) married **Rictrudis** (c. 612-88) against the wishes of her family. The couple moved to Flanders where for sixteen years they practiced a life of prayer and charity. When Adalbald returned on one occasion to the family homestead, Rictrudis' unforgiving family ambushed and killed him. Rictrudis refused her family's request that she re-marry. Instead she founded a monastery of men and women and ruled there as abbess for forty years. The mother advised her daughter **Eusebia** (d. c. 680) to enter the convent, where her great grandmother Gertrude was abbess. Eventually the three other children, **Adalsind** (d. c. 715), **Clotsind** (c. 635-714) and **Mauront** (d. 701), also entered monastic life.

Walbert (d. c. 678) and **Bertilia** (d. c. 687) raised two daughters, **Aldegundis** (630-84) and **Waldetrudis** (d. c. 688). When the parents agreed to a life of continence, Walbert joined a monastery and Bertilia became a religious hermit. The daughters became Benedictine nuns at Mons, but before doing so, Waldetrudis married, raised four children, and like her parents, separated so that she and her husband could enter monasteries.

Vincent Madelgarius (d. 677) and **Waldetrudis** (d. c. 688) raised four children, all of whom are regarded as saints. About 653 the parents decided to separate so that each might become Benedictines. He founded a monastery and she, a convent. **Landericus** (7th century), the oldest child, served as bishop of Meaux for ten years before succeeding his deceased father as abbot of Soignies. His brother **Dentelinus** (7th century), the youngest child, died at age seven. The sisters **Aldetrudis** (d. c. 696) and **Madalberta** (d. 706) succeeded each other as abbesses.

Stephen, King of Hungary (975-1038), his wife **Bl. Gisella** (d. 1095) and their son **Emeric** (1007-31) are described in this chapter.

Bl. John Naisen (d. 1626), his wife **Bl. Monica** (d. 1626) and their son **Louis** (1619-26) were martyred in Nagasaki. John and Monica were tortured to death and their son was beheaded.

Thérèse of Lisieux (1873-97) and her father **Louis Martin** (1823-94) and mother **Zelie** (1831-77) are described in this chapter.

MOTHER AND CHILD(REN)

Mary (1st century), the mother of **Mark** (d. c. 74), also known as John Mark, opened her home in Jerusalem as a gathering place for the apostles. There Peter fled when he was released from prison. Mark accompanied his cousin Barnabas on the first missionary journey of Paul. At Pamphylia on the way to Cyprus, Mark abandoned Paul. He did not accompany Paul on his second or third journeys. Mark returned to Paul's good graces by visiting him during his house-arrest at Rome. He was the disciple whom Peter affectionately calls "my son" (1 P 5:13). Mark wrote the first Gospel based on his conversations with Peter.

Mary Salome (1st century) requested of Jesus that her sons **James the Elder** (d. 42) and **John the Beloved Disciple** (c. 6-c. 104) receive the top positions in the kingdom (Mt 20:20-23). She stood at the foot of the cross and was among the women who discovered the empty tomb of Jesus. Her two sons made a living as Galilean fishermen. They abandoned their nets, however, to follow Jesus who selected these two brothers along with Peter to accompany him on the Mount of the Transfiguration, at the raising of the daughter of Jairus from the dead, and during his agony in the Garden of Gethsemane. James the Elder was the first of the apostles to be martyred. John the Beloved Disciple of the Lord was the last of the apostles to die. At Golgotha Jesus left his mother in the care of John, and asked that she accept John as her son.

Priscilla (d. c. 98) and her son **Pudens** (1st century) allowed their home on the Via Salaria to serve as Peter's headquarters in Rome. Catacombs were constructed later under the home. These catacombs bear her name and are still visited by pilgrims to Rome. The son became a senator and one of the earliest Christians listed among the aristocracy.

Helen (c. 250-328) is regarded as a saint in both the Eastern and Western Churches, but her son **Constantine the Great** (c. 285-337) does not enjoy unanimous agreement about his sanctity. She converted to Christianity in 313, when her son promulgated the tolerant Edict of Milan. She won renown for prayerfulness, charity and evangelization. She passed her final years between Rome and the Holy Land, where she oversaw the construction of many churches and allegedly discovered the true cross on which Christ died. Constantine trained at the court of Diocletian. He seems to have had, however, a religious experience at the Milvian Bridge in 312. This event changed his and history's course. He adopted Christianity, nonetheless remaining an unbaptized catechumen until his deathbed. He henceforth forbade the persecution of Christians and the erection of pagan temples, promulgated the Edict of Milan, established Christian cathedrals throughout the Empire, helped to reconcile the Church's internal and external difficulties, and convened the pivotal ecumenical Council of Nicea in 325. While the East regards Constantine as the "thirteenth apostle," the

West suggests that Constantine exploited Christianity by fostering religious unity as a means of achieving and sustaining political unity. Representatives from the Eastern Churches comment that Helen and Constantine provided "a mother-son influence on Christianity that has never been duplicated."[7]

Macrina the Elder (c. 270-340) and her son **Basil the Elder** (d. 370) lived in Pontus, Cappadocia. Both possessed a deeply religious spirit and both were forced to flee for safety during separate periods of persecution.

The relationship between **Monica** (c. 331-87) and her son **Augustine** (354-430) is described in this chapter.

Paula (347-404) and her husband raised five children. When he died in 379, she renounced terrestrial treasures and dedicated herself to helping the poor. Her daughter **Blesilla** (363-83) married, but after seven months her husband contracted a fever and died. Blesilla joined her mother in serving the poor. Four years later Blessilla died. Another daughter, **Eustochium Julia** (d. c. 419), accompanied the mother on a pilgrimage throughout the Holy Land. In Jerusalem Paula built a hospice and monastery. Eustochium assisted Jerome in his translation of the Scriptures. The mother and then the daughter directed three monasteries which Jerome had founded.

Probably at Cerny near Lyons, **Celina** (5th century) raised in the faith her son **Remigius** (c. 437-530), who was ordained bishop of Rheims at age twenty-two and served in that position for more than seventy years. This "Apostle of the Franks" instructed and baptized the pagan king Clovis, his family, chiefs, and 3,000 followers.

Sylvia (6th century) and her husband raised two sons, one of whom became pope, **Gregory the Great** (c. 540-604). She was from Sicily. Her husband was a Roman patrician. After he died, she lived for twenty years as a quasi-monastic. Gregory is one of only two popes to receive the appellation "great." He established political stability by persuading the Lombard invaders to spare Rome, thereby overriding and eliminating the authority of the Byzantine emperor, which led to the Church's acquisition of political power which continued into medieval times. He reformed the clergy, religious orders, and the liturgy. Gregorian chant originated from his support of this musical form.

Sexburga (d. c. 699), daughter of the king of East Anglia and wife of the king of Kent, bore four children: two sons who became princes and two daughters who became saints, **Ercongota** (d. c. 660) and **Ermenilda** (d. c. 700). After her husband's death, Sexburga retired to monastic life. Both daughters became nuns: Ercongota under her holy aunt, Ethelburga; and Ermenilda, like her mother, in widowhood. Sexburga and Ermenilda were successive abbesses, first at Minster and then at Ely. Sexburga and her husband had built the monastery at Minster.

Ermenburga (d. c. 700), princess of Kent, married the king of Mercia. This couple gave birth to three daughters: **Milburga** (d. 715), **Mildred** (d. c. 700) and **Mildgytha** (d. c. 676). The first child died last and the last child died first. All four women entered Benedictine convents, the mother in her old age and her daughters in their youth. The mother and the first two daughters served as abbesses. Little is known about the third daughter.

Matilda (c. 895-968) married a Germanic king. After her husband died, she repeatedly had to reprimand two of her sons, who fought incessantly for the throne of their father. Her youngest son, **Bruno of Cologne** (925-65), served at the court of his brother the emperor, first as secretary and then as chancellor. He became a priest and later archbishop of Cologne, insisting on high standards in both monastic life and institutions of education. He played a leading role in imperial and ecclesiastical affairs. **Wilfrida**, queen of England (d. c. 988), retired to Wilton Abbey with her daughter **Edith** (962-84) shortly after the child's birth. Numerous allusions to scandalous circumstances suggested that the king was not the father. The mother eventually became a nun and abbess. The pre-1970 Roman Martyrology says of Edith:

"She rather knew not this world than forsook it."[8] At her vow ceremony a man appeared who tempted her by laying on the chapel's floor gold and silver jewelry. She chose to live the simple life of a nun, performing the most menial tasks of the convent and refusing the position of abbess in three monasteries. She likewise declined the throne of queen.

Margaret of Scotland (1045-93) was born and raised in the royal court of her uncle, King Stephen of Hungary. She and her exiled parents had sought refuge there. At age twelve, she and her family fled to the courts in England. At age twenty-one she and her family fled again, this time to Scotland, where four years later she married the king who had given her refuge. She established charities for the poor, reform synods against simony and usury, regulations for marriages, and funding for the arts and education. Her son **David I of Scotland** (1084-1153) went as a child to the Norman court in England, where he married and later returned home to succeed his brother as King of Scotland. David fought for justice, practiced charity and established many sees and monasteries. David was never officially canonized; however, he is listed in both Protestant and Catholic calendars of saints.

Bl. Joan of Aza (d. c. 1190) raised four sons, two of whom are saints. **Dominic** (1170-1221), who started out as an Augustinian canon regular, eventually founded the Order of Preachers to convert the Albigensians and to forestall conversions from Christianity. **Bl. Mannes** (d. c. 1230) joined the new community as one of its sixteen charter members. At Paris, he made the first French Dominican foundation and became chaplain for many convents.

Elizabeth of Hungary (1207-31) married at age fourteen, bore four children in the six years before she was widowed, was forced out of the landgrave's castle, became an exemplary Franciscan tertiary, and died before her twenty-fourth birthday. Her daughter **Bl. Gertrude** (1227-97) was born two weeks after her Crusader father died. At age two Gertrude was placed in a Praemonstratensian abbey. At age twenty-two, she was elected abbess, which post she held for fifty years. She built a church and an almshouse near the monastery and introduced the feast of Corpus Christi into Germany through her monastery.

Bridget of Sweden (1303-73) and her daughter **Catherine** (c. 1331-81) are described in this chapter.

FATHER AND CHILD(REN)

Saturninus (d. 304), a priest of Abitina in North Africa, and forty-nine members of his congregation were arrested during Mass. The charge was possession of a Bible, which the Emperor Diocletian had forbidden. The group was transported to Carthage, where they were tortured and martyred. The congregation included four of his children: **Felix** and **Saturninus**, who were lectors, **Mary** and the young child **Hilarion**.

Both **Nerses I the Great** of Armenia (d. c. 373) and his son, **Isaac the Great** (d. 439), became monks after their wives died at young ages. Each man eventually became the Katholikos of Armenia. Each reformed the clergy and constructed many churches, schools and hospitals. The father suffered exile after he denounced the king for murdering his wife. A new king invited Nerses to a banquet under the guise of healing the division. But the king poisoned to death the revered Katholikos. When Isaac became Katholikos, he continued the moral reforms and institutional developments of his father. He supported the creation of the Armenian alphabet and the Armenian translation of the Bible along with works of the Greek and Syrian doctors of the Church. He developed a national liturgy and the beginnings of a national literature. Isaac, who served as Katholikos for forty-nine years, is regarded as the founder of the Armenian Church.

Father and son, **Hormisdas** (d. 523) and **Silverius** (d. c. 537), were popes who struggled against the Monophysite heresy. Hormisdas composed a creed acceptable to the Monophysites. Part of the "Formula of Hormisdas" provided the "landmark statement on the authority and primacy of the Pope and has been quoted down through the ages to substantiate that claim."[9] Six other popes served during the intervening 13 years before Silverius' term. The son's reign lasted only 17 months. "The new pope was now caught in a fatal web of intrigue."[10] Silverius resisted the restoration of a Monophysite bishop to the see of Constantinople, for which he was banished to the island of Palmaria where he died of starvation.

Ethelbert, king of Kent (560-616), converted to Christianity by the influence of his wife. His daughter **Ethelburga** (d. c. 647) similarly influenced her husband. Ethelbert, the first Christian king of England, "granted religious freedom to his subjects, believing conversion by conviction was the only true conversion."[11] He ruled justly and wisely for fifty-six years. Ethelburga married Edwin of Northumbria, who was baptized by his wife's chaplain, Paulinus.

Authaire (7th century) and his son **Ouen** (c. 610-84) were courtiers for king Dagobert I of France. Ouen served virtuously as lay chancellor, opposing simony and promoting charity. Eventually he became a priest and archbishop of Rouen. He built monasteries and sent missionaries throughout his see.

Arnulf of Metz (d. c. 643) fathered two famous sons. One married Begga (d. 693) and their offspring began the Carolingian dynasty. The other was **Clodulf** (c. 605-c. 696), who followed in his father's footsteps by becoming a priest and a bishop. When Arnulf's wife entered the convent, he entered the monastery, but the citizenry successfully urged him to accept the episcopacy. Clodulf succeeded his father and ruled wisely for forty years. **Richard of Lucca** (d. 720), prince of the West Saxons, raised three saintly children. He made a pilgrimage to Rome with two of his sons, but he died at Lucca, just short of the destination. The sons, **Willibald** (c. 700-86) and **Winebald** (d. 761), later helped their uncle Boniface in the evangelization of the Franks. Their sister

Walburga (d. 779) was appointed abbess of Heidenheim, where she administered a school for the children of nobles.

John (d. c. 1002) and his son **Euthymius** (d. 1028) from Georgia, left home with the family's permission to live as monks on Mount Olympus in Bithynia. Later they founded the Iviron Monastery, whose first two abbots were this father and son. **Vladimir I of Kiev** (c. 975-1015) was introduced to Christianity and the Christian woman whom he would marry, while he was engaged in battle in the Crimea. His conversion in 989 marked the beginning of Christianity in Russia. "He reformed his life, putting aside his five former wives, built schools and churches, destroyed idols, brought Greek missionaries to his realms, exchanged ambassadors with Rome, and aided Boniface with his mission to the Pechangs."[12] In the same year in which their father died, his Christian sons **Boris** (d. 1015) and **Gleb** (d. 1015) were killed by their non-Christian step-brothers, who were rivals for the throne.

King Canute IV (d. c. 1086) and his son **Bl. Charles the Good** (1081-1127) were both slain in church forty-one years apart. The king aided missionaries by building churches but alienated nobles by imposing heavy taxes to support his wars. Revolutionaries followed the royal entourage to the church of St. Alban. After the king had gone to confession and was kneeling at the altar, he was slain. His five-year-old son was raised by his grandfather. Charles ruled justly and charitably as the Count of Flanders. He opposed the profiteers who surfaced during times of famine. While Charles was praying in the church of St. Damian, the profiteers murdered him.

Theodore (d. 1299), Duke of Yaroslav in Russia, ruled in an exemplary Christian way. He gave particular attention to the care of the poor and the propagation of the faith. His two sons by his second marriage, **David** (d. 1321) and **Constantine** (d. 1321), were like the father, "forgiving of injuries, and more mindful of their own obligations than of the delinquencies of others."[13] A few days before his death, Theodore put on the habit of a monk.

Some Japanese parent-and-child saints were martyred during anti-Christian persecutions. **Bl. Michael Cozaki** (d. 1597) and his son **Bl. Thomas** (1582-97) died in support of the faith at Nagasaki.

Notes for Chapter 3

1   *The Confessions of Saint Augustine*, Book 9.10-11, as found in *The Liturgy of the Hours*, vol. IV, pp. 1352-54.

2   *Butler's Lives of the Saints*, vol. IV, p. 266.

3   *The Liturgy of the Hours*, vol. IV, pp. 1328-29.

4   Quoted in Anthony Butkovich, *Revelations*, p. 4.

5   Thérèse of Lisieux, *The Autobiography of St. Thérèse of Lisieux*, pp. 68-69.

6   *Bibliotheca Sanctorum*, art. Guistiniani, Niccolo e Anna Michela.

7   George Poulos, *Orthodox Saints*, vol. II, p. 135.

8   *The Book of Saints*, p. 174.

9   Delaney, *Dictionary of Saints*, p. 290.

10   *The Oxford Dictionary of Popes*, p. 59.

11   Delaney, p. 201.

12   Ibid., p. 578.

13   Ibid., p. 602.

CHAPTER 4

SIBLING SAINTS

Brothers

1. Peter and Andrew
2. James the Elder and John the Beloved Disciple
3. James the Younger and Jude Thaddeus
4. Heraclas and Plutarch
5. Gregory Thaumaturgus and Athenodorus
6. Paphserios, Theodotion and Paul of the Suez
7. Donatian and Rogatian
8. Cosmas and Damian
9. Justus and Pastor
10. Orentius and six brothers
11. Manuel, Sabel and Ismael
12. Honoratus and Venantius
13. Martinian and Saturian
14. Romanus and Lupicinus
15. Vincent of Lerins and Lupus of Troyes
16. Laserian and Goban
17. Fursey, Foillan and Utlan
18. Chad and Cedd
19. Votus and Felix
20. Cyril and Methodius
21. Boris and Gleb
22. Dominic and Bl. Mannes
23. Bl. Ceslau and Hyacinth

Sisters

24. Irene, Agape and Chionia
25. Bl. Blesilla and Eustochium Julia
26. Ermengilda and Ercongota
27. Begga and Gertrude of Nivelles
28. Waldetrudis and Aldegundis
29. Milburga, Mildgytha and Mildred of Portugal
30. Cyneburga and Cyneswide
31. Cuthburga and Quenburga
32. Benedicta and Cecilia
33. Bl. Teresa, Bl. Sanchia and Bl. Mafalda
34. Clare of Assisi and Agnes of Assisi
35. Bl. Cunegund and Bl. Jolenta
36. Bl. Teresa Soiron and Bl. Catherine Soiron
37. Edith Stein and Rosa Stein*

Brother(s) and Sister(s)

38. Martha, Mary and Lazarus of Bethany
39. Basil the Great, Gregory of Nyssa, Peter of Sebastea, and their sister Macrina the Younger
40. Gregory Nazianzen, Caesarius and their sister Gorgonia
41. Ambrose and Marcellina
42. Patrick of Ireland and Tigris
43. Honorata and Epiphanius of Pavia
44. Enda and his sister Fanchea
45. Gibrian's six brothers: Tressan, Helan, Germanus, Veran, Abran and Petran; and three sisters: Franca, Promptia and Possenna
46. Caesarius of Arles and Caesaria

---

* Edith Stein was beatified in 1987, but Rosa Stein has no cause for canonization pending.

47. Benedict and Scholastica
48. Isidore of Seville, Leander, Fulgentius and their sister Florentina
49. Ebba the Elder and her brother Oswald, king of Northumbria
50. Aldetrudis, Dentelinus, Landericus and Madelberta
51. Erconwald and his four sisters: Etheldreda, Ethelburga, Sexburga and Withburga
52. Mauront and his sisters: Eusebia, Adalsind and Clotsind
53. Winebald, Willibald and their sister Walburga
54. Bl. Vitalis and Bl. Adeline
55. Bernard of Clairvaux's four siblings: Bl. Guy, Bl. Gerard, Bl. Nivard and their sister Bl. Humbeline
56. King Louis IX of France and Bl. Isabel
57. Bl. John of Rieti and Bl. Lucy of Amelia
58. Bl. Amadeus da Silva and Bl. Beatrice da Silva

Brothers and Sisters in the Lord: Sibling Saints

Brothers and sisters are the fruit of the same family tree. They bear resemblances based in nature and nurture. "Biologically, brothers and sisters are more closely connected than any other humans, and experts believe the emotional attachment carries a similar impact."[1] They live with and learn from each other. They grow together in the context of family life. This relationship lasts a lifetime. "Some researchers believe that it is psychologically impossible to disassociate oneself from a sibling as one might from a friend or spouse. The relationship is too fundamental, the severing is too wrenching."[2] The sibling relationship forms an irrevocable bond.

The Old and New Testaments relate numerous stories about siblings. On the one hand many brothers and/or sisters manipulated, betrayed, fought with and even killed one other. On the other hand many siblings aided one another in human life for the fulfillment of a divine mission. Jesus used the analogy of the brother and/or sister relationship as the criterion for judgment, the model for caring, and the description of his own relationship with people: "I assure you, as often as you did it for one of my least brothers (and sisters), you did it for me" (Mt 25:40). The sibling-like intimacy demonstrated in the early Christian community led members to refer to one another as brothers and sisters in the Lord. All except two of the twenty-three non-Gospel books of the New Testament witness to this practice.[3]

Sibling saints are especially numerous among all the relationships which we will discuss. Siblings supported each other in the principles and practice of the Christian life. They journeyed together as pilgrims along the path of holiness. This journey was to end face to face with God. The way was easier when a brother or sister shared the way.

Particular examples

1. BASIL THE GREAT AND THREE SIBLINGS

Basil the Great's (329-79) saintly siblings include Gregory of Nyssa (c. 330-c. 395), Peter of Sebastea (c. 340-91) and their sister Macrina the Younger (c. 330-79), who had been named after her grandmother Macrina the Elder.

These four children, like their six other siblings, were well educated. The three brother saints became bishops. They disputed Arianism. They dealt with the hardships caused by famine. Basil, who had been a teacher of rhetoric, became a hermit and later organized his own monastery. Gregory, who also had been a professor of rhetoric, married, was widowed, and then gave himself to religious life. Peter, the youngest of the ten children, entered a monastery founded by his parents and headed by his brother Basil. Macrina, after her father's death, joined her mother in forming a Christian community on the family's country estate.

Gregory of Nyssa was asked by a priest friend to describe his extraordinary sister, Macrina the Younger. Gregory wrote that she often engaged in philosophical discussions with her brothers, spoke forthrightly with them, and as the eldest among the ten children, challenged and corrected them oftentimes. Gregory credits Macrina with keeping their brother Basil's feet on the ground. Basil was deservedly one of the more outstanding persons in his times. He knew it and, at home, he flaunted it. Macrina brought him back down to earth, in ways that only a brother or sister can do! She poked fun at his pride. She mocked his interest in worldly fame. She challenged Basil to renounce passing pleasures in favor of Christian asceticism and eternal life. The brother Gregory writes:

> After the mother had decorously arranged the sisters' affairs, in accordance with what seemed suitable for each one, the great Basil, the brother of the aforesaid woman, returned from school where he had been trained in rhetoric for a long time. She indeed detected that he was enormously puffed up with pride over his rhetorical abilities; he despised all the worthy people and exalted himself in self-importance among all the illustrious men of the province. Yet she drew him with such speed to the goal of philosophy that he renounced worldly renown. He expressed contempt at being an object of marvel on account of his rhetoric. He deserted to this laborious [monk's] life of manual labor to prepare himself by complete poverty and unfettered life directed toward virtue.[4]

2. Clare and Agnes of Assisi

Clare of Assisi (1194-1253) ran away from home on Palm Sunday in 1212 to enter the convent. She had been inspired to commit her life to Christ after hearing a homily preached by Francis of Assisi. This seventeen-year-old girl was followed two weeks later by her fifteen-year-old sister Agnes (c. 1197-1253). The father was furious. He sent armed men to bring his daughters home. They were hiding in a Benedictine convent. The strongmen failed. They could neither persuade nor force the girls to return home. Soon Clare founded the Poor Clares. Not only Agnes but also another sister and their mother eventually joined the community. After seven years in community life, Clare and Agnes became separated when Clare asked Agnes to serve as foundress and abbess in four successive monasteries. The sisters corresponded, but the exchange of numerous letters hardly satisfied Agnes. She had expected to spend the whole of her religious life together with her older sister. After living apart for thirty years in different countries, they came together at the death bed of Clare. Three months later, they were united for eternity when Agnes died. Their relationship exemplifies the anonymous saying: "God made us sisters. Love made us friends." Only one of their letters is extant. The pain of separation permeates the words of Agnes to Clare:

> The lot of all has been so established that one can never remain in the same state or condition. When someone thinks that she is doing well, it is then that she is plunged into adversity. Therefore, you should know, Mother, that my soul and body suffer great distress and immense sadness, that I am burdened and tormented beyond measure and am almost incapable of speaking, because I have been physically separated from you and my other sisters with whom I had hoped to live and die in this world. This distress has a beginning, but it knows no end. It never seems

to diminish; it always gets worse. It came to me recently, but it tends to ease off very little. It is always with me and never wants to leave me. I believed that our life and death would be one, just as our manner of life in heaven would be one, and that we who have one and the same flesh and blood would be buried in the same grave.[5]

3. ISIDORE OF SEVILLE AND THREE SIBLINGS

Isidore of Seville (c. 560-636) and his three siblings, Leander (c. 534-c. 600), Fulgentius (d. c. 633) and their sister Florentina (d. c. 636) accomplished unparalleled achievements for the Church in Spain.

Leander, the oldest of the four children, and a papal diplomat, was appointed archbishop of Seville in 584. Responsible for the conversion of the king, the king's two sons and many of the Visigoths from Arianism, he conducted synods, reformed the liturgy, and unified the Church in Spain. In 600 Leander was succeeded as archbishop by Isidore.

Isidore served as archbishop of Seville for the next thirty-seven years, continuing his brother's work on the unification and revivification of the Church. He completed the composition of the Mozarabic liturgy, convoked additional councils and, although never a monk himself, implemented the renewal of monastic life. One of his councils decreed that every diocese should develop its own seminary. Isidore "was himself an encyclopedic writer on theology, scripture, biography, history, geography, astronomy and grammar."[6] He was a voracious reader and voluminous writer. "St. Isidore seems to have foreseen that unity of religion and a comprehensive educational system would weld together the heterogeneous elements which threatened to disintegrate his country, and it is mainly thanks to him that Spain was a centre of culture when the rest of Europe seemed to be lapsing into barbarism."[7]

Fulgentius and Florentina also dedicated their lives to God and the service of the Church. Fulgentius served as bishop of Ecija in Andalusia. Florentina, who grew up under the guardianship of Leander after her parents had died in her youth, entered a monastery for which Leander had written a rule of life. She eventually became abbess of that and other monasteries. Leander tenderly instructed and encouraged her along the path of holiness:

> Meditate like the dove, holiest sister, and think extensively of the glory that awaits you in the future, in that you have not given in to flesh and blood nor surrendered that most holy body to corruption. Yea, even dare to hope, and realize with what embraces Christ desires to receive you, who have trodden upon the enticements of the world; with what longing the virgin band awaits you, whom the heights of heaven behold hastening up those steps by which that virgin band reaches Christ. Mary, Mother of God, rejoices, too, the supreme example of virginity, mother of incorruption, who by her example bore you and remains pure: she bore you a living proof, yet knew not pain; she bore the Bridegroom, yet is a Virgin.
>
> Realize that your brother's heart desires your safe journey, realize that your brother's most fervent desire is that you should be with Christ. Although I do not have within myself what I wish you to achieve, and may grieve that I have lost what I want you to keep, yet, meanwhile, I shall have some portion of forgiveness if you, the better part of our body, do not walk "in the way of sinners," if you hold most firmly to that which you have.
>
> Finally, I beg you, dear sister, to remember me in your prayers, and do not forget our younger brother Isidore, for his parents rejoiced to leave him in the care of God and of his remaining brothers and sister, and when they journeyed to the Lord, they had no fear for his infancy. Although I love him as my own son and would place nothing on earth above my concern for

him and would give my life for love of him, you should
love him the more dearly and pray to Jesus for him
more sincerely because you know that his parents
were so tenderly fond of him. I am sure that your
prayer as a virgin will win the divine ears to our
attention, and if you keep the pact which you made
with Christ, your good deeds will win you the crown
and Leander's exhortations will achieve your pardon,
and if you persevere so to the end, you will be saved.
Amen.[8]

4. EDITH STEIN AND ROSA

Edith Stein (1891-1942) and Rosa (c. 1884-1942)
died together in the Nazi concentration camp at Auschwitz.
Both women converted to Catholicism, Edith from atheism
as a twenty-six-year-old and Rosa from Judaism two years
before she died. Both women fled their native Germany
and took refuge in a Carmelite convent in Holland. Edith
was a nun in the cloister. Rosa found sanctuary as a visitor
inside the same convent but outside the cloister.

Edith, an intellectual genius, excelled throughout
school in all subjects except mathematics. At age twenty-
five she attained her doctoral degree in philosophy. She
then worked as a graduate assistant to Edmund Husserl,
the famed father of phenomenology. She taught on campus by day and lectured off campus by night. She wrote
two books relating traditional philosophical approaches to
current philosophy and women's issues. She began an
autobiography but completed only the first half of her life
story when the Nazis captured and killed her.

Edith had stopped practicing her Jewish religion even
though her mother remained a devout Jew all her life. At
age thirteen, Edith claimed that she was an atheist. At age
twenty-six she went to console a Christian friend whose
young husband had just died. The widow possessed great
calm because of her faith. Edith later wrote of this incident:

"It was then that I first came face to face with the cross and the divine strength which it gives to those who bear it."[9] While visiting other friends, Edith noticed the autobiography of St. Teresa of Avila. She borrowed the book, read it through the night and finished the text. The next day she bought a Catholic catechism and read that from cover to cover. The following day she went to her first Mass, and after Mass asked the priest to baptize her. The priest inquired about where she had received instructions. She smiled and invited the priest to quiz her. He quizzed her. He baptized her. She wanted to enter the Carmelite order immediately but her concern for her mother's reaction and the advice of her spiritual director persuaded her to wait a dozen years. In 1934, one year after Hitler came to power, Edith entered Carmel where she took the name Sister Teresa Benedicta of the Cross.

Edith wrote that her sister, Rosa, was nicknamed "the Lion":

> It was inspired by her loud roar of rage whenever she was provoked. Of all the children, she was the most difficult to raise. Although in no way lacking talent, she was always a poor student. The most undisciplined boys in the house or in the neighborhood were her best friends. With them she tore through the streets, rang doctors' doorbells, and joined in other pranks boys usually play.[10]

Edith commented that Rosa developed the habit of focusing all her affection and attention on one person. The object of attention changed throughout the years but Edith remained the constant choice with Rosa:

> As I was always rather plain and anemic, she made me the object of particular solicitude. When I accompanied her to the city on errands, she rarely omitted taking me to a small coffee shop where she saw to it that I had a piece of apple cake with whipped cream,

or, in the summer, a dish of ice cream likewise topped with whipped cream. I never begged her for this; but, unintentionally, as we came near our usual haunt (Illgen's Coffee Shop in the Schmiedebrucke, where such marvelous things could be had for fifteen Pfennige) I would peep at the store window out of the corner of my eyes, and immediately, without saying a word, she would head for the entrance.[11]

Edith mentions that "as I grew older I came to have more and more influence on my sister without having made any effort to do so."[12] Edith provides an example of their mother wanting to celebrate another sister's wedding anniversary in the home which the mother and Rosa shared. The mother, knowing Rosa would resist this idea, requested that Edith might suggest it, since Rosa would respect any suggestion that came from Edith. Edith intended to write more about her relationship with Rosa, ending her chapter on family relations by stating: "How it came about that my sister, so much older than myself, allowed herself to be led by me so willingly, and how her path eventually joined my own, I must recount later in the proper context." The translator adds: "The sentence indicates Edith's expectation of completing the story to include her own entrance into Carmel and her sister Rosa's subsequent acceptance into the Catholic Church."[13] Unfortunately, Edith was never able to complete her autobiography.

General Observations

Some siblings encouraged their brothers or sisters to follow the way of the Lord. Andrew led Peter to Jesus. Bernard of Clairvaux led four brothers and a sister to the Cistercian life. Honoratus persuaded his older brother Venantius to become a Christian.

Siblings came to sainthood according to the spirituality of their day. Jesus called to discipleship Andrew and Peter, James and John, and enjoyed the friendship of Mary, Martha and Lazarus. Martyred siblings during the Roman persecutions include the brothers Cosmas and Damian, Heraclas and Plutarch, Donatian and Rogatian who watched his brother being martyred and stepped forward to embrace the same fate, Justus and Pastor, Martinian and Saturian, and the sisters Irene, Agape and Chionia. During the French Revolution Bl. Teresa Soiron and her sister Bl. Catherine Soiron were martyred.

Hermits followed the martyrs as the new Christian heroes. Siblings included the brothers Honoratus and Venantius, Romanus and Lupicinus, and Votus and Felix.

Monastic life attracted many siblings. Brothers include Lupus of Troyes and Vincent of Lerins; the missionaries Fursey, Foillan and Utlan; Goban and Laserian; Chad and Cedd; and Cyril and Methodius. Sisters include Begga and Gertrude; Waldetrudis and Aldegundis; Cuthburga and Quenburga; Benedicta and Cecilia; Teresa, Sanchia, and Mafalda; Clare of Assisi and Agnes; Bl. Cunegund and Bl. Jolenta; Aldetrudis and Madalberta; and Ethelreda, Ethelburga, Sexburga and Withburga. Brother and sister members of monastic orders include Bernard of Clairvaux and his sister Bl. Humbeline; Enda and his sister Fanchea; Bl. Vitalis and his sister Bl. Adelina; Winebald, Willibald and their sister Walburga; Bl. John of Rieti and Bl. Lucy of Amelia; and Bl. Amadeus da Silva and Bl. Beatrice.

The new orders of itinerant friars were represented by the brothers Ceslau and Hyacinth, and brothers Dominic and Bl. Mannes. Many monks had taken marriage vows before religious vows. Bl. Amadeus da Silva had been married briefly before he and his wife agreed to separate so that he could enter religious life. The nuns Waldetrudis, Cuthburga, Etheldreda and Humbeline separated from their husbands to enter religious life. Begga, Sexburga, and the sisters Cunegund and Jolenta were widowed and then entered religious life. The sisters Teresa and Mafalda had their marriages nullified on grounds of consanguinity, thereby enabling them to enter religious life.

These saints represent a variety of careers. The brothers Peter and Andrew, as well as the brothers James the Elder and John were fishermen before becoming apostles. The brothers Cosmas and Damian were physicians as were Caesarius of Nazianzen, and probably Walburga. Gregory Thaumaturgus and his brother Athenodorus were law students. Methodius was governor of the Slavic people. Vincent of Lerins and Gerard of Clairvaux were former soldiers. Oswald of Northumbria and Louis IX of France were kings. Princesses include the sisters Cuthburga and Quenburga; sisters Cunegund and Jolenta; sisters Teresa, Sanchia and Mafalda; Ebba, and Imelda. Bishops include Erconwald, Landericus, the brothers Malachy and Christian, three brothers from one family: Basil the Great, Gregory of Nyssa and Peter of Sebastea; and three brothers from another family: Isidore of Seville, Leander and Fulgentius.

Great frankness characterized the relationships between the sibling saints. No other relationship witnesses to the same direct talk. For example, Martha criticized her sister Mary to Jesus because Martha was busy about household chores and Mary was not. Basil the Great was "puffed up" with pride over his abilities, and his older sister Macrina the Younger verbally corrected him and brought him back down to earth. Scholastica scolded her twin brother Benedict because he interpreted too strictly the rule which limited the time of their conversation. Bernard of Clairvaux chided his sister Humbeline for excessively valuing material possessions. In all these cases, the sibling's challenge proved effective; it was peer counselling at its best.

Among the sibling saints, one brother or sister usually stands out above the others: namely, Peter, John the Beloved Disciple, Malachy, Dominic, Gertrude of Nivelles, Clare of Assisi, Cunegund, Basil the Great, Gregory Nazianzen, Ambrose, Patrick, Isidore of Seville, Bernard of Clairvaux, and Louis IX.

The chapter on parent-child saints mentions that in some families all the living children became recognized as saints, namely: Gregory Nazianzen and his brother Caesarius and sister Gorgonia; the sisters Aldetrudis and Madelberta and their brothers Dentelinus and Landericus; and Winebald, Willibald and their sister Walburga. A situation in which all the siblings are saints, but neither parent is, are the sisters Etheldreda, Ethelburga, Sexburga and Withburga and their brother Erconwald.

In other families many but not all siblings became renowned for sanctity. The chapter on parent-child saints already named four saints among the ten children in the family of Basil the Great, Gregory of Nyssa, Peter of Sebastea and their sister Macrina the Younger. Of Bernard of Clairvaux's six brothers and sisters, three were saints: the brothers Gerard and Nivard and their sister Humbeline. Of Isidore of Seville's four siblings, three were saints: the brothers Leander and Fulgentius and their sister Florentina.

In some large families only one of the siblings became a saint. These persons cannot be included in our list. Interestingly, each of the saints in mind was the youngest in the family; Catherine of Siena was the youngest of twenty-five children; Ignatius of Loyola, of thirteen children; and Thérèse of Lisieux, of nine. None of these saints enjoyed a sibling saint.

Some saints have no chance to be included here because they were the only child. Most notable are John the Baptist, Pope Gregory the Great and John Chrysostom.

There are three pairs of twins who are saints: Cosmas and Damian, the brother physicians who cared for the poor gratuitously; John and Benignus, monks under Hildulphus; and the monk Benedict, and his nun sister Scholastica. Three other saints were twins, but in each case their twin was not recognized as a saint: Thomas Aquinas, whose sister was struck by lightning as an infant as the two lay side by side; Catherine of Siena, whose sister died in infancy; and Thomas the apostle, of whose twin nothing is known.

Application Of The Theme:

Common Vision: These brothers and sisters had a similar outlook on life. They wanted to follow the will of God as revealed in the person of Jesus Christ. Oftentimes an older sibling even educated a younger one to these sacred matters.

Common Way: Similar vision led to similar mission. Similar goals led to similar means. They walked or ran together along the way of righteousness. They eschewed the way of evil. Oftentimes they did together what they did for God and God's people.

Common Bond With Each Other: The reality of common challenges and crises forced them to turn to each other for support. Together they had fled from home, careers, wealth or safety in order to seek ineffable and immeasurable spiritual treasures. These similar experiences led to similar feelings. They were *simpatico* with each other.

Common Bond With God: What originally motivated and ultimately satisfied these siblings was life with each other and especially life with God. Success was measured by union with God. They supported each other to leave all things for God.

APPENDIX: SIBLING SAINTS

BROTHERS

The fishermen **Peter** (d. c. 64) and **Andrew** (1st century) lived in Bethsaida near Lake Tiberias. Andrew, a disciple of John the Baptist, met Jesus when he was being baptized at the Jordan River. Andrew, who was Jesus' first disciple, invited Simon to hear Jesus. The brothers were busy with their fishing nets when Jesus called them. Jesus gave Simon the name Peter, meaning Rock. Peter is mentioned in the Gospels more frequently than any other apostle.

The fishermen **James the Elder** (d. 42) and **John** "the disciple whom Jesus loved" (c. 6-c. 104) were repairing their nets at Lake Genesareth when Jesus called them. These two along with Peter accompanied Jesus at his Transfiguration, the Agony in the Garden, and various miracles. James, the oldest of the apostles, was the first apostle to be martyred. John, the youngest of the apostles, was the only one among the Twelve not martyred. John alone stood at the foot of the cross and received Mary into his care.

James the Younger (d. 62) and **Jude Thaddeus** (1st century), relatives of Jesus, were apostles. James became head of the Christian community at Jerusalem. To him Peter sent news of his escape, and Paul sent news of his missionary journeys. James decreed that Gentile converts did not have to observe the usual array of Jewish laws. Jude, also known as Thaddeus, served in Mesopotamia and Persia.

The Egyptians **Heraclas** (c. 180-247) and **Plutarch** (d. c. 202) were the first students and converts at Origen's catechetical school in Alexandria. Many of the students were arrested and executed during the persecution of Emperor Septimus Severus. Plutarch died at this time. Heraclas escaped. He became Origen's assistant and successor as head of the school. He was appointed patriarch in 231. When Origen, who had been condemned by the previous patriarch for his theological views, returned to Alexandria, Heraclas excommunicated him.

While **Gregory Thaumaturgus**, "the wonder worker," (c. 213-68) and **Athenodorus** (d. c. 269) were traveling from their native Neocaesarea to Beirut to continue their legal studies, they met Origen at Caesarea. The brothers changed their career plans and entered Origen's catechetical school. They became converts. Gregory returned home about 238 and was soon elected bishop, reportedly by the seventeen Christians of the city, and at his death there were only seventeen non-Christians left in Neocaesarea.[14] Athenodorus became a bishop in Pontus and was martyred during the reign of Emperor Aurelian.

Paphserios (d. 3rd century), **Paul** (d. 3rd century) and **Theodotion** (d. 3rd century) were raised as Christians in their native Suez region of Egypt. When their parents died, two of the brothers entered a monastery while Theodotion opted to make his way as a highway robber. All were successful at what they did! Eventually the brother monks were seized for martyrdom as Christians. Theodotion returned to the city to rescue his brothers. When he saw that their release was impossible despite his skill at nefarious undertakings, he broke through the crowd to join his brothers in declaring the faith and greeting death.

Donatian (d. 289 or 304) and **Rogatian** (d. 289 or 304) were martyred in their native Nantes, Brittany during the persecution of Emperor Maximian. After Donatian was arrested, he refused to offer incense to the Roman gods. Rogatian, who had not yet formally converted to Christianity, then stepped forward to stand with his brother and declared his faith. Both were beheaded.

Cosmas (d. 303) and **Damian** (d. 303), who are traditionally believed to be twins, were born in Arabia, studied medicine in Syria and practiced in Cilicia. Reportedly they offered their medical skills free of charge to those in need. They were arrested and beheaded during the Diocletian persecution. Some sources say that three of their brothers — Anthimus, Euprepius and Leontius — were martyred with them.

Justus (d. c. 304) and **Pastor** (d. c. 304), when thirteen and nine years old respectively, were scourged and beheaded at Alcala in Spain during the general persecution of Emperor Diocletian.

In approximately 304 during the persecution of Maximian seven brothers died for the faith. All were Roman soldiers. When the leader of the opposing Scythians challenged one soldier to step forward to do battle in order to avoid needless loss of others' lives, **Orentius**, the strongest of the siblings and of the entire camp, volunteered. Just before exchanging the first blows, Orentius fell to his knees in prayer. He easily defeated his opponent. Orentius was hailed as champion but he claimed that Jesus should be hailed for the strength he gave him. The six brothers agreed. All were exiled to northern Armenia where they suffered mistreatment and died. The other brothers are named **Heros**, **Pharnacius**, **Firminus**, **Firmus**, **Cyriacus** and **Longinus**.

In the year 362, Persian political leaders selected three brothers to serve as ambassadors of peace in the on-going conflict with the Roman emperor Julian the Apostate. The brothers **Manuel**, **Sabel** and **Ismael** happened to be Christians. At the banquet before negotiations, all the guests were invited to pay homage to the Roman gods. The Christian brothers humbly declined. Julian became enraged and had them beheaded.

As a youth **Honoratus** (d. 429) renounced paganism and dedicated himself to live as a Christian hermit. He persuaded his older brother **Venantius** (d. c. 400) to do the same. The two settled on an island near Cannes, then traveled to the East to study the monastic life. Upon returning to their native Gaul, they encouraged their relative Hilary of Arles and their friend Caprasius to join them in the monastic life. Honoratus later founded the famous Lerins monastery and was named archbishop of Arles. Venantius died as a young monk at Modon in Morea.

Four brothers who grew up in the African region of Mauretania served as slaves to three successive masters before being martyred. During the first enslavement, **Martinian** (d. 458), **Saturian** (d. 458) and their two brothers were converted to Christianity by a slave woman named Maxima. The slave master insisted that Martinian and Maxima marry. She, however, had taken a vow of virginity. She and Martinian fled. When they returned, they were beaten. All five Christians were later sold to a Vandal. He released Maxima, who then entered a convent. He re-sold the four men to a Berber chief. Because the four slaves converted many Berbers to Christianity, the master dragged them by horses until they died.

Romanus (d. c. 460) at age thirty-five became a hermit in the Jura Mountains between Switzerland and France. **Lupicinus** (d. 480) and their sister and other women joined him in the eremetical life. The brothers built two monasteries for men, over which they ruled jointly, and a women's monastery, St. Romain de la Roche, over which their sister was appointed abbess.

Lupus of Troyes (c. 383-478) and **Vincent of Lerins** (d. c. 445) are probably brothers. Vincent abandoned his military career in order to enter the Lerins abbey where he wrote his *Commonitorium* which contains the fundamental teaching that the only doctrines to be held true are those that have been held "always, everywhere and by all the faithful."[15] Lupus was a monk at Lerins and missionary to Britain before serving as bishop of Troyes.

Goban (7th century) served as a missionary to England and France before becoming abbot of Leighlin monastery in southern Ireland. **Laserian** (d. 639), who had lived at the monastery of Iona, was ordained by Pope Gregory the Great, served as papal legate to Ireland, defended the use of the Roman instead of the Celtic liturgy, and became bishop of Leighlin, succeeded Goban as abbot.

Irish missionary monks include **Fursey** (d. c. 648), **Foillan** (d. c. 655) and **Utlan** (d. 686). Fursey had founded a monastery in Ireland where he lived for a dozen years before going to England. All three brothers moved to England to evangelize the East Angles. When their monastery was attacked after many years, they moved to France and established a monastery there.

The Englishmen **Chad** (d. 672) and **Cedd** (d. 644) studied at Landisfarne before returning to the East Angles as missionary monks where they later were appointed bishops. Cedd abandoned the Celtic rite in favor of the Roman observances.

Votus (d. c. 750) and **Felix** (d. c. 750) left their native Saragossa to establish a hermitage in the Pyrenees near Aragon. John of Atares accepted them into his laura. All three saints died there.

Cyril (c. 825-69) and **Methodius** (c. 826-84) evangelized the Slavic people, created an alphabet to translate liturgical texts into the vernacular, and laid the foundation for Slavic literature. Cyril was a deacon who many years later was ordained a priest. Shortly before his death, he took the habit of a monk and at that time changed his name from Constantine to Cyril. Methodius had studied for a position in the imperial government before becoming a monk. Both brothers had served as missionaries to the Jewish Khazars before they were appointed as missionaries to the Slavs. Their ministry among the Slavs was hindered by tension with German missionaries who resented the brothers' use of the vernacular. The German bishop even refused to ordain the brothers' candidates for priesthood. In 863 Cyril and Methodius traveled to Rome, at whose initiative is not clear, and there the pope authorized that the two brothers be ordained bishops, that they ordain their candidates to priesthood, and that the Slavic vernacular be used in the liturgy. Some question remains whether or not Cyril was ordained bishop. The brothers continued their ministry in the midst of opposition, which lasted until their deaths.

Boris (d. 1015) and **Gleb** (d. 1015), sons of Vladimir, were murdered in separate incidents by an older and pagan step-brother who wished to eliminate them as rivals for the family's inheritance. The two victims, following their Christian calling to be peaceful persons, refused to vie with physical force for what was rightfully theirs.

Before **Dominic** (1170-1221) founded the Order of Preachers, he was an ordained Augustinian canon regular. He accompanied his bishop into the regions where Albigensianism flourished. His preaching won many converts. In fact, some Albigensian nuns provided the model of his later community of friars. He founded his community in 1214 and two years later it received Roman approval. His brother **Bl. Mannes** (d. c. 1230) was one of the original sixteen members. Immediately after taking vows, Mannes and six other friars were missioned to Paris to establish the first French Dominican house. The next year he was sent to Madrid, where he remained the rest of his life as chaplain to Dominican nuns. Dominic was canonized thirteen years after his death. Mannes' cult was approved 604 years after his death.

Hyacinth (1185-1257) and **Bl. Ceslau** (d. 1242) appear to have been brothers. They were born in Poland, traveled to Rome and were received as Dominicans by Dominic. They evangelized the peoples of Eastern Europe. Ceslau was elected provincial of the Polish province. Hyacinth was regarded as one of Poland's great apostles.

SISTERS

Irene (d. 304), **Agape** (d. 304) and **Chionia** (d. 304) of Thessalonica along with many companions were burned to death during the persecution of Emperor Diocletian. The sisters were charged with possessing scriptural texts. They refused to offer sacrifice to the pagan gods. Irene's death was delayed for two days while she was sent to a brothel.

Bl. Blesilla (363-83) and **Eustochium Julia** (d. c. 419), daughters of Paula, were members of the prayer group led by Jerome at Rome.

Ermengilda (d. 703) and **Ercongota** (d. c. 660) are the daughters of the king of Kent and Sexburga. Ermengilda, like her mother, married and then separated from her husband to enter the convent. Ermengilda went to her mother's convent, succeeded her as abbess, and eventually joined her mother at a second convent. Ercongota traveled to Gaul, where she lived as a nun under her aunt Ethelburga at the abbey of Faremoutier.

Begga (d. 693) and **Gertrude** (626-59) became saints like their parents. Begga married the son of Bishop Arnulf of Metz. Their son founded the Carolingian dynasty in France. After her husband died in 691, Begga built a church and convent, which she entered just before her death. When Gertrude was thirteen years old, her father died and her mother built a monastery of men and women at Nivelles. Mother and daughter entered the same monastery and Gertrude became its first abbess.

Waldetrudis (d. c. 688) and **Aldegundis** (630-84) became saints like their parents. Waldetrudis' husband and four children also became saints. After eight years of marriage Waldetrudis and her husband separated in order to enter religious life. He became a monk and she founded a convent at Mons. Aldegundis joined her older sister in the convent. The younger sister's hermitage developed into the Benedictine monastery of Mons.

The princesses of Mercia, **Cyneburga** (7th century) and her sister **Cyneswide** (7th century), both entered the convent. The latter succeeded the former as abbess. Cyneburga was married and widowed before she became a nun.

Milburga (d. c. 700 or 722), **Mildgytha** (d. c. 676) and **Mildred** (d. c. 700 or 725), daughters of Ermenburga, all became nuns. The latter two entered the convent founded by their mother and succeeded her as abbess. The first daughter was the founding abbess of another convent.

Cuthburga (d. c. 725) and **Quenburga** (8th century), sisters of the king of Wessex, co-founded the abbey at Wimborne which later provided many of the nuns who evangelized Germany. Cuthburga became the first abbess of this Benedictine convent. She had married in 688 but the couple later separated so that she might enter the convent.

The princesses **Benedicta** (10th century) and **Cecilia** (10th century), daughters of the king of Lorraine, entered religious life and served as successive abbesses of Susteren in the Rhineland.

Bl. Teresa (d. 1250), **Bl. Sanchia** (1182-1229) and **Bl. Mafalda** (1204-52) were daughters of the royal family of Portugal. Sanchia (c. 1180-1229) helped to develop the first Franciscan and Dominican houses in Portugal, and then she joined the Cistercians at Cella. Teresa (d. 1250) married her cousin the king of Leon, but the Holy See declared the marriage null on grounds of consanguinity. She returned to Portugal and entered the Cistercian convent at Lorvao. Mafalda (1203-52) married the king of Castile when she was only twelve. This marriage was later nullified by the Holy See on the grounds of consanguinity. She then entered the Cistercian convent of Arouca.

The lives of **Clare of Assisi** (1194-1253) and her sister **Agnes** (c. 1197-1253), are described in this chapter.

The Hungarian princesses **Bl. Cunegund** (1224-92) and **Bl. Jolenta** (d. 1299) entered the Poor Clare convent after their husbands died in 1279. Cunegund passed her widowhood at the convent at Sandeck. Jolenta entered religious life at Sandeck but later joined the convent at Gnesen. Cunegund generously built churches, hospitals and convents, and ransomed Christians from the Turks. She raised Jolenta from her childhood. Jolenta is known also as Helen of Poland.

Bl. Teresa Soiron (d. 1794) and **Bl. Catherine Soiron** (d. 1794) died together during the French Revolution. Teresa had been working as a maid in the service of one of the king's daughters until the royal family fled the city for safety's sake. Teresa and her sister then attached themselves to the Carmelite convent at Compiegne. The two worked as doorkeepers. They were not in vows but were guillotined nonetheless with the Carmelite Sisters in 1794.

Edith Stein (1891-1942) and her sister **Rosa** (c. 1884-1942) are presented in this chapter.

BROTHERS AND SISTERS

Mary (1st century), **Martha** (1st century) and **Lazarus** (1st century) appear many times in the Gospels. They lived in the family home at Bethany. Martha was busy about many household chores when Jesus visited on one occasion. Martha also ran outside to greet Jesus, who came to their home after he heard that Lazarus had died. Mary has oftentimes been identified with Mary Magdalene but insufficient evidence exists to support this. Lazarus was a dear friend of Jesus, and was raised from the dead by him.

Basil the Great (329-79), **Gregory of Nyssa** (c. 330-c. 395), **Peter of Sebastea** (c. 340-91) and their sister **Macrina the Younger** (c. 330-79) are treated in this chapter.

Gregory Nazianzen (c. 329-89), **Caesarius** (c. 329-69) and their sister **Gorgonia** (d. c. 372) were the children of sainted parents. Gorgonia, the oldest of the three, married and raised three children of her own. She and her husband were baptized well after the middle years of their lives. Gregory eulogized at her funeral that she loved the spiritual services of the Church, made generous donations to the Church, and freely gave of her time and wealth to the poor. Caesarius served as physician to two emperors and as treasurer for a third emperor. He was baptized while serving as treasurer. He willed that at his death that his wealth be distributed to the poor. Gregory studied with Basil the Great in Cappadocia and Athens. After completing studies, Gregory went home for a short while, then rejoined Basil for two more years in the solitary life. When his octogenarian father became ill, Gregory again returned home. His father, a bishop, insisted on ordaining Gregory a priest, who reluctantly submitted. Gregory assisted his father for ten years before being appointed bishop of Sasima by Basil. Gregory never went to his see which had been created to infringe on the jurisdictional claims of an Arian bishop. Sasima was a hotbed of Arianism. Gregory stayed at home where his preaching won many converts from Arianism and Apollinarism. At age forty-six he suffered an apparent break-down. After five years' recovery and the lessening of imperial persecution he returned to public life as archbishop of Constantinople. Within months, however, hostilities began anew. He convoked the Council of Constantinople in 381 and months later resigned his see in the hope that his absence would help to restore peace. He spent the last eight years of his life in private retirement.

Ambrose (c. 340-97), bishop of Milan, dedicated his treatise on virginity to his sister **Marcellina** (d. c. 398). These two were born in Trier to the prefect of Gaul. They moved to Rome when they were children. Marcellina entered religious life. She practiced great austerities which her brother repeatedly encouraged her to moderate. Ambrose consistently confronted emperors and Arians who were on the verge of restoring paganism and Arianism to the Empire. "More than any other man he was responsible for the rise of Christianity in the West as the Roman Empire was dying."[16]

Patrick of Ireland (c. 389-c. 461) and one of his five sisters, **Tigris** (5th century), are renowned; he is regarded as the Apostle of Ireland, and she is esteemed as the mother of five sons, all of whom became bishops. Fact and fiction are difficult to distinguish in Patrick's life. He was born in Britain as the son of a Roman official. At age sixteen he was captured and carried off to Ireland to do slave labor. Six years later he escaped. He studied for three years at the monastery of Lerins, and for another two years at Auxerre. After fifteen years of priesthood at Auxerre, he was ordained a bishop in 432 by Germanus to replace Paulinus in Ireland. Patrick converted practically the whole island to Christian belief and practices. He lived there for about thirty years.

Epiphanius (439-96) and his sister, **Honorata** (d. c. 500) came from Pavia in northern Italy. Epiphanius was elected bishop of Pavia in 467. He became known as the "Peacemaker" for his successful interventions with the invading Ostrogoths, Visigoths and Burgundians. He converted many people by his faith-filled words and charitable deeds, especially for the hungry. Honorata, a nun, who along with many other townsfolk was taken hostage by the Ostrogoths, was ransomed by her brother.

Enda (d. c. 530) and his sister **Fanchea** (d. c. 530) entered monastic life. She had repeatedly encouraged him to cease his warring, settle down and marry. He finally agreed but his fiancée died before they could marry. He decided to become a monk. He made a pilgrimage to Rome, was ordained, returned to Ireland and there built many churches and monasteries. With Finnian, Enda is regarded as the founder of monasticism in Ireland. Fanchea is believed to have been the founding abbess of a convent.

Gibrian (d. c. 515) led his six brothers and three sisters from Ireland to Brittany where all ten became solitaries and saints. They lived separately but close enough together so that they could visit from time to time. Gibrian, the oldest and a priest, was their leader. The brothers were named **Tressan**, **Helan**, **Germanus**, **Veran**, **Abran** and **Petran**. The sisters were named **Franca**, **Promptia** and **Possenna**.

Caesarius of Arles (470-543) and his sister **Caesaria** (d. c. 529) contributed immensely to the development of the Church in Gaul. She served as abbess in a monastery he had founded. She supervised several hundred nuns and cared for the poor, the sick and children. Caesarius became a monk at age twenty and a bishop at age thirty. He reformed ecclesiastical discipline, presided at numerous Church councils, protected the faith against Arianism and semi-Pelagianism, and defended the city of Arles against the Visigoths and Ostrogoths. "During the distress caused by the siege of Arles in 508 he sold the treasures of his church to relieve the poor."[17]

The twins **Benedict** (c. 480-c. 547) and **Scholastica** (d. 543) were born in Nursia, Italy. Benedict studied in Rome but the immorality of city life repulsed him. In 500 he fled to Subiaco where for three years he lived a hermit's life in a cave. Word of his holiness and learning spread. Neighboring monks invited him to be their abbot. He agreed and applied to them his own strict rule. They disagreed with that, and tried to poison him. He returned to his cave. Another group of disciples urged him to be their spiritual leader. He organized them into twelve monasteries. Again he applied his strict rule of life. Again some tried to undermine his work. Finally he fled in 525 to Monte Casino. There he reconverted the townspeople to Christianity and founded the monastery which is the birthplace of Western monasticism. He developed his rule of prayer, work and study in the context of a stable and obedient community which lived the ascetical life in moderation. Scholastica founded a convent nearby under her brother's direction. They visited each other once a year.

The family of **Isidore of Seville** (c. 560-636), **Leander** (c. 534-c. 600), **Fulgentius** (d. c. 633), and their sister **Florentina** (d. c. 636) is described in this chapter.

Ebba the Elder (d. 683) was sister to **Oswald**, king of Northumbria (c. 605-42). Oswald fled to Scotland in 617 when his father was killed in battle. There at Iona he converted to Christianity. In 634 Oswald became king of Northumbria. He attributed his military success to a vision of St. Columba and to a large cross he had erected the night before a great battle. The king wanted to convert his people to Christianity. For this purpose he invited Aidan to preach the Gospel, gave Aidan the island of Lindisfarne as his see, and built many churches and monasteries. Ebba refused to marry the king of Scotland because she preferred to be a nun at Lindisfarne. She built two monasteries, the second of which included both men and women. She became its first abbess. Her monasteries later became notorious for their laxity of discipline.

Aldetrudis (d. c. 696), **Dentelinus** (7th century), **Landericus** (seventh century) and **Madelberta** (d. 706) are the children of sainted parents. Aldetrudis and Madelberta were confided to the care of their aunt Aldegundis, who founded the monastery of Maubeuge. The older sister became the second abbess of the Benedictine monastery, and the younger sister became the third abbess. Dentelinus died as a seven-year-old child. Landericus served as bishop of Meaux from 641-50. When his father Vincent died, Landericus resigned his see to succeed his father as abbot of Soignies.

Erconwald (d. c. 686) and his sisters **Etheldreda** (d. 679), **Ethelburga** (d. c. 678), **Sexburga** (c. 635-d. c. 699) and **Withburga** (d. c. 743) became Benedictines, and all except the youngest sister served as heads of their respective monasteries. The brother was appointed bishop of London in 675. Etheldreda claims an unusual distinction: "twice married, she remained a virgin."[18] She later entered the nunneries at Coldingham under Ebba, and at Ely where she herself became abbess. Ethelburga became the first abbess of a double monastery founded by her brother at Barking. Sexburga married the king of Kent and begot two daughters who in turn were renowned for sanctity: Ermengilda and Ercongota. When Sexburga was widowed in 664, she entered the convent of Minster which she had founded; and fifteen years later she transferred to Ely, where she became abbess. Withburga, the youngest of the four sisters, lived a solitary life at Holkham, Norfolk for several years. After her father was killed in battle, she entered the convent which she had founded at East Dereham. To provide for the numerous disciples who gathered around her, she constructed a church and convent.

Mauront (d. 701) and his three sisters **Eusebia** (d. c. 680), **Adalsind** (c. 715) and **Clotsind** (c. 635-714), like their widowed mother, entered Benedictine monasteries. The mother founded the double monastery at Marchiennes, where her oldest son, Eusebia and Clotsind joined her. When Eusebia was elected abbess back at Hamage, where she had lived prior to joining her mother at Marchiennes, Adalsind joined her older sister at Hamage.

Winebald (d. 761), **Willibald** (c. 700-86) and their

sister **Walburga** (d. 799) left England to assist their cousin, Boniface, in missionary work with the German people. In 721, while the brothers had been traveling with their father to Rome, Winebald became ill and remained at Rome, while Willibald continued on pilgrimage and became the first Englishman to visit the Holy Land. After many years of study and prayer, both brothers entered monastic life. Around 740 they joined Boniface. In 748 the brothers were joined by Walburga, who had been educated, apparently in medicine, in the monastery in England. The brothers later founded a double monastery at Heidenheim. Willibald appointed Winebald and Walburga abbot and abbess at the double monastery. When Winebald died, Willibald became abbot. When Willibald died, Walburga became abbess of both monasteries until her death thirteen years later. Willibald served also as bishop of Eichstatt for forty-five years,

 Bl. Vitalis (c. 1063-1122) and his sister **Bl. Adeline** (d. 1125) descended from their good but not canonized grandfather William the Conqueror. Vitalis lived for seventeen years as a hermit before founding a Benedictine monastery at Savigny in Normandy, which monastery then served as the motherhouse for numerous monasteries throughout France and England. Adeline was abbess of one of the houses in Normandy.

 In 1112 **Bernard of Clairvaux** (1090-1153) persuaded thirty-one of his friends and family members, including four brothers, to enter the monastery of Citeaux which had been founded just fourteen years earlier. Bernard was the third son in a family of six sons and one daughter; his sister was the middle child. Bernard's second brother **Bl. Gerard** (d. 1138) was too engrossed in military life to enter the monastery. A severe wound and a long imprisonment, however, helped to convince him: *"sic transit gloria mundi."* Upon his release from military prison, Gerard joined his brother and became Bernard's confidant. Little is known of Bernard's oldest and youngest brothers, namely, **Bl. Guy** (12th century) and **Bl. Nivard** (c. 1100-c. 1150). When the troupe was first leaving home, Guy allegedly shouted back to his youngest brother who was remaining home: "You will have all the estates and lands to yourself," whereas Nivard retorted: "What! you then take heaven and leave me only the earth. The division is too unequal."[19] Nivard soon followed. He eventually became novice master in the community. **Bl. Humbeline** (1092-1135) too remained home when her brothers first left for the monastery. She later married a wealthy man and lived a very comfortable life. She visited her brother at Clairvaux and he criticized her for her ostentatious dress and worldly lifestyle. This encounter led to her conversion. She received from her husband consent to become a nun. She entered the Benedictine convent near Troyes and eventually became abbess. She founded a Cistercian monastery for others although she remained a Benedictine herself. She died in Bernard's arms.

Louis IX, king of France, (1214-70) has gained the reputation of being one of the greatest of the French kings. While he went to war on some occasions, he generally developed skill as an arbitrator. He achieved much political peace between warring factions and nations, worked for justice between lords and vassals, and founded numerous religious and educational institutions. His sister **Bl. Isabel** (d. 1270) refused many suitors in order to dedicate her virginity to God. She founded and entered a monastery, although she never became a nun. She spent her life ministering to the sick and poor.

Bl. Lucy of Amelia (d. 1350) and **Bl. John of Rieti** (d. 1350) embraced the Augustinian spirit. He joined the Hermits of St. Augustine and became famous for his concern for all people, especially the sick. She joined the local Augustinian monastery, became their abbess and was famous for her austerities.

Bl. Amadeus da Silva (1420-82) and his sister **Bl. Beatrice da Silva** (1424-90) abandoned the frivolities of the Portuguese courtly life in order to pursue the monastic life. He had recently married but soon decided instead to enter a monastery. He joined the Franciscans. He became a reformer among the order and confessor to the pope. She had been raised at court with the famous Isabel. While Isabel became queen, Beatrice chose to become a Cistercian nun. Beatrice founded a women's community in a castle donated by Isabel.

Notes for Chapter 4

[1]   "Brothers and Sisters," *Christopher News Notes*. July, 1991, p. 2.

[2]   Ibid., p. 3.

[3]   The exceptions are Titus and 2 John.

[4]   Quoted by Elizabeth Clark, *Women in the Early Church*, p. 241.

[5]   *Clare of Assisi: Early Documents*, pp. 105-6.

[6]   *The Book of Saints*, p. 286.

[7]   *Butler's Lives of the Saints*, vol. II, p. 26.

[8]   *Iberian Fathers*, pp. 188-89, and pp. 27-28.

[9]   Ann Ball, *Modern Saints*, p. 375.

[10]   Edith Stein, *Life in a Jewish Family: 1891-1916*, p. 50.

[11]   Ibid., p. 51.

[12]   Ibid., p. 114.

[13]   Ibid., p. 475, n. 27.

[14]   Butler, vol. IV, pp. 363-64.

[15]   Delaney, *Dictionary of Saints*, p. 575.

[16]   Ibid., p. 49.

[17]   *The Book of Saints*, p. 106.

[18]   Ibid., p. 191.

[19]   Butler, vol. III, p. 361.

CHAPTER 5

SAINTLY RELATIVES

Grandparent(s)-Grandchild(ren)

1. Joachim and Anne for Jesus
2. Macrina the Elder for Basil the Great, Macrina the Younger, Gregory of Nyssa and Peter of Sebastea
3. Melania the Elder and Melania the Younger
4. Clotilde and Clodaldus
5. Gertrude of Hamage and Eusebia
6. Romaricus and Gertrude of Remiremont
7. Adele and Gregory of Utrecht
8. Ludmilla and Good King Wenceslaus
9. Olga and Vladimir

Aunt/Uncle-Niece/Nephew

10. Heliodorus and Nepotian
11. Eustochium Julia and Melania the Younger
12. Honoratus and Hilary of Arles
13. Patrick of Ireland and Mel
14. Patrick of Ireland and Loman
15. Tarsilla and Emilianna were nieces to Pope Felix II
16. Tarsilla and Emilianna were aunts to Pope Gregory the Great
17. Gall of Clermont and Gregory of Tours
18. Columba and Colman of Lann Elo

19. King Edwin and Hilda
20. King Edwin and King Oswald of Northumbria
21. Arnulf and Goercius
22. Eugene of Toledo and Ildephonsus
23. Gregory of Utrecht and Alberic of Utrecht
24. Ottilia and Remigius
25. Ottilia and Gundelindis
26. Plato of Bithynia and Theodore Studites
27. Adalbero and Ulric
28. Edith of Polesworth and Edith of Wilton
29. Alphege and Dunstan
30. Emperor Henry II and his wife Cunegund for Emeric
31. King Stephen of Hungary and Queen Margaret of Scotland
32. King Stephen of Hungary and Margaret's son David
33. Alexis Falconieri and Julianna Falconieri
34. Hedwig and Elizabeth of Hungary
35. Elizabeth of Hungary and Elizabeth of Portugal
36. Bl. James Duckett and Bl. John Duckett

Cousins

37. Mary and Elizabeth
38. Jesus and John the Baptist
39. Jesus and James the Younger, Simon, Jude Thaddeus
40. Mark and Barnabas
41. The sisters Cyneburga and Cyneswide to Tibba
42. Boniface and Lull
43. Boniface and Lioba
44. Lioba and Thecla
45. The brothers Hyacinth and Bl. Ceslau to Bl. Bronislava
46. Ven. Charles de Foucauld and Marie de Bondy*

---

* Charles de Foucauld was declared Venerable in 1978. Marie de Bondy has no cause for canonization pending.

In-laws

47. Hilary of Arles was brother-in-law to Lupus of Troyes
48. Pope Agapitus I was distant relative to Pope Gregory the Great
49. King Stephen of Hungary was brother-in-law to the couple, Emperor Henry II and Cunegund

The Tree of Life: Saintly Relatives

Relatives provide deep roots for the full flowering of any family tree. They are part of one's family before one's birth and remain so after one's death. Relatives connect us physically, emotionally and spiritually with a ready made community. Friends may come and go but the blood relation continues forever.

Throughout the Scriptures frequent references are made to kin. According to the Old Testament kinship provides a sense of belonging, security and responsibility. Successive generations received and handed on the covenant between Yahweh and Israel "so that you and your son and your grandson may fear the Lord, your God" (Dt 6:2). According to the New Testament Jesus' relatives provided his earliest disciples and the context whereby his neighbors knew him. The local folk wondered how he had ever gained so much knowledge and wisdom. "Is this not the carpenter, the son of Mary, a brother of James and Joses and Judas and Simon? Are not his sisters our neighbors here?" (Mk 6:3).

Numerous grandparents and grandchildren, aunts and uncles with nieces and nephews, cousins and in-laws are counted among the saints. Saintly relatives supplied not only familial but also religious identity. They provided personal example and encouragement on behalf of religious values. Oftentimes one extended family member influenced another member so positively that the latter followed the former's path of sanctity.

Particular examples

1. HILARY OF ARLES AND HIS UNCLE HONORATUS

Hilary of Arles (c. 400-49) was converted from pagan ways to the Christian faith by his uncle and good friend Honoratus (c. 350-429). Hilary had busied himself with high public office in Lorraine until Honoratus convinced Hilary to visit the monastery of Lerins which Honoratus had recently founded. Hilary resisted. Honoratus insisted: "I will obtain from God what you will not concede."[1] A few days later Hilary acquiesced and followed Honoratus to Lerins. There Hilary delighted in the experience of the monastic life, sought Christian baptism, sold his belongings and gave the money to the poor. Uncle and nephew lived the monastic life in exemplary fashion. In 426 Honoratus was appointed bishop of Arles. The uncle took his nephew along with him to serve as his secretary. Three years later Honoratus died. As Hilary was leaving the city to return happily to the monastic life at Lerins, the townspeople caught up to him and popularly hailed him as the people's choice to be the new archbishop. Hilary served heroically, combining his pastoral duties with monastic practices. On the anniversary of the death of Honoratus, Hilary preached the homily which is excerpted below:

> For on this day that virtuous and priestly bishop of this Church, of blessed memory, Honoratus by name, laid aside his mortal life. Whatever I add as a fitting tribute of praise will undoubtedly be considered out of place. For if I say: He has journeyed to the stars — why even while he lived on earth he was numbered

among the most brilliant stars of God. Shall I add: He is standing at the side of Christ? But, when in his life did he not stand at His side? His entire life fulfilled that word of Elias: 'The Lord liveth, before whom I stand this day.' Shall I say: He left the things of earth, when, as the Apostle says, his conversation always was in heaven. Similarly, therefore, whatever my soul feels, whatever occurs to it to say about such a man, cannot be a tribute befitting his personal worth.

Joy and grief are in conflict in my heart. It is a delight to recall such a man; to be deprived of his presence is a deep sorrow. Therefore, a twofold motive urges me on. On the one hand, the charm of his praises draws me aside to overwhelming grief. And so, be indulgent when these two affections distract my attention, if the organ of speech, as it were, refuses proper obedience to two masters. Whatever my memory suggests along the lines of praise, grief entirely assumes, reckoning it among its losses. Moreover, even if I had calmness of mind at my command, and though my tongue obeyed my thoughts with fitting service, could his praises be sung more fully by my words than they remain fixed in our very senses? There is no one, I think, who does not feel the charm of this great man more fully than could be expressed by the most splendid eloquence of any orator.[2]

2. Pope Gregory the Great and his Aunt Tarsilla

Gregory the Great's (c. 540-604) two saintly aunts, Tarsilla (d. c. 550) and Emiliana (d. c. 550), lived in the home of their brother, Gregory's father. The two women were renowned for their prayer, austerities and visions. They felt at home with Gregory's mother Silvia who also is recognized as a saint. These holy women produced a tremendous impact on this only child in the home. This patrician family had previously given two popes to the Church, Agapitus I and Felix III. It now produced in

Gregory one of the most outstanding persons in world history.[3] He is one of only two popes — the other is Leo I — heralded as "great." The two aunts died around the year 550, twelve days apart. One of Tarsilla's visions is recounted by her famous nephew:

> Sometimes our Creator and Redeemer Himself appears to a departing soul to offer it consolation. As an example of this I wish to repeat here what I wrote in the homilies on the Gospels about my aunt Tarsilla. She and her two sisters had reached a high degree of sanctity together through a life of constant prayer, recollection and severe self-denial. On one occasion my grandfather Felix, Bishop of Rome, appeared to her in a vision and showed her the home of eternal bliss, saying, 'Come! I will receive you into this dwelling of light.' Shortly after, she was struck down by a fever and brought to death's door. Many people came to console the near relatives, as is the custom when one of the nobility is about to die. Consequently, a goodly number of men and women had gathered round her bed at the time of her death. Suddenly she looked up and saw Jesus coming. She turned to her visitors with a look of great concern. 'Stand back! Stand back!' she exclaimed. 'Jesus is coming.' While she directed her gaze intently on the vision, her holy soul took its leave from the body. With this, a refreshing fragrance filled the room, indicating to all the presence of Him who is the source of all that is fragrant and refreshing.[4]

3. GOOD KING WENCESLAUS AND HIS GRANDMOTHER LUDMILLA

Ludmilla (c. 860-921) was grandmother to "Good King Wenceslaus" (c. 903-29). Ludmilla, the daughter of a Slav prince, married Borivoy, Duke of Bohemia. When her husband converted to Christianity and was baptized by the saintly Methodius, she followed him into the Church.

Together they sponsored the building of the first Christian Church in Bohemia, which is in the present-day Czech Republic. Borivoy tried to force Christianity on his people and met with a mixed reception. Upon his death his two sons succeeded him. The younger son's son, Wenceslaus, was entrusted to the grandmother Ludmilla for upbringing since the mother was only nominally Christian. Ludmilla had Methodius baptize him. "She was now about fifty years of age, a woman of virtue and learning, and it was to her unfailing care and interest that Wenceslaus in a large measure owed his own sanctity."[5]

When Wenceslaus' father died in battle against the Magyars, his queen regent mother felt threatened on the throne both by her popular mother-in-law Ludmilla and the queen's own son Wenceslaus. The queen regent hired assassins to strangle Ludmilla to death. With the deed accomplished, the Slav population reacted with horror, drove the queen assassin from her throne and acclaimed Wenceslaus as king.

The young king accepted his position and then forgave and recalled his murderous mother from her place of refuge. She never again did him or others any harm. Wenceslaus' political and religious policies, however, aroused the ire of his enemies. His brother soon joined the opposing political faction. The peace-loving and pious Wenceslaus was invited by his conspiring brother to attend a religious celebration. The day after the celebration ended, Wenceslaus was making his way to the chapel to attend Mass when the brothers met unexpectedly. Wenceslaus thanked his brother for his kind hospitality. The brother replied, "Yesterday I did my best to serve you fittingly, but this must be my service today." With that being said, Wenceslaus' brother and other cohorts struck him. Dying, he fell to the chapel floor. He murmured, "Brother, may God forgive you."[6] Grandmother and grandson are both regarded as saints and martyrs for their practice and propagation of the faith, and for their deaths at the hands of secularist powers. Grandmother and grandson were murdered just eight years apart.

4. CHARLES DE FOUCAULD AND HIS COUSIN MARIE DE BONDY

Charles (1858-1916) led such a dissolute life that he was expelled even from the French Foreign Legion for "indiscipline and notorious misconduct."[7] He was so lazy that he was expelled from military school. He was so fat that he could not fit into officer's clothing. He refused to take orders. He refused to respect women, telling them: "I rent by the day, not by the month." He was gifted but not a well directed person. After military reinstatement and an eight-month stint in Algeria, he resigned his commission, and returned home by way of Morocco. In the Moroccan desert he made geographical studies and wrote two books that won gold prizes from the French Geographical Society in 1885. At twenty-eight years of age, he returned to Paris where he found lodging close to his relatives. He also found a new meaning in life; he underwent a conversion. Perhaps the usual rebelliousness of youth had been exacerbated by the fact that both his parents had died by the time he was seven years old, or that a rich uncle had died and left him independently wealthy at age twenty-two. In any case, of all his relatives only his cousin Marie (1850-1934) could influence him positively.

Marie influenced him by respecting him, accepting him and praying for him. She never reprimanded him. She converted him without speaking a word; it was her kindness and goodness that beckoned him. Charles wrote about Marie's role in his conversion: "A beautiful soul assisted you, God, but by its silence, its gentleness, its kindness, its perfection; she allowed me to see myself; she was beautiful and exuded an enticing perfume, and she did nothing else."[8] He wrote to his cousin: "You have brought me back to Jesus."[9]

Marie was a daily communicant, with a passionate love of the Eucharist and devotion to the Sacred Heart. She was eight years Charles' senior, married with four children. When Charles made his first communion at age fifteen, just before he lost his faith at age sixteen, Marie gave him Bossuet's *Elevations sur les Mysteres*, which Charles later heralded as the first Christian book that he read, and which led to his conversion. When Charles was on the verge of conversion, Marie introduced him to her spiritual director. Marie and Charles prayed together at the altar of the Holy Virgin in their parish church on the morning of his conversion. They prayed together at the same altar on the day of his departure to a Trappist monastery. She had encouraged him to make a retreat there to decide, with the help of God, his vocation. When he entered the Trappists, she wrote him weekly. He in turn made frequent entries addressed to her in his journal, 800 in all. His relatives kept the faith, and because of his love of and association with his relatives, especially Marie, he was led back to the faith. The way in which Marie converted Charles framed his way for converting others: not by preaching but by a loving presence.

> A thousand times thank you for your letters, my dear cousin: four arrived at once! The good God is good! I have to thank God for having put so much kindness in your heart! I believed myself to have been damned when God enabled me to see in you God's goodness. . . . You have given me an infinite confidence in God . . . a confidence in myself and a confidence in others.

> Despite everything you are sad, sad over difficulties and anxieties, sad because of the sufferings of the Abbe (Huvelin) and the trials of this coast, sad because of the burdens of life . . . that is why my letter begins sadly, my dear cousin, however, we ought to rejoice because Our Lord has risen, our beloved, our fiancé, our divine spouse who loves us is infinitely happy. . . . But, Lord, bless your daughter through

whom you yourself have ordered that I beseech you more than any others, accomplish in her the will of your heart, sanctify her, console her, bless her intentions that they may conform to yours.[10]

General Observations

Many grandparents, cousins, in-laws and especially uncles and aunts served as saintly influences upon their blood relations.

Some grandparents directly influenced their grandchildren. Adele encouraged Gregory of Utrecht to become, like herself, a disciple of Boniface. Both then served as abbess/abbot of a monastery. The Frankish Queen Clotilde spirited away Clodaldus from murderous political intrigue; his two brothers had been killed by an uncle fearing rival claimants to the throne. When Clodaldus came of age for the throne, he, like his grandmother, publicly eschewed political ambitions. This peaceful young man became a hermit instead. In Czech society Ludmilla similarly rescued Wenceslaus from warring factions of the family, especially his murderous mother, and raised him in the faith. He eventually ascended the throne and continued his grandparents' mission of evangelization of the Czechs. "Good king Wenceslaus," however, ruled only briefly as he was killed by his brother who himself wished to ascend the throne. Olga too protected her grandson Vladimir from the political and religious rebellion of his father and his own step-brothers.

Interestingly all four of the above mentioned grandmothers succeeded in converting their husbands and grandsons, but not their own sons. In all four situations it was the grandmothers who initiated Christian evangelization, and the grandsons who succeeded in accomplishing the mission.

Some grandparents never met their grandchildren but

stories of the grandparents' lives influenced the young relatives. Melania the Elder and her namesake typify that kind of influence. Melania the Elder, one of the first Roman Christians to visit the Holy Land, built a monastery at the Mount of Olives. About seven years after her death, the granddaughter, Melania the Younger, likewise traveled to the Holy Land. She convinced her husband and mother to remain there in complete dedication to God. Melania the Younger lived in Jerusalem twenty-two years.

Notice that almost all of the saintly grandparents we know are grandmothers, except for Joachim, who is traditionally regarded as the grandfather of Jesus, and Romaricus, who is the grandfather of Gertrude of Remiremont.

Cousins played supporting roles in each other's lives. Mary visited Elizabeth for about three months while both women were pregnant. The second cousins John the Baptist and Jesus acclaimed each other. John said of his cousin: "Look! There is the Lamb of God who takes away the sins of the world! . . . This is God's chosen one" (Jn 1:29, 34). Jesus said of John: "History has not known a man born of woman greater than John the Baptizer" (Mk 11:11). Mary the mother of Jesus was consoled at the foot of the cross by her cousin Mary Cleophas. Jesus' cousin James the Younger received the responsibility of leading the first Christian community in Jerusalem. The cousins Barnabas and John Mark traveled with Paul on the latter's first missionary journey until a dispute arose between the volatile Paul and young Mark. Barnabas sided with his cousin, and both separated themselves for a while from Paul. Melania the Younger followed her cousin Paula to the desert to join the monastery which her cousin had founded. The brothers Hyacinth and Bl. Ceslaus along with their cousin Bl. Bronislava won many followers to Christ, they as Dominican missionaries to Silesia and Scandinavia, and she as a Norbertine nun.

The largest number of saintly relatives is found among uncles/aunts and their nephews/nieces.

Many younger relatives literally followed in the footsteps of their uncle or aunt. Many nephews of bishops became bishops. Honoratus of Lerins was uncle to Hilary of Arles. The missionary Patrick was uncle to Mel of Armagh. Gall of Clermont raised his nephew Gregory on the death of the father, and later saw the nephew ordained bishop of Tours. Many uncles and nephews were successive bishops of the same see: Heliodorus and Nepotian in Altinum, Eugene and Ildephonsus in Toledo, Gregory and Alberic at Utrecht, Arnulf and Goercius at Metz, and Adalbero and Ulric in Augsburg. Plato of Bithynia and his nephew Theodore Studites were successive abbots of Sakkudion. Ottilia and her niece Gundelindis were successive abbesses at Niedermunster. Edith of Polesworth and her niece Edith of Wilton were Benedictine nuns and abbesses, however, of two different monasteries.

Edwin and his niece Hilda were baptized together. The same Edwin and his nephew Oswald were successive kings of Northumbria. Alphege the bishop of Winchester and his nephew the abbot Dunstan reformed the English Church and English monasticism. James and John Duckett, uncle and nephew, were martyred by hanging at Tyburn Prison but forty-one years apart. Alexis Falconieri and his niece Julianna respectively founded a men's and a women's community of Servites. Emperor Henry II and his wife Cunegund, parents of the sainted Emeric, raised at their castle their niece Margaret, later queen of Scotland, and parent herself to the sainted David. Pope Gregory the Great was blessed with two saintly aunts Tarsilla and Emiliana who themselves were grand-nieces of Pope Felix. Elizabeth of Hungary was the grand-aunt of Elizabeth of Portugal. The two had never met but the grand-niece lived her life intentionally in imitation of her holy namesake. Both women were princesses who married kings, became mothers, and in widowhood became Franciscan tertiaries famous for their poverty and practical service of the poor.

Blood is thicker than water, in itself, and analogously in relationships. The strength of consanguinity is demonstrated time and again among the saints. When Jesus separated three apostles to be present with him in special moments like the Transfiguration, the Agony in the Garden and certain miracles, he chose Peter, the leader; John, his beloved; and James the Younger, his cousin. When Mary the mother of Jesus wept at the foot of the cross, she counted on the support of her cousin Mary Cleophas. In the dispute between Paul and John Mark, Barnabas sided with his cousin and the pair together abandoned Paul. In Jerusalem Melania the Younger was strengthened in her resolve to remain there by the support of her cousin Paula. The grandmothers Clotilde, Ludmilla and Olga rescued their respective grandsons Clodaldus, Wenceslaus and Vladimir from political intrigue. James Duckett was inspired to die for his belief in God by the martyrdom of his Uncle John.

Application Of The Theme

Common Vision: Older relatives embodied for younger ones a living vision. What the grandparents, aunts, uncles and cousins lived clearly, grandchildren, nieces, nephews and younger cousins could see plainly. Younger relatives saw with their eyes and felt with their hearts the elders' unconditional love for God and themselves.

Common Way: Older relatives protected, provided for, instructed and encouraged younger relatives. Elders wished younger relatives to make right choices. Relatives, unlike parents however, had the luxury of loving unconditionally without demanding accountability from their young relatives.

Common Bond With Each Other: Oftentimes relatives lived and learned together. They accepted and assisted each other. They loved being with each other. Their blood-relationship provided a pre-existing, permanent and dependable bond. Younger relatives felt full of love for their elders who had first loved them.

Common Bond With God: The joy of union with each other was surpassed only by the joy of union with God. Relatives prayed for each other. They prayed with each other. They believed that their relationships which began on earth would continue in eternity. Saintly relatives believed in the communion of saints on earth and in heaven.

APPENDIX: SAINTLY RELATIVES

GRANDPARENT(S) - GRANDCHILD(REN)

Joachim (1st century) and **Anne** (1st century) are regarded traditionally as the parents of the Blessed Virgin Mary and hence as the grandparents of Jesus.

Macrina the Elder (c. 270-340) was grandmother to **Basil the Great** (329-79), **Macrina the Younger** (c. 330-79), **Gregory of Nyssa** (c. 330-c. 395) and **Peter of Sebastea** (c. 340-91). "In more than one of his letters St. Basil the Great refers to his father's mother, Macrina, by whom he was apparently brought up, and to whose care in giving him sound religious instruction he attributes the fact that he never imbibed any heterodox opinions which he had afterwards to modify."[11] Grandmother and grandchildren deepened their faith in times of great trial. She kept the faith during repeated Roman persecutions, during one of which she hid in exile for seven years. The grandchildren struggled faithfully against the Arian heresy.

Melania the Elder (c. 342-c. 410) was grandmother to **Melania the Younger** (383-439). The Elder possessed a great wealth and great interest in the Holy Land. She was one of the first Roman Christians to visit there. She built a monastery at the Mount of Olives. Her granddaughter and namesake, daughter of a Roman senator, was married against her will at age fourteen to Pinian (d. 432). This young couple is treated in the chapter on husbands and wives.

Queen **Clotilde** (c. 474-545) was grandmother to **Clodaldus** (d. c. 560). She had converted the king on Christmas Day in 496. The king had made intercession to "Clotilde's God" to help him win a battle that seemed all but lost. When he won, he became a believer. After the king died, the three sons feuded over their inheritances. Clotilde abandoned the political machinations of Paris in favor of Tours, where she spent her last years caring for the sick and poor. She raised Clodaldus and his two brothers. Their father had killed one cousin, and was killed by another. Clodaldus' two brothers were assassinated at ages ten and seven by an uncle who wished to eliminate all rival claimants to the throne. Only eight years old, Clodaldus was saved when his grandmother whisked him away to a secure hiding in Provence. He became a priest and abbot and forsook all claims on the royal throne.

The last wish of **Gertrude of Hamage** (d. 649) was that her twelve-year-old great granddaughter **Eusebia** (d. 680) would succeed her as abbess of the convent which the grandmother founded. This wish followed the custom that abbesses would come from noble families in order to ensure financial and political support for the convents. Eusebia's mother Rictrudis intervened and took the nuns from Hamage to her convent at Marchiennes to allow Eusebia to mature for her position as abbess, which she soon attained.

Romaricus (d. 653) became a Christian through the influence of Amatus (c. 567-630). The widowed Romaricus founded an abbey on his estate, became a monk, and succeeded Amatus as abbot. Romaricus' granddaughter

Gertrude of Remiremont (d. c. 690) became a nun in the convent near Remiremont. Her brother Adolphus and her aunt Clare are also recognized as saints.

Adele (d. c. 734) and her grandson **Gregory of Utrecht** (c. 703-76) were both disciples of Boniface. A letter among Boniface's correspondence is addressed to her. After her husband died and she had provided for her son, she founded a monastery near Trier, becoming its first abbess. Her son fathered Gregory. Gregory was so inspired by a homily preached by Boniface that he volunteered to join the missionary. Boniface appointed Gregory an abbot and soon an administrator of the diocese. He ruled there for twenty-two years while remaining an abbot and without ever being appointed bishop. Gregory forgave and freed the murderers of his two step-brothers.

Ludmilla (c. 860-921) and her grandson "Good King Wenceslaus" (c. 903-29) are presented in this chapter.

Olga (c. 879-969) and her grandson **Vladimir** (c. 975-1015) began the evangelization of Russia. After her husband was assassinated in 945, and before her conversion to Christianity, Olga captured his murderers. She had them scalded to death and was responsible for the murder of hundreds of their followers. She embraced the faith in 957 and requested missionaries to evangelize her people. She was not very successful in this venture, being unable to convert even her own son. Her son's illegitimate son Vladimir, however, converted in 989 and did succeed in Christianizing Russia. Before his conversion, Vladimir was involved in internecine wars and murders, and was husband simultaneously to five wives. After a successful foray into the Crimea he was impressed by the cultural advancement brought by Christianity. He married the daughter of the Byzantine emperor and one year later became a Christian. He reformed his life and spread the faith by building churches and schools, by supporting missionaries including Boniface, and by exchanging ambassadors with Rome. Two of his sons, Romanus and David, became saints.

AUNT/UNCLE - NIECE/NEPHEW

Heliodorus (c. 332-90) and his nephew **Nepotian** (d. 395) joined the circle of St. Jerome at Jerusalem. Heliodorus financed the production of the Vulgate. He was named bishop of Altinum, near Venice. Nepotian resigned an esteemed position in the imperial bodyguard in order to become a priest. The uncle ordained the nephew to the priesthood. The nephew later succeeded his uncle as bishop of Altinum. Jerome dedicated to Nepotian a treatise on priestly life.

In the Holy Land **Melania the Younger** met her aunt **Eustochium Julia** (d. c. 419), who was the sole surviving daughter of Paula. Eustochium Julia introduced Melania to the Christian community at Bethlehem, which Jerome led. Melania and Jerome proceeded to become friends until his death three years later. Melania was "one of the great religious philanthropists of all time."[12] She built monasteries on three continents and aided the poor and sick wherever she went.

Hilary of Arles (c. 400-49) and his uncle **Honoratus** (c. 350-429) are described in this chapter.

Patrick of Ireland (c. 390-461) is alleged to have been uncle to numerous nephew-bishops. One sister is said to have had fifteen sons, ten of whom became bishops and one of whom is **Mel** (d. c. 488). Mel was the first abbot-bishop of Armagh and Brigid was his disciple. One author comments: "The evidence, however, concerning him and his brothers is hopelessly entangled and conflicting."[13] **Loman** (d. c. 450), another bishop, is said to have been a son of a second sister of Patrick. Loman was the first bishop of Trim in Meath. "Some scholars believe that in reality Loman was a bishop of Trim in the seventh century and in no way related to Patrick."[14]

Tarsilla (d. c. 581) and **Emilianna** (d. c. 550) were the paternal aunts of the pope, **Gregory the Great** (c. 540-604). Their relationship is described in this chapter.

Tarsilla and Emilianna were related not only as aunts

to Gregory but also as nieces to Pope **Felix II** (d. 492). Gregory was great-nephew to Pope Felix II through one of the pope's two children. Felix had served as pope from 483 to 492. His papacy was fraught with fighting against the heresies of Monophysitism and Eutychianism and in dealing with apostasies occasioned by the Vandals' persecution in North Africa.

Gregory was mayor of Rome before entering monastic life. He was appointed papal nuncio to Constantinople. Upon his return to Rome in 590, he was chosen pope which position he held for fourteen years. He continued the evangelization of the Anglo-Saxons by sending Augustine of Canterbury and forty monks to them. He undertook the conversion of the barbarian Lombards in Italy and of the Goths in Spain. He personally developed popular liturgical texts and chants. He cared for the poor in Rome, Ravenna and on his estates in Sicily and authored numerous treatises on spiritual theology. He is one of only two popes and a handful of other saints who have been given the exalted title of "great."[15]

Gregory of Tours (540-94), after the early death of his father, was raised by his uncle **Gallus of Clermont** (c. 489-554). Gregory eventually became the bishop of Tours. He rebuilt the cathedral and several churches and successfully converted many heretics. He wrote books on the martyrs, the Fathers, the saints, and is remembered especially for his *History of the Franks,* which is "one of the outstanding original sources of early French history."[16] His uncle Gallus, who was Gregory's teacher, was ordained by the saintly bishop Quinctian. Quinctian chose Gallus as his representative at the royal court and as his successor in the see of Clermont.

Columba (c. 521-97) greatly influenced his nephew **Colman of Lann Elo** (c. 555-611). The great Columba managed to found at Iona "the greatest monastery in Christendom."[17] It was a rocky road getting there, however, for this Irish monk. He left his original monastery in Ulster when plague prohibited inhabitation. For the next fifteen years or so he preached and founded monasteries all over Ireland. He made two significant mistakes. One, he copied a manuscript without permission of the owner and was forced to hand over his copy. Two, he precipitated a battle in which 3,000 persons lost their lives. In penance, he left Ireland and went to live among the Scots whom he converted in large numbers. He propagated the use of the Celtic rite which was later replaced by the Roman rite. Colman of Lann Elo founded two monasteries, becoming the abbot of each and eventually a bishop.

Edwin, king of Northumbria (c. 585-633), and **Hilda** (614-80), the daughter of his nephew, were baptized by Paulinus. After Edwin's first wife died, he married in 625 a Christian woman of Kent who brought with her entourage her confessor Paulinus. Two years later the king, after much encouragement from his wife, decided to be baptized. So did many others in the royal court. Thus began Christianity in Northumbria. Hilda was thirteen. She lived as a noblewoman until her thirty-third year when she joined her sister in the nunnery, eventually being named abbess in two successive convents. "She became renowned for her spiritual wisdom, and her monastery for the caliber of its learning and of its nuns."[18] The famous council at Whitby, which adopted for England the Roman liturgical and Benedictine monastic observances, was convened by her even though her monastery had favored the Celtic rule and observances.

Oswald of Northumbria (604-42) became king when his uncle and predecessor **Edwin** (c. 585-633) was killed. Oswald returned from Scotland, where he had fled for his life in 617 when his father was killed in battle. In Scotland Oswald converted to Christianity. From Scotland he battled his way back to England and the throne. Oswald continued Edwin's tradition of evangelization and charity. Oswald invited Aidan to assist in evangelization and gave to Aidan the island of Landisfarne for his see. Oswald is usually regarded as a martyr, since he died doing battle against the pagan Mercians.

Arnulf (d. c. 640) and **Goercius** (d. 647) were relatives and successive bishops of Metz. Both had held positions
at the royal court. When Arnulf's wife became a nun, he
planned to enter a monastery, but instead was persuaded to
become bishop. He served from about 610 to 626 when he
resigned in order to retire to a hermitage. His famous
grandson began the Carolingian line of kings. Goercius, who
had become a priest in thanksgiving for suddenly recovering
his sight after having gone blind, succeeded Arnulf.

Eugene of Toledo (d. 657) and **Ildephonsus** (607-
67), uncle and nephew, served as successive bishops of the
same see. Eugene, who was renowned for his poetry and other
writings, was blessed with many saintly influences. He was a
cleric under Helladius, a monk under Engracia, and archdeacon for Braulio. Ildephonsus was blessed with his uncle,
and possibly with Isidore as his instructor at Seville.
Ildephonsus became a monk, abbot and archbishop at Toledo. He is regarded in Spain as a Doctor of the Church. "He
was responsible for the unification of the Spanish liturgy and
excelled as a writer, chiefly on Our Lady."[19]

When **Gregory of Utrecht** (c. 703-76) died, his nephew
Alberic (d. 784) became bishop of the see. Alberic, who was
very well educated, was appointed to the episcopacy, a
distinction not enjoyed by his uncle. His apostolate among
the barbarians was very fruitful.

Ottilia (d. c. 720) was the aunt of **Remigius** (d. 783)
and **Gundelindis** (d. c. 750). All were born of noble families
in the Alsace region. Tradition tells us that Ottilia was born
blind and for that reason the family disowned her. When she
was twelve years old, she was accepted as a charity case into
a convent. There she recovered her sight. She went on to
found two monasteries: one at Hohenburg, and the other at
Niedermünster. Her nephew Remigius served as abbot of
Münster before being appointed bishop of Strasburg. Her
niece Gundelindis served as abbess of the monastery of
Niedermünster.

Plato of Bithynia (d. 813) and his nephew **Theodore**

Studites (759-826) opposed the divorce and remarriage of the Byzantine emperor. Because of their opposition, they twice suffered imprisonment and exile. Despite the fact that Plato had served for twelve years as abbot at Sakkudion and that he had been raised by his uncle the imperial treasurer, he did not escape exile. Theodore succeeded his uncle as abbot at Sakkudion. In addition to the exile because of his involvement in the marriage controversy, he twice more suffered exile because of the iconoclast controversy and his defense of the primacy of the bishop at Rome. Between his first and second exiles, Theodore moved to Constantinople, where he revitalized the 300-year-old Studios Monastery which had been allowed to become rundown and was inhabited by only a dozen monks. Theodore built it up into a community of over 1,000 monks and established it as a center of Eastern monastic life famous for its liberal and fine arts and its revivified monastic rule.

Ulric (c. 890-973) succeeded his uncle **Adalbero** (d. 909) as bishop of Augsburg. Adalbero was a Benedictine monk who became abbot of Ellwangen monastery and abbot-restorer of Lorsch before being named bishop of Augsburg in 887. Ulric led the populace in restoring the cathedral and the city after the Magyars had plundered both. When Ulric was ready to retire, he handed over the see to his nephew. Ulric's canonization was the first one presided over by a pope.

Edith of Polesworth (d. c. 925) and **Edith of Wilton** (961-84) reportedly were aunt and niece. The elder Edith was sister to an English king and married a Viking king. When her husband died one year after marriage, she became a Benedictine nun and perhaps an abbess. The younger Edith was brought to the convent when she was very young and, in the words of the pre-1970 Roman Martyrology, "she rather knew not this world than forsook it."[20] She declined the position of abbess in three monasteries, and refused to leave the convent to become queen when her half brother was murdered. She was attended by Dunstan in her last days.

Alphege (d. 951), a monk and later the bishop of Winchester, ordained to priesthood his nephew **Dunstan** (909-988) who was responsible for reviving monasticism in England. Alphege was renowned for his gift of prophecy. Dunstan is remembered as a great reformer of Church and State. In his capacity as a Benedictine abbot, he reformed Glastonbury Abbey and surrounding abbeys. In his capacity as advisor to five successive kings, he restored ecclesiastical discipline, rebuilt monasteries which had been destroyed by Danish incursions and replaced inept priests with able monks.

The Holy Roman Emperor **Henry II** (972-1024) and his wife **Cunegund** (d. 1039) were blessed with two saintly relatives. Henry's sister married King **Stephen of Hungary** (975-1038) and begot Henry's and Cunegund's nephew **Emeric** 1007-1031).

Stephen was ten years old when he and his father were baptized. After his father's death and a series of battles against rival leaders, Stephen was crowned in 1001 the first king of Hungary. The pope sent the crown. Stephen reorganized the Magyar people and introduced many political, social and ecclesiastical reforms.

Stephen raised Emeric in the Christian faith. After Emeric died at fourteen years of age in a hunting accident, the father's final years were burdened with political struggles over the right of succession to the throne.

In the same court where he raised Emeric, Stephen also raised his niece **Margaret of Scotland** (1045-93). Her exiled parents and Margaret left Hungary in 1057 and traveled to England to seek refuge with their relatives. After the Battle of Hastings in 1066, Margaret fled to Scotland. There she met and married the Scottish king four years later. She is renowned for her life of prayer and fasting, care for the poor, ecclesiastical and liturgical reforms, and encouragement for the arts and education. On her deathbed, she received news that her husband and son had been killed by warring rebels. She died with a broken heart.

Another son of Margaret was **David** (1084-1153), who

had been sent in 1093 to England to escape the bloodshed current in Scottish politics. He returned home as king in 1124, established a system of civil law and provided for the expansion of the Church. "Though listed in both Catholic and Protestant calendars, he has never been formally canonized."[21]

The Florentines **Alexis Falconieri** (c. 1200-1310) and his niece **Julianna Falconieri** (1270-1341) were early members of the Servite community. Alexis was one of the seven holy founders. Julianna was among the first women Servites. Tradition tells us that she had been raised from childhood by her mother and uncle after her father died. At age fifteen she was vested with the Servite habit. One year later she became a Servite tertiary. After her mother died, Julianna headed the community of women dedicated to prayer and charitable works. This band of women later became the Servite nuns, with Julianna who was outstandingly regarded not as their foundress but as the *mater en caput*, or "the head mother."

Hedwig (c. 1174-1243), the aunt of **Elizabeth of Hungary** (1271-1336), studied with the Benedictine nuns. At age twelve she married the eighteen-year-old head of the Polish royal family. They begot seven children, six of whom predeceased Hedwig. The parents founded hospitals and houses for religious communities. Their convent for the Cistercians at Trebnitz was the first monastery for women in Silesia. Hedwig's sole surviving child became the abbess of the monastery to which Hedwig retired as a widow. Hedwig's sister's daughter was the renowned Elizabeth of Hungary.

Elizabeth of Hungary (1207-31) provided a name and an example for her niece **Elizabeth of Portugal** (1271-1336). Both women grew up as princesses, married kings and, in widowhood, lived as Franciscan tertiaries. Elizabeth of Hungary married at age fourteen, bore three children, and became a widow at age twenty when her husband was killed in a Crusade. She then devoted herself to living with and for the poor. She died at age twenty-four, and was canonized three years later. The niece tried to emulate her aunt. Elizabeth of Portugal married when she was twelve years old and bore two children. She spent much time trying to reconcile her husband with the surrounding kings in Castile and Aragon, as well as dealing with the political rebellions led twice by their son and another time by her brother. She earned the title "Peacemaker." Daily she prayed the Divine Office and assisted at Mass. She "founded convents, hospitals, foundling homes and shelters for wayward girls."[22]

Bl. James Duckett (d. 1602) and his nephew **Bl. John Duckett** (1613-44) were both hanged at Tyburn Prison in London, England only forty-two years apart. James was raised a Protestant but he refused to attend services because he held doubts about the denomination. For his refusal he served two prison terms. Upon release from prison he took religious instructions and became a Catholic. He printed and distributed Catholic materials, for which he spent nine of the next twelve years in prison; he was charged with the felony of possessing Catholic books. He died at the gallows. Eleven years later John was born. He studied at Douai, where he was ordained a priest. He studied at Paris for three more years and after one year of ministry in England he was arrested. At Tyburn John was hanged, drawn and quartered.

Cousins

Mary (1st century) visited her cousin **Elizabeth** (1st century) when both were pregnant. The baby in the womb of Elizabeth leapt when he heard Mary's greeting. "Elizabeth was filled with the Holy Spirit and cried out in a loud voice: 'Blest are you among women and blest is the fruit of your womb. . . . Blest is she who trusted that the Lord's words to her would be fulfilled'" (Lk 1:41-42, 45). Mary in turn praised God in the prayer that comes to us as the Magnificat. "My soul proclaims the greatness of the Lord, my spirit finds joy in God my Savior, for he has looked upon his servant in her lowliness" (Lk 1:46-48). We read no more of Elizabeth in the Scriptures.

The sons of Mary and Elizabeth were **Jesus** (4 B.C-30 A.D) and **John the Baptist** (1st century). They were second cousins. John lived as a hermit in the desert. He preached "a baptism of repentance which led to the forgiveness of sins" (Lk 3:3). On the banks of the Jordan River John baptized Jesus, protesting: "I should be baptized by you, yet you come to me" (Mt 3:14). John later indicated to his disciples that Jesus was the long-awaited Messiah: "Look! There is the Lamb of God who takes away the sin of the world!" (Jn 1:29). When John was in prison awaiting death for his censure of the king's incestuous marriage, Jesus said of him: "History has not known a man born of woman greater than John the Baptizer" (Mt 11:11).

Jesus was related to many men and women but it is difficult to ascertain the precise degree of relationship (cf. Mt 13:55-56). **James the Younger** (d. 62) has been identified traditionally as son of Alphaeus, one of the twelve apostles, author of one of the epistles, and head of the early Christian community at Jerusalem. Today, however, some scholars suggest that there may have been two persons: one of them, the son of Alphaeus and an apostle; and the other, the author and bishop. **Joseph** (1st century) is mentioned twice as one of the brethren of the Lord. He is described as son of another Mary and brother to James. **Simon** (d. c. 107) is named in the Roman Martyrology as the son of Cleophas, the brother of Joseph, who was the foster father of Jesus. Simon succeeded James as bishop of Jerusalem. **Jude Thaddeus** (1st century) is generally but not universally believed by scholars to be an apostle and author of an epistle. Luke (6:16) and Acts (1:13) speak of an apostle Jude, and Matthew (10:3) and Mark (3:18) speak of an apostle Thaddeus. The liturgical memorial of Simon and Jude is celebrated jointly in accord with the tradition that these relatives of Jesus ministered and died jointly in Persia.

The cousins **Mark** (d. c. 74) and **Barnabas** (1st century) accompanied Paul on his first missionary journey. John Mark was probably a Levite and perhaps a minor minister in the synagogue. Barnabas was one of the earliest converts to the burgeoning Christian community. He persuaded the local community in Jerusalem to accept the erstwhile persecutor Paul. On Paul's first journey a falling out occurred between Paul and Mark at Pamphylia. They separated company. Barnabas chose to accompany his cousin back to Jerusalem. The two traveled together again on mission to Cyprus. Mark later visited Paul during his imprisonment in Rome.

Tibba (7th century) was cousin to the Anglo-Saxon sisters **Cyneburga** (7th century) and **Cyneswide** (7th century). Tibba joined her cousins at the convent founded by Cyneburga after her husband went to war against his father and never returned. The sisters were successive abbesses.

The missionary and martyr **Boniface** (c. 680-758) enjoyed the companionship of many relatives. These Britons left their homeland to evangelize the German people. Boniface in 718 was missioned to Germany by the pope. Four years later Boniface was named regional bishop of Germany and after nine more years he was named metropolitan bishop of the entire German territory. His cousin **Lull** (d. 786) joined Boniface as an assistant, emissary and eventual successor when Boniface resigned his see four years before his death in order to focus his energies on reconverting the lapsed Germans. **Lioba** (d. 780) began a correspondence with Boniface when he was appointed bishop. In her first letter to him she reminded Boniface that he had met her father and was related by blood to her mother. Lioba added: "I am the only child of my parents and, unworthy though I be, I should like to look on you as my brother, for I can trust you more than anyone else of my kinfolk."[23] Twenty-six years later Boniface requested the abbess of Lioba's convent to send some missionaries.

Lioba, who was Boniface's relative, and **Thecla** (d. c. 790), who was Lioba's relative, were among the thirty or more nuns sent in response to the request. Boniface immediately appointed Lioba the abbess of the newly arrived English nuns. Lioba in turn appointed Thecla abbess of two other convents. Lioba's native town of Wimborne was not very far from Boniface's native Crediton. The relatives were so close not only in blood but also in spirit that Boniface requested successfully that Lioba be buried beside him.

Bl. Bronislava (d. 1259) was cousin to the brothers **Hyacinth** (1185-1257) and **Bl. Ceslaus** (d. 1242). These three evangelized their native Poland. Bronislava became a Premonstratensian nun and eventually a hermit near Cracow. The brothers are discussed in the appendix on siblings.

Charles de Foucauld (1858-1916) and his cousin **Marie de Bondy** (1850-1934) are described in this chapter.

IN-LAWS

Lupus of Troyes (c. 383-478) married the sister of **Hilary of Arles** (c. 400-49). Lupus and Hilary eventually entered the recently founded and later famous Lerins monastery. Lupus and his wife of six years agreed to a separation so that he could enter the monastery. Hilary forsook his high position in local government in order to enter Lerins. Both brothers-in-law were soon named bishops: Hilary to the see of Arles, and Lupus to the see of Troyes where he served for over half a century.

Gregory informs us that he was related to another pope, **Agapitus I** (535-36), although the degree of relationship is not known. Agapitus' tenure lasted only eleven months. He deposed the Monophysite patriarch of Constantinople. Six popes and fifty-four years separated the pontificates of Agapitus I and Gregory I.[24]

King Stephen of Hungary (975-1038) married the sister of emperor **Henry II** (972-1024), whose wife **Cunegund** (d. 1033) is also a saint. These leaders pursued policies of Christianization which the popes supported but local political and religious leaders sometimes opposed because of the usurpation of power by Stephen and Henry.

Notes for Chapter 5

1. *Butler's Lives of the Saints*, vol. II, p. 237.
2. *Early Christian Biographies*, pp. 361-62.
3. *The Oxford Dictionary of Popes*, p. 65; and Butler, vol. I, p. 566.
4. *St. Gregory the Great: Dialogues*, pp. 21-22.
5. Butler, vol. III, p. 570.
6. Ibid., p. 664.
7. *Silent Pilgrimage to God*, p. 91.
8. Charles de Foucauld, *Lettres a Mme de Bondy*, p. 13.
9. Ibid.
10. Ibid., pp. 34-35.
11. Butler, vol. I, p. 82.
12. Delaney, *Dictionary of Saints*, p. 404.
13. *The Book of Saints*, p. 395.
14. Delaney, p. 362.
15. The other pope was Leo I. The other saints were Albert the Great, Basil the Great, Gertrude the Great, Nerses the Great and his son Isaac the Great.
16. Delaney, p. 270.
17. Ibid., p. 155.
18. Ibid., p. 287.
19. *The Book of Saints*, p. 281.
20. Ibid., p. 174.
21. Delaney, p. 174.
22. Ibid., p. 195.
23. Butler, vol. III, p. 669.
24. *The Oxford Dictionary of Saints*, pp. 58-59.

CHAPTER 6

SAINTLY FRIENDS

Best Friends

1. Jesus and John the Beloved Disciple
2. Jesus and Mary, Martha and Lazarus
3. The Four Mary's at the Foot of the Cross: Blessed Virgin Mary, Mary Cleophas, Mary Salome and Mary Magdalene,
4. Antony and Athanasius
5. Basil the Great and Gregory Nazianzen
6. John Chrysostom and Olympias
7. John Chrysostom and Maro
8. Jerome and Liberius, Valerian, Chromatius, Heliodorus, Paulinus of Nola, Gregory Nazianzen, Epiphanius of Palestine, Damasus, Marcella, Asella, Albina, Lea, Melania the Elder, Fabiola, Pammachius, Paula, Blesilla and Eustochium Julia
9. Augustine and Alipius
10. Paulinus of Nola and Ambrose, Martin of Tours, Augustine, Jerome, Delphinus, Melania the Elder, Melania the Younger, Pinian, Nicetas of Remesiana
11. Patrick and Brigid
12. Symeon and John
13. Gregory of Tours and Agricola
14. Eligius and Bathildis
15. Rictrudis and Amandus

16. Elfleda and Cuthbert
17. Boniface and Lioba
18. Lioba and Bl. Hildegard of France
19. Edward the Confessor and Gervinus
20. Gregory VII and Hugh of Cluny
21. Malachy and Bernard of Clairvaux
22. Robert of Newminster and Godric
23. Edmund Rich and Richard de Wyche
24. Francis of Assisi and Clare of Assisi
25. Clare of Assisi and Bl. Agnes of Prague
26. Thomas Aquinas and Bonaventure
27. King Louis IX and Bl. Isabel with Bonaventure and Thomas Aquinas
28. Catherine of Siena and Catherine of Sweden
29. Philip Neri and Charles Borromeo, Ignatius of Loyola and John Leonardi
30. Bl. Peter Favre and Alphonsus Rodriguez
31. Rose of Lima and Martin de Porres
32. Martin de Porres and John Massias
33. Vincent de Paul and Louise de Marillac
34. Pope Pius X and Bl. Louis Guanella

Celibate Friends

35. Jerome and Paula
36. Bl. Jordan of Saxony and Bl. Diana d'Andalo
37. Catherine of Siena and Bl. Raymond of Capua
38. Francis de Sales and Jane de Chantal
39. Margaret Mary Alacoque and Claude de la Colombière

Soul Friends

40. Queen Radegund and John of Chinon
41. Bl. Ida of Boulogne and Anselm

42. Bruno of Rheims and Hugh of Grenoble
43. Bl. Ceslau and Hedwig
44. Peter of Verona and the Seven Founders of the Order of Servites
45. Raymond of Peñafort and Peter Nolasco
46. John of Avila and John of God, Peter of Alcantara, Francis Borgia, Teresa of Avila and John of the Cross
47. Teresa of Avila and her successive directors: John of Avila, Peter of Alcantara and John of the Cross
48. Charles Borromeo and Alexander Sauli
49. Philip Neri and Bl. Juvenal
50. Alphonsus Rodriguez and Peter Claver
51. Robert Bellarmine and Aloysius Gonzaga
52. Vincent de Paul and Jane de Chantal
53. Joseph Cafasso and John Bosco
54. Louis IX and Bl. Giles of Saumur

United in Mind and Heart: Saintly Friends

"A friend doubles one's joy and divides one's sorrow," observes Francis Bacon.[1] Friends share life: visions and values, interests and activities, thoughts and feelings. Friends may pass the whole day together and then go home and write or telephone each other to talk about the delight of having been together. They confide in each other what is most private and personal. Because they share deeply, they influence each other deeply.

The Book of Sirach in the Old Testament states: "A faithful friend is a sturdy shelter; whoever finds one finds a treasure. A faithful friend is beyond all price, no sum can balance his worth. A faithful friend is a life-saving remedy, such as one who fears God finds" (Si 6:14-16). Jesus said of his disciples: "I no longer call you servants, I call you friends" (Jn 15:13). Jesus elevated human friendship to the dignity of sacred relationship. Blessed are those who make friends in the Lord and become friends with the Lord.

Friends satisfy us in countless ways; but perhaps most characteristically, friends, like God, faithfully and lovingly accept us. Friends accept us as we are, while inviting us to become our best selves. Fidelity to one's friend is so essential that Jerome writes: "Friendship which can end was never true friendship."[2] Aelred of Rievaulx so esteemed friendship that he wrote in his twelfth century book on *Spiritual Friendship* that: "God is friendship."[3]

Particular examples

1. ANTONY AND ATHANASIUS

Antony (251-356), the desert hermit, and Athanasius (c. 296-373), the urban bishop, chose very different but mutually supportive ways to live the Gospel. Their separate paths crossed many times and they became best friends.

Antony lived as a hermit since age twenty-one. "He lived a life of prayer, penance, and the strictest austerity, ate only bread and water once a day, and engaged in struggles with the devil and temptations that are legendary."[4] He desired complete solitude and eventually abandoned his hermitage around which other monks and faithful gathered for instruction and edification. Twenty years later he emerged from his solitude to form a community of solitaries who came together weekly for common worship. In 311 he traveled to Alexandria to aid the Christians suffering persecution from the pagan emperor. Antony returned to the desert to form another community, but later sought solitary retirement from it. In 325 he attended the Council of Nicea which condemned Arianism and excommunicated Arius. In 355 he traveled again to Alexandria to aid Christians suffering from the Arian-led persecution. There he worked with his friend Athanasius.

Athanasius served as the bishop's secretary, then as bishop and, finally, as archbishop of cosmopolitan Alexandria. He was well educated in scripture and theology. He attended the ecumenical Council of Nicea in 325. He struggled the remainder of his life against Arianism and its defenders. He spent seventeen years in on-again off-again exiles that were imposed on five different occasions.[5] He spent about seven of those seventeen years with the desert monks, becoming their public defender. He has provided for posterity the definitive biography of his 105-year-old friend, Antony. An excerpt describes the turning point in Antony's life:

> Now, you have also asked me for an account of the life of the blessed Antony: you would like to learn how he came to practice asceticism, what he was previous to this, what his death was like, and whether everything said about him is true. You have in mind to model your lives after his life of zeal. I am very happy to accede to your request, for I, too, derive real profit and help from the mere recollection of Antony; and I feel that you also, once you have heard the story, will not merely admire the man but will wish to emulate his resolution as well. Really, for monks the life of Antony is an ideal pattern of the ascetical life. Upon his parents' death he was left alone with an only sister who was very young. He was about eighteen or twenty years old at the time and took care of the house and his sister. Less than six months had passed since his parents' death when, as usual, he chanced to be on his way to church. As he was walking along, he collected his thoughts and reflected how the Apostles left everything and followed the Savior; also how the people in Acts sold what they had and laid it at the feet of the Apostles for distribution among the needy; and what great hope is laid up in Heaven for such as these.

With these thoughts in his mind he entered the church. And it so happened that the Gospel was being read at that moment and he heard the passage in which the Lord says to the rich man: "If thou wilt be perfect, go sell all that thou hast, and give it to the poor; and come, follow me and thou shalt have treasure in Heaven."[6]

2. BASIL THE GREAT AND GREGORY NAZIANZEN

Basil (329-79) and Gregory Nazianzen (329-89) enjoyed a lifelong friendship. They first met as students of rhetoric in Caesarea in Cappadocia, where they spent two years together. They met again as law students in Athens, where they passed an additional ten years together. They separated for a few months when Basil went to Pontus to pursue a hermit's life. Basil soon invited Gregory to join him, which he did. The two friends spent two more years together, this time dedicated to monastic prayer and study. Gregory left Basil and the quiet of the monastic life to assist his octogenarian father who was a bishop. "Not content, however, with the help his son could give him as a layman, the aged bishop, with the connivance of certain members of his flock, ordained him priest more or less by force."[7] Gregory felt torn between a sense of personal unworthiness and an inexpressible esteem for the priesthood. He fled to his best friend, Basil. Basil encouraged Gregory to accept the office conferred on him by others. Ten weeks later Gregory accepted his new responsibility.

Basil and Gregory could not help but become involved in the disputes of their day. Gregory busied himself in confronting the Arians and trying to reconcile the semi-Arians, eventually calling upon Basil for assistance. Basil did all he could to help his friend and was soon named archbishop of Caesarea. Basil then attempted to assign his friend to a see that was full of theological and political controversy. Basil trusted Gregory to restore the see to religious orthodoxy and political peace. Gregory, who had reluctantly accepted ordination to both priesthood and the episcopacy, had no desire to occupy this hotseat. Basil could not understand Gregory's hesitation. "In reply to the reproaches of Basil, who accused him of slackness, he declared that he was not disposed to fight for a church. Gregory was deeply hurt at the treatment he had received, and although he became reconciled to St. Basil, the friendship was never again the same."[8]

Gregory remained in Nazianzus as his father's coadjutor until the aged man died in 374 and a new bishop was appointed. Gregory won numerous converts by his excellent preaching and was invited to Arian-dominated Constantinople to support the orthodox struggle there. He suffered an apparent nervous breakdown in 375 and he spent the next five years recuperating in Seleucia. In 380 the newly baptized emperor appointed Gregory bishop of Constantinople. He acceded. Within a few months, however, new hostilities arose. At the Council of Constantinople in 381, over which Gregory presided, opponents made allegations regarding his election as bishop. In the hope of restoring peace, Gregory resigned his see and retired to a private austere life, which he enjoyed until his death in 389.

Gregory wrote about his and Basil's classical friendship:

> Basil and I were both in Athens. We had come, like streams of a river, from the same source in our native land, had separated from each other in pursuit of learning, and were now united again as if by plan, for God so arranged it.

> I was not alone at that time in my regard for my friend, the great Basil. I knew his irreproachable conduct, and the maturity and wisdom of his conversation. I

sought to persuade others, to whom he was less well known, to have the same regard for him. Many fell immediately under his spell, for they had already heard of him by reputation and hearsay.

What was the outcome? Almost alone of those who had come to Athens to study he was exempted from the customary ceremonies of initiation for he was held in higher honor than his status as a first-year student seemed to warrant.

Such was the prelude to our friendship, the kindling of that flame that was to bind us together. In this way we began to feel affection for each other. When, in the course of time, we acknowledged our friendship and recognized that our ambition was a life of true wisdom, we became everything to each other: we shared the same lodging, the same table, the same desires, the same goal. Our love for each other grew daily warmer and deeper.

The same hope inspired us: the pursuit of learning. This is an ambition especially subject to envy. Yet between us there was no envy. On the contrary, we made capital out of our rivalry. Our rivalry consisted, not in seeking the first place for oneself but in yielding it to the other, for we each looked on the other's success as his own.

We seemed to be two bodies with a single spirit. Though we cannot believe those who claim that "everything is contained in everything," yet you must believe that in our case each of us was in the other and with the other.

Our single object and ambition was virtue, and a life of hope in the blessings that are to come; we wanted to withdraw from this world before we departed from it. With this end in view we ordered our lives and all our actions. We followed the guidance of God's law and spurred each other on to virtue. If it is not too boastful to say, we found in each other a standard and rule discerning right from wrong.

Different men have different names, which they owe
to their parents or to themselves, that is, to their own
pursuits and achievements. But our great pursuit, the
great name we wanted, was to be Christians, to be
called Christians.[9]

3. FRANCIS DE SALES AND JANE DE CHANTAL

Francis de Sales (1567-1622) and Jane Frances de
Chantal (1572-1641), spiritual writers and religious leaders, shared an affection that was common knowledge to all
who knew them. For eighteen years they called each other
dearest and best friends. They exchanged hundreds of
letters, visited frequently for up to ten days at a time, and
traveled together to each other's family estates where they
walked and talked tirelessly for hours. When they could
not speak with each other face to face, they wrote voluminous and very affectionate letters. Two excerpts included
below were written by Francis to Jane during the first five
years of the foundation of the community of the Visitation
Sisters. He missed her greatly and longed to have his heart
joined with hers:

> Oh God! my dearest daughter, I protest, but I protest
> with my whole heart, which is more yours than mine,
> that I feel keenly the privation of not having seen you
> today. Tomorrow, with God's help, I will come and
> speak with you a good hour before the sermon and we
> will speak of our challenge, which, my dear daughter,
> you will find very agreeable and worthy of our heart
> which is so indivisible. And so, good night, my very
> own daughter, I wish that you could experience the
> feelings that I had today, while taking Communion, of
> our precious unity because it was immense, perfect,
> sweet, powerful and almost like a vow or consecra-
> tion.[10]

> I have been here in Thonon (Francis' family home) for
> three days, my dearest daughter, where I am happily

and without any feelings of weariness. Oh God, my dearest daughter, I don't know which road I took, the one to Thonon or the one to Burgundy (Jane's family home) but I know very well that I am more in Burgundy than I am here. Yes, my daughter, as it pleases the divine Goodness, I am inseparable from your heart and speaking with the words of the Holy Spirit, we now have only one heart and one soul, because I find that what is said of all the Christians of the early Church is, thanks be to God, now true of us.[11]

Francis was upset sometimes because the extent of the display of Jane's affection poured out in her letters prohibited him from showing them to the Visitation sisters. He writes:

In your covering letters, when you write to me you should not call me, "My father, my dear love" because I want to be able to show them to those to whom you send greetings in order to comfort them. . . Now for my niece de Brechard, she well knows that I am wholly yours, because she has seen the notes that contain that truth. However, I have not wanted to show her the last three letters either in whole or in part.[12]

4. POPE PIUS X AND BL. LOUIS GUANELLA

Both Pope Pius X (1835-1914) and Bl. Louis Guanella (1842-1915) hailed from the north of Italy. Pius, born Giuseppe Sarto, came from the neighborhood of Venice where his father was a shoemaker and postman. Louis was born in the rugged Italian Alps, where his parents were farmers. Pius was the second of ten children, and Louis was the ninth of thirteen.

Louis dedicated himself to the service of disabled persons, the mentally and physically handicapped, the abandoned elderly and young orphans. He gathered these needy people into residences which he established as Centers of Providence. He trusted in the goodness of God and of Christian people to provide food, clothing and shelter for these persons in greatest need. He was not disappointed. He founded religious communities for both men and women to assist in the ministry to the poorest. He ran afoul of the political leaders because he criticized their ironic "liberalization" of the country by the suppression of all religious communities. Louis was forbidden to teach and write, and he was kept under political surveillance while celebrating Mass.

Giuseppe Sarto also ran afoul of the political leaders because he rejected their modernism, which disguised their political interference in Church administration, their confiscation of Church property, and a narrow nationalism. Both men advocated participation by the laity at daily Mass and daily communion. Louis was the first to promote this practice for which Pius X later became famous.

> After the construction of one home for the retarded, he (Louis) asked Pope Pius if he might name the new home in honor of His Holiness. Laughingly the pope replied, "Yes, yes, put me at the head of your retarded patients. Immortalize me through them; call it the Pius X Home." These two great men of their age often joked in this manner while carrying out numerous works of charity. When the pope asked Don Guanella if all his responsibilities did not worry him a great deal, the priest replied: "I worry until midnight and from then on I let God worry. I even sleep too much. Sometimes when I am in the streetcar and should get off at [one place], I sleep and it takes me to [another place]. And then quietly, and well rested, I return without telling anyone so they will not make fun of me."[13]

General Observations

Friendships between the saints abounded within every category of familial and ministerial relationships. These friendships may be divided into three kinds: best friends, soul friends and celibate friends. At times the lines of these three overlap. At other times all three are embodied in one relationship.

Best friends provided mutual support. During the disputes involved in the Arian heresy Antony and Athanasius publicly defended the same theological positions, and repeatedly visited each other in their respective desert and city locations. Basil the Great and Gregory Nazianzen studied together for a dozen years, lived together as monks for two years, and spent the rest of their lives as bishops in neighboring dioceses. John Chrysostom and Olympias encouraged each other, he in advocating moderation in her ascetical practices and she in his fidelity to the truth during his three periods of exile. Jerome and Paula met in Rome but longed for the desert's solitude and eventually settled there. Augustine and Alipius were boyhood friends. They studied together at Tagaste, Carthage, Rome, Milan and Cassiciacum. Together they became successively Manicheans, catechumens, Christians, priests and then bishops. Patrick and Brigid were family friends who together evangelized Ireland. Gregory of Tours and Agricola were neighboring bishops who shared the same goal and method of evangelization: individual spiritual growth fostered through institutional expansion. Eligius was lay advisor to the Queen Regent Bathildis. Both generously donated their wealth to the financial needs of the Church and the poor. He became priest and bishop. She resigned her regency and entered a convent. When Rictrudis' husband was killed, her good friend Amandus interceded with the king to cease pressuring her to marry and allow the noblewoman to enter a convent.

Edward, the English king, and Gervinus, the renowned French abbot, frequently exchanged visits. Pope Gregory VII and Hugh of Cluny commiserated in poignant letters about the weight of their responsibilities in promoting Church reform. Bonaventure and Thomas Aquinas studied together for three years at the University of Paris and later taught there for another seven. Bonaventure remained at the same school for a total of thirty-one years and often was a dinner guest, along with Thomas Aquinas, of King Louis IX and his sister Bl. Isabel. In the same city but four centuries later Vincent de Paul and Louise de Marillac developed a tender bond of affection for each other and the poor whom they served. Vincent was also friend to Francis de Sales and spiritual director to Francis' best friend, Jane de Chantal. Teresa of Avila and John of the Cross provided mutual support for the development of their spiritual life and institutional reform. Philip Neri attracted many friends through his great sense of humor. Among those friends were counted Charles Borromeo, Ignatius Loyola and Pope Gregory XIII. Peter Favre was a family friend of the father of Alphonsus Rodriguez who, as a widower, entered Peter's community. Alphonsus was assigned to Montserrat in Spain and served there for three years as spiritual director of the seminarian Peter Claver.

Numerous saints chose saints as their spiritual directors. The director saw and guided the soul which the directee bared. These friends were called soul friends.[14] Besides the list of soul friends, many best friends and all the listed celibate friends were also soul friends. Chrysostom was spiritual director for Olympias. After John of Avila and Peter of Alcantara died, Teresa asked John of the Cross to serve as her spiritual director, which he did for the next twenty-four years. Vincent de Paul served as spiritual director for Louise de Marillac and Jane de Chantal.

Celibate friends were best friends who also experienced mutual romantic attraction and transcended that by spiritual union with God and each other. Beautiful letters attested to the deep affection and care which these saints held for one another. Bl. Jordan of Saxony, successor to Dominic as general superior, enjoyed a profound relationship with Bl. Diana d'Andalo. Catherine of Siena and Raymond of Capua, stalwart defenders of Church unity during the Avignon Papacy, delighted in a deep celibate friendship. Francis de Sales and Jane de Chantal shared openly before family, friends and community members their mutual attraction and affection. Margaret Mary Alacoque and Bl. Claude de la Colombière enjoyed a similar bond.

Other saints may have experienced this kind of platonic union but the nature of the relationship calls for great discretion both by the couple and the historians identifying these relationships. Other saints whose lives give some evidence of enjoying this celibate and delicate relationship may include Jerome and Paula, Chrysostom and Olympias, Vincent de Paul and Louise de Marillac, and numerous Irish saints.

Application Of The Theme

Common Vision: Saintly friends focused their relationship on union with and action for God and God's people. More than mutual natural attraction was necessary to sustain this kind of friendship. Their Christian values formed the foundation of the friendship. Friends shared a love of human life and a desire for eternal life.

Common Way: They shared conversation, correspondence, solace in sufferings, safe haven in exile, insight and inspiration, sense of the needs of the Church and foresight for the direction of the Church. They challenged and encouraged each other in individual and common pursuits for the Lord.

Common Bond With Each Other: They loved and trusted their friends more than anyone else. These friends shared their most profound and personal movements of the heart. They grew together as they walked and talked. Whether present or absent, a friend was a life-support for another friend's being and activity.

Common Bond With God: God was their mutual friend. God was their best friend. Friendship in this present life was a foretaste of friendship in the afterlife. These friends believed that the providence of God had brought them together. Even when alone neither friend felt lonely because of their friendship with each other and with God.

APPENDIX: SAINTLY FRIENDS

BEST FRIENDS

John the Evangelist (c. 6-c. 104) four times refers to himself as "the disciple whom **Jesus** loved" (Jn 13:23, 19:26, 20:2, 21:7). He accompanied Jesus together with Peter and James during significant moments. He alone among the apostles remained with Jesus at the foot of the cross.

Jesus visited the home at Bethany of **Mary** (1st century), **Martha** (1st century) and **Lazarus** (1st century). He sat down and chatted with them, came to console them in their suffering, and raised Lazarus from the dead. The Gospel writer commented: "Jesus loved Martha and her sister and Lazarus" (Jn 11:5).

The **four Mary's** at the foot of the cross include the **Blessed Virgin Mary**; **Mary Cleophas**, the mother of John Mark; **Mary Salome**, the mother of James the Younger and John the beloved disciple; and **Mary Magdalene**. All four women were disciples of Jesus.

Antony (251-356) and **Athanasius** (c. 297-373) are described in this chapter.

Basil the Great (329-79) and **Gregory Nazianzen** (329-89) are described in this chapter.

The friendship which **John Chrysostom** (c. 347-407) and the deaconess **Olympias** (c. 361-408) enjoyed is described in the chapter on the Benefit of Saintly Companions.

John Chrysostom was best friends too with **Maro** (d. 433), the Syrian hermit and founder of the Bait-Marun monastery from which it is believed the Maronite rite takes its name. These two friends supported each other by correspondence in the controversy over the Monothelite heresy. While Chrysostom was in exile, he begged for the prayers of Maro.

Jerome (342-420) enjoyed saintly friends wherever he lived: Rome, Aquilea, Antioch, Constantinople and Bethlehem.

At Rome he was baptized as an eighteen-year-old by Pope **Liberius** (d. 366). At Aquilea he participated in a prayer-and-study group which was directed by **Valerian** (d. 389), and attended by the priest **Chromatius** (d. c. 407) and the bishop **Heliodorus** (c. 332-c. 390). Here Jerome met Rufinus who was "first the bosom friend and then the bitter opponent of Jerome."[15] At Antioch he lived a hermit's life until **Paulinus** (c. 354-431) ordained him, although Jerome never once officiated at Mass. He traveled to Constantinople where he studied the scriptures under **Gregory Nazianzen** (c. 329-89). Jerome then traveled to Rome in the company of Paulinus and **Epiphanius** (c. 315-403) to attend a council convoked by Pope **Damasus** (304-84). Jerome remained in Rome as Damasus' secretary; here he produced his extraordinary scriptural translations, and guided a community of noble women ascetics. Only after Damasus died did Jerome and many of the women ascetics make their way to the Holy Land where he lived out his days.

The young widow **Marcella** (d. 410) had co-founded with Jerome at Rome the community of women ascetics. Her sister **Asella** (d. c. 406) and their mother **Albina** (5th century) lived with Marcella and her house guest Jerome. The widows **Lea** (d. 384) and **Melania the Elder** (c. 342- c. 410) who was the first Roman woman to visit the Holy Land, also belonged to Marcella's community.

Fabiola (d. 384) belonged to the community until she divorced her husband for his dissolute life and she remarried. After her second husband died, she returned to the Church and renewed her practice of social and ecclesiastical charities, including building the first public hospital in the western part of the Empire. She traveled to Bethlehem where she supported Jerome and his activities but declined to join Paula's monastic community. Fabiola returned to Rome and with **Pammachius** (d. 410) opened a hospice for pilgrims. **Paula** (347-404) and two of her daughters belonged to the community at Rome. After one of her daughters died, she and the second daughter left Rome with Jerome and traveled to the Holy Land.

Augustine (354-430) and **Alipius** (c. 360-430) were lifelong friends. They grew up together in Tagaste, North Africa. At Carthage they became Manicheans. At Rome they studied law. At Milan they took instructions from Ambrose and were baptized by him at the same ceremony. At Cassiciacum they joined a monastic community. They returned to Africa to live in a Christian community founded by Augustine. Three years later they traveled to Hippo and were ordained priests. Augustine became coadjutor bishop of Hippo. Alipius was named bishop of Tagaste. "[There Alipius] served for more than three decades and was the confidant and aid of Augustine for the rest of his life."[16]

Paulinus of Nola (c. 354-431) enjoyed his best friendship with **Ambrose** and **Martin of Tours**. He corresponded with **Augustine** and **Jerome**. Paulinus was very well educated, a successful lawyer and high public official. He traveled extensively throughout the western Empire. He married a Spanish noblewoman and settled near Bordeaux. There bishop **Delphinus** (d. 404) baptized him. He moved to Spain where his newborn son died after one week. Paulinus and his wife then began practicing great austerities. They distributed their wealth to the Church and the poor. In 393 the bishop of

Barcelona, acting on popular demand, ordained Paulinus to the priesthood. Two years later the couple moved, via Milan as Ambrose's guest, to an estate at Nola near Naples. There Paulinus built a basilica and church, an aqueduct and a hospice for travelers. **Melania the Elder** and later **Melania the Younger** and her husband **Pinian** stayed as guests of Paulinus. **Nicetas of Remesiana** (c. 335-c. 414) stayed twice with Paulinus. Paulinus provided shelter in his home for the city's poor. He was elected bishop of Nola and served until his death twenty-two years later. He is famous for his poetry and letters, many of which remain extant.

　　Patrick (c.389-c.461) baptized the parents of **Brigid** (c. 450-525) and befriended her. These two were buried together at Downpatrick. He converted to Christianity virtually the whole population and laid the foundation for a system of education for "the land of saints and scholars." She founded at age twenty the double monastery at Kildare where she became famous for her prayerfulness and compassion for those in distress.[17] These two saints and Ita are considered the most famous saints of Ireland.

　　The story is told that the good friends **Symeon** (d. 570) and **John** (d. 6th century) left behind in Edessa of Mesopotamia Symeon's widowed mother and John's young bride in order to make a pilgrimage to the Holy Sepulchre in Jerusalem. They never returned home. They went instead to the Jordan River where they dedicated their lives first as monks and eventually as hermits. After thirty years Symeon left John at the Jordan in order to minister in Syria.

　　Gregory of Tours (538-94) wrote about the exemplary life and austerities practiced by his friend **Agricola** (c. 497-580). Agricola served forty-eight years as bishop of Chalon-sur-Saone. Gregory's episcopal tenure in Tours lasted twenty-one years. Both men built and/or beautified many of the churches in eastern France. **Eligius** (c. 590-c.660), friend and counsellor to the Frankish Queen Regent **Bathildis** (d. 680), alone supported her independence when other courtiers were pressuring the widow to remarry. He had been a highly skilled and generous goldsmith before age fifty when he was ordained priest and then bishop. Bathildis, born in Britain and brought as a slave to the royal palace, married the king and bore him three sons, all of whom became kings. She ruled as regent for eight years. "She ransomed many captives, helped promote religion in the realm, and endowed and founded numerous monasteries."[18]

When **Rictrudis** (c. 612-88) was widowed, she was ordered by the king to remarry. She, however, wished to become a nun. Her old friend and spiritual director **Amandus** (7th century) interceded for her. The king relented and she then entered the double monastery which she had founded at Marchiennes. Three of her four children eventually joined her there, where she served as abbess for forty years.

The co-abbess **Elfleda** (d. 714) and bishop **Cuthbert** (d. 687) were great servants of the Church and great friends. Both won fame as peacemakers among opposing ecclesiastical as well as political factions. Elfleda and her mother succeeded Elfleda's abbess Hilda as co-abbesses.

When **Boniface** (c. 680-754) was ordained bishop, **Lioba** (d. 780) began a long-lasting correspondence with him. She introduced herself as "Liobgetha" whose parents he knew. When he requested missionary assistance, she volunteered. They worked together for thirty-two years. He appointed her abbess in Mainz, where he lived as archbishop. He requested that she be buried beside him.

Lioba was friend also to **Bl. Hildegard** (d. 783). Hildegard befriended and financially assisted many monks and nuns, but the closest of all these relationships was her friendship with Lioba.

King Edward the Confessor (1003-66) and the abbot **Gervinus** (d. 1075), although separated by the English Channel, developed a close friendship by frequent correspondence and visits. Edward built an abbey at Westminster which is the site of the present cathedral. Gervinus traveled widely in response to the popular demand for his preaching and spiritual counseling.

Pope **Gregory VII** (c. 1021-85) and **Hugh of Cluny** (1024-1109) lived as Benedictine monks at Cluny for two years (1047-49) under the abbot Odilo. These two ecclesiastical giants led the spiritual and institutional revival of the Church in the eleventh century. Both advised numerous popes; Hugh advised nine popes, and Hildebrand (the baptismal name for Gregory VII) served as archdeacon for five popes, until he himself was named pope in 1073. Gregory's lifelong opposition to lay investiture, simony and clerical concubinage gained for him many enemies. He even spent the last years of his life in exile. Hugh's advice was sought not only by popes but also by virtually all the sovereigns of Europe. He ruled over 1,000 monasteries and dependent houses.

Malachy (1095-1148) died in the arms of his friend **Bernard of Clairvaux** (1090-1153). They had met six years earlier, when the Irish bishop visited Clairvaux on his way to Rome. Malachy wished to become a Cistercian but the pope refused him permission and instead appointed him papal legate to Ireland. Bernard at age twenty-five had persuaded thirty-one friends and relatives to enter the monastery at Citeaux, from which sixty-eight other monasteries eventually originated. His advice was sought by popes and kings, and his preaching and miracle-working were solicited by countless thousands.

The hermit **Godric** (d. 1170) was oftentimes visited by **Robert of Newminster** (1100-59), a Cistercian monk. The two shared much conversation and mutual encouragement. Before Godric retired to a monastery for the last sixty years of his life, he spent some years as a store merchant and sixteen years as a sailor. He made three pilgrimages: to St. Giles' shrine in Provence, to Rome and to Jerusalem.

Edmund Rich (c. 1180-1240) and **Richard de Wyche** (c. 1197-1253) were lifelong friends as well as master and disciple.

Clare of Assisi (1194-1253) enjoyed the friendship not only of her younger sister Agnes but also of **Francis of Assisi** (c. 1181-1226) and **Bl. Agnes of Prague** (1205-82). Clare wrote to Agnes of Prague that she should see herself daily in the mirror as the bride of Christ, as reflected in the imagery of the Canticle of Canticles. Clare wrote to her: "I have indelibly written your happy memory into my heart, for you are dearer to me than all the others."[19]

Two of the Church's greatest scholars, **Bonaventure** (1221-74) and **Thomas Aquinas** (c. 1225-74), were classmates, fellow faculty members and friends. At the University of Paris they studied and received together their doctoral degrees and for six years more they taught together in the same department. "The assumption of intimate friendship is based on the fact that they were members of the newly founded mendicant orders which fostered special mutual friendship among the members, and that the bull of Bonaventure's canonization, *Superna caelestis patria*, of April 14, 1482, strongly intimates their close friendship."[20]

There are numerous anecdotes about their friendship. Each one wished the other to receive his degree first. The issue was decided on age, Bonaventure being four years older than Thomas. Pope Urban IV commissioned Bonaventure and Thomas to compose a suitable Office and Mass for the feast of Corpus Christi. Allegedly, Bonaventure visited Thomas, saw his antiphon, *O Sacrum Convivium*, returned home, and cast into the fireplace the work that he himself had been preparing. Another story relates that the Dominican asked the Franciscan to show him the books from which he had learned so much. Bonaventure simply pointed to a crucifix and said: "It is from this well-spring of light and love that I have drawn whatever is to be found in my lectures or writings."[21]

King Louis IX of France, (1214-70), who rebuilt Saint Chapelle and supported the establishment of the Sorbonne, enjoyed unusual dinner guests: **Thomas Aquinas** during the ten years that he was at the University of Paris; **Bonaventure** (1221-74) during the thirty-one years he spent teaching there; Louis' sister **Isabella** (13th century), and the king's chaplain **Bl. Giles of Sannur** (d. 1266). Table conversations are recorded in which the king repeatedly reveals his desire to know and accept God's will in personal and public matters. Bonaventure recounts that he refused to use his close friendship with the king for intercession for others. Two years after Louis died, Bonaventure introduced the liturgical memorial of King Louis IX.

Catherine of Siena (1347-80) and **Catherine of Sweden** (c. 1331-81) fought the same fights: against the immoral lives of the kings, queens and popes whom they criticized publicly and powerfully, and against the pope's remaining in Avignon instead of returning to Rome. Once the pope wished to send them together on a mission to encourage the queen of Naples to support him and not the anti-pope; Raymond of Capua dissuaded the pope because of the great danger to the women which this plan presented. Catherine of Sweden came to Rome in 1350 because she terribly missed her mother. She remained there for the next thirty years except for two brief absences from the city. Catherine of Siena attracted many people, including Catherine of Sweden, to the causes of prayer, community and public morality. Catherine of Siena traveled extensively in carrying out her missions in the cause of peace and reconciliation.

Philip Neri (1515-95) was known as the most popular person in Rome as well as "the second apostle of Rome."[22] He stood on street corners and visited marketplaces in order to meet people where they were most comfortable and most easily found. "He [Philip] was consulted by rich and poor, powerful and helpless for his spiritual wisdom and his ability to look into men's minds."[23] He "was venerated by popes, cardinals, rulers, and ordinary people."[24]

He attracted even the famous but not sainted Palestrina, who prepared music for afternoon services and "excursions" to other churches and community picnics. Other friends whom he met in ministry included **Charles Borromeo** (1538-84) and **Ignatius Loyola** (1491-1556). Charles Borromeo spent much time in the eternal city assisting his uncle the pope as papal ambassador, and back in Milan as the bishop and reformer of ecclesiastical and civil society. He rescued Milan during a three year plague by organizing and paying for the feeding of 3,000 people daily. Ignatius Loyola spent much time in Rome from 1541 when he founded the

Jesuit community until his death. He missioned the society's members to works of evangelization and education. **John Leonardi** (c. 1550-1609) was encouraged in his community by Philip.

Bl. Peter Favre (1506-46), a great friend of the father of **Alphonsus Rodriguez** (1533-1617), prepared the son for First Communion. Teacher and student became great friends. Peter emphasized that the reform of the Church ought to begin with reform of the clergy and laity rather than with the return of the Protestants. Alphonsus, a widower, applied at age fifty for entrance into the Jesuits. Uneducated, he was refused. He returned to school and at age fifty-four took his vows as a lay brother.

The families of **Rose of Lima** (1586-1617) and **Martin de Porres** (1579-1639) lived three blocks apart. His monastery and her home were located another three blocks apart in another direction.[25] His chapel served as her parish church. When he was fifteen years old and entered the monastery, she was nine years old; at that time began their frequent, if not virtually daily, visits.

Rose was baptized Isabel but, because of her beauty, family and friends nicknamed her Rose, which name she then chose for confirmation. She built a hut in her back yard to use as an infirmary for the sick and as a prayer place where she practiced austerities and enjoyed mystical experiences. Numerous pilgrims visited her. Rose was the first canonized saint of the New World. Martin was an illegitimate child of a black Panamanian mother and a Spanish soldier who acknowledged responsibility for his mulatto child but soon abandoned him, his mother, and his sister. As a lay brother, Martin built a home for orphans, distributed food to the hungry, and ministered medically and spiritually to the African blacks who had been transported to Lima's slave markets. Martin was loved by all ages, kinds and classes of people. "His pallbearers were the bishops and nobility of Peru."[26] Besides the usual mystical gifts of prayer, Martin was blessed with bilocation and aerial flight.[27] "Martin was a mystic of the highest order."[28]

Martin de Porres was close friends with **John Massias** (1585-1645), who also was a Dominican lay brother in a neighboring convent. John was orphaned as a child in Spain. He traveled to the New World in search of a new life where he worked on a cattle ranch before moving to Lima and becoming a monk. Both men were mystics. Both served the poor in practical ways. Since John was the monastery's porter, he received and begged alms for the poor. When he died, virtually the whole city attended his funeral.[29]

The friendship between **Vincent de Paul** (1580-1660) and **Louise de Marillac** (1591-1660) sanctified them and was manifested in practical service for the poor and the Church. In 1625, the same year in which he founded the Vincentian community, Louise de Marillac asked Vincent to be her spiritual director. At thirty-four years of age she had been married for thirteen years. She lacked confidence in herself, her abilities, and her relationship with God. Her diffident spirit may be traced to her status as an illegitimate child who, although acknowledged by her nobleman father, was not treated equally at home. One year after she met Vincent, her husband died, leaving her with one son. Vincent encouraged Louise to forget her excessive worry and self-preoccupation by busying herself in the practical care of the hungry, the sick and the unevangelized. Louise took his advice. She organized a group of wealthy women into the Ladies of Charity and founded the community of the Daughters of Charity.

CELIBATE FRIENDS

Throughout the two millennia of the Church's history, several members of the opposite sex not only have been best friends but also have experienced a romantic attraction to one another. These celibate friends had a genuine affection for each other that transcended the limitations and expectations of simple romantic love. While there may have been many more relationships of this kind, those included here are commonly accepted as being "more than just friends."

Jerome (c. 342-420) and **Paula** (347-404) met in Rome while he was secretary to Pope Damasus. After her daughter Blesilla (363-83) died, Jerome consoled her. Vicious rumors circulated about the propriety of their relationship and Jerome then left Rome. Paula and her daughter Eustochium Julia (d. c. 419) left with him. The trio traveled throughout the Holy Land and eventually settled in Bethlehem where they established four monasteries. "She [Paula], who became Jerome's closest confidante and assistant taking care of him and helping him in his biblical work, built numerous churches which were to cause her financial difficulties in her old age."[30]

Bl. Jordan of Saxony (d. 1237) and **Bl. Diana d'Andalo** (c. 1201-36) shared a great love for God and each other. She wanted to be a nun but her family forcibly prohibited her. Jordan, successor to Dominic as master general, suggested that the family build a convent right on the family's property so that they would not lose their only daughter. Jordan wrote to Diana: "You are so deeply engraven on my heart, the more I realize how truly you love me from the depths of your soul, the more incapable I am of forgetting you, the more constantly you are in my thoughts. For your love of me moves me profoundly and makes my love for you burn more strongly."[31]

Catherine of Siena (1347-80) and **Raymond of Capua** (1330-99) met when she was twenty-seven years old and he, forty-three. She asked him to be her spiritual director. Before she died, six years later, he became convinced of her mystical relationship with God. He wrote her biography. Catherine wrote to Raymond about their "close particular love" which "cannot believe nor imagine that one of us wishes anything else than the other's good" while "seeking ever in the other the glory of the name of God and the profit of his holy soul."[32]

The relationship between **Francis de Sales** and **Jane de Chantal** is described in this chapter.

Margaret Mary Alacoque (1647-90) and **Bl. Claude de la Colombière** (1641-82) met in 1675, when he was appointed superior of the Jesuit house at Paray-le-Monial, where she lived in the Visitation convent. She had experienced numerous visions and revelations regarding devotion to the Sacred Heart of Jesus, which had been rejected by her religious community, her previous spiritual director and theologians. Only Claude, her new spiritual director, supported her. Beginning in 1684, a new administration in her religious community and a revelation released in a book by Claude created a new appreciation of Margaret Mary. She was vindicated in her community and the Church, and devotion to the Sacred Heart of Jesus prospered.

Soul Friends

Queen Radegund (518-87), daughter of a pagan king, suffered terrible calamities from the men in her life: her father was murdered by his brother, her uncle lost a military battle in which the twelve-year-old Radegund was claimed by a king who six years later forced her to marry him, and some years later killed her brother. The queen could endure no more. Her spiritual director, **John of Chinon** (6th century), who had supported her in all her adversities, now advised her to leave her husband. She did. She entered a convent in 557 and for the next thirty years dedicated herself to prayer, poverty and a peaceful spirit.

Bl. Ida of Boulogne (1040-1113), a descendant of Charlemagne, sought out **Anselm** (c. 1033-1109) as her spiritual director. When her husband died, she disbursed her significant wealth to the poor and built and restored monasteries, living out her last years as a Benedictine oblate.

Bruno of Rheims (1030-1101) initiated the Carthusian spirit and practice of prayer, poverty and manual labor. His friend **Hugh of Grenoble** (1052-1132) worked zealously as a layman and later as bishop for the reform of the Church through restoration of clerical discipline. He became frustrated at the lack of cooperation he met, resigned his see and became a Benedictine. The pope ordered him back to his episcopal see. Subsequent popes refused Hugh's repeated requests to resign his see. As bishop, he provided land to Bruno for establishment of the first Carthusian monastery.

Bl. Ceslau (d. 1242) served as spiritual director for **Hedwig** (c. 1174-1243). Some authors claim that they may have been brother and sister. Ceslau, a native of Silesia, returned there for his priestly ministry. Hedwig married at age twelve the duke of Silesia who was then eighteen. They had seven children. Only one daughter survived the mother. Hedwig influenced her husband to construct houses for many religious communities. When her husband died, she entered the convent at Trebnitz where she took the habit but not the vows "in order that she might be free to administer her own property in her own way for the relief of the suffering."[33]

Peter of Verona (1205-52) served as spiritual director for the **Seven Founders of the Order of the Servites**. He was received into the Dominican order by Dominic himself. Peter became famous for his preaching, was appointed Inquisitor for northern Italy, and paid the price of martyrdom for his fidelity to his charge. He guided the Servites in their founding phase.

Raymond of Peñafort (1175-1275) and **Peter Nolasco** (c. 1189-1258), spiritual director and directee respectively, traveled the whole of Spain preaching and seeking the ransom of Christian prisoners from the Moors. Some say, although others dispute it, that they co-founded the Order of Our Lady of Ransom, popularly known as the Mercedarians. The community's fourth vow is to give themselves in exchange for a slave, if necessary.

John of Avila (1499-1569) guided the spiritual lives of many people, among whom were John of God, Peter of Alcantara, Francis Borgia, Teresa of Avila and John of the Cross. John of Avila had been born into great wealth but forsook that for priesthood. Upon his parents' deaths, he distributed his inheritance to the poor. He won both fame and enmity as a preacher.

John of Avila helped **John of God** (1495-1550) to change his life radically. John of God had lived a dissolute life as a soldier in France, Spain and Hungary; he was at one time an overseer of slaves in Morocco, and in his youth a shepherd near Seville. At age forty he resolved to do penance by traveling to Africa to rescue Christian slaves. He got as far as Granada, where his noble intentions turned to mercenary ones. He became a dealer in religious goods. In 1538 after hearing John of Avila preach, John of God became filled with remorse for his sins. He went berserk and was put in an insane asylum where John of Avila met, befriended and assisted him. When John of God left the asylum, he began works of charity for the sick and poor which led to the founding of the Order of the Brothers Hospitalers.

Francis Borgia (1510-72) served for ten years as advisor to Emperor Charles V and later as administrator for Charles' son. Francis married, raised eight children, and when his wife of seventeen years died, he joined the Jesuits. He was ordained a priest in 1541. Within fourteen years he was elected superior general of all Jesuits. He opened the Gregorian and the Gesù universities in Rome and established the foreign mission apostolate, beginning with the American mission. "So successful was he in revitalizing and reinvigorating the Jesuits that he is often called their second founder."[34]

Peter of Alcantara (1499-1562) was spiritual director for Teresa of Avila for five years until his death. This relationship began just two years after her initial experience of visions and voices.

Teresa of Avila (1515-82) is known as the saint of good sense and good humor. She was the first woman to be named a Doctor of the Church. In 1557 she met **Louis Bertrand** (1526-81), who encouraged her in her vision of reform for the Carmelite community. Louis was the Dominican novice director, which position he held for thirty years. In 1562 Teresa founded a convent for the strict observance of the Carmelite rule. Five years later she received permission to expand her company.

While building the second convent she met **John of the Cross** (1542-91). These two immediately discovered that they were kindred spirits who shared a similar longing for

God. They ignited each other's soul and the soul of the Church during the Counter-Reformation. John confided to Teresa that he was considering transferring from the Carmelites to the Carthusians to satisfy a desire for deeper prayer. She persuaded him to remain in the Carmelites and to join her in a reform movement. She asked him to be her spiritual director. Teresa affectionately referred to John as her "half a friar," since John stood just under five feet tall. He founded numerous men's monasteries. She founded sixteen women's convents. These two best friends and confidantes wrote unparalleled spiritual and mystical classics.

In 1568 John and four brother Carmelites founded the first reform Carmelite monastery, the Discalced Carmelites. In 1577 John was arrested and imprisoned for nine months. In 1590, at a General Assembly, John was stripped of all community offices and was exiled to a monastery in Andalusia. His most fervent enemies wanted him expelled from the order altogether. He soon contracted a fever, never recovered and died the following year.

The great **Charles Borromeo** (1538-84) chose as his spiritual director **Alexander Sauli** (1534-92). The pope, who was Charles' uncle, made him a cardinal at age twenty-two and appointed him Secretary of State. Charles was an heroic reformer. He even suffered a wound in an assassination attempt by a disgruntled priest whose community had been asked to cease their laxity. He asserted the rights of the Church against the encroachments of political leaders and won many converts from Protestantism to Catholicism. He personally organized and assisted the clergy and religious to aid the famine and plague stricken poor of the city of Milan, whose political leaders had fled out of fear for their own health. Alexander was a Barnabite priest and teacher, and eventually the provost general of his community. He supported in word and deed the reform movement of the Church and Charles.

Philip Neri (1515-95) served as spiritual director to several persons, one of whom was **Bl. Juvenal** (1545-1604). Juvenal left his double career of education and medicine to join Philip's Oratorians in 1575. He was ordained a priest and bishop of Saluzzo where he became famous for his service of the poor. He did not last long as bishop. "On his return (from his first episcopal visitation) he was poisoned by a friar whose evil life he had rebuked."[35]

The "old man" **Alphonsus Rodriguez** (1533-1617), who took the vows of a lay brother when he was fifty-four years old, was assigned the humble position of hall porter at Montesion College on Majorca. He became popular with the students during his twenty-four years of service there. One student, **Peter Claver** (1588-1654), chose Alphonsus as spiritual director. Peter was missioned to the New World where he was ordained a priest in the seaport slave-trading center of Cartagena, Colombia. Peter provided the slaves with food, medicine, instruction in the faith and baptism. He made 300,000 converts during his forty-year ministry. Alphonsus Rodriguez and Peter Claver were canonized together in 1888.

Robert Bellarmine (1542-1621) lived in Rome as provincial of his Jesuit community at the same time that the young **Aloysius Gonzaga** (1568-91) was studying there. Aloysius asked the saintly provincial to be his spiritual director. Robert served in that capacity for three years. The young and sickly Aloysius died in the arms of Robert.

Jane Frances de Chantal (1572-1641) followed for many years the spiritual direction of her very good friend, Francis de Sales. She later sought out **Vincent de Paul** (1580-1660) in this capacity.

Joseph Cafasso (1811-60) and **John Bosco** (1815-88) studied and then worked in Turin. Cafasso encouraged Bosco in his vocation of ministering to young boys. Cafasso was serving then as chaplain at a hospice for young girls and permitted Bosco to utilize a building on the grounds as a shelter for his boys. Bosco asked Cafasso to serve as his spiritual director and Cafasso encouraged the founding of Bosco's new religious community.

The spiritual director and palace chaplain for **Louis**

IX (1214-70) was **Bl. Giles of Saumur** (d. 1266). Giles accompanied Louis on the Seventh Crusade. Giles was named bishop of Damietta in Egypt and later of Tyre in Syria. He died back in Belgium.

Notes for Chapter 6

1.   *Dictionary of Quotations*, p. 258.7.
2.   Jerome, *Letter* 3:6, *PL* 22:395, as in Aelred of Rievaulx, *Spiritual Friendship*.
3.   Aelred of Rievaulx, ibid., p. 65.
4.   Delaney, *Dictionary of Saints*, p. 65.
5.   Athanasius was exiled in 336 to Trier, between 339-46 to Rome, between 356-62 to the desert, during 362-63 and for another four months in 363 to the desert, and finally for the period 365-66 to the desert again; cf. *The Book of Saints*.
6.   St. Athanasius, *The Life of Saint Antony*, pp. 17, 19.
7.   *Butler's Lives of the Saints*, vol. II, p. 256.
8.   Ibid., p. 257.
9.   From a sermon by St. Gregory Nazianzen, *The Liturgy of the Hours*, vol. I, pp. 1285-87.
10.   Wendy M. Wright, *Bond of Perfection*, p. 149.
11.   Ibid., p. 150.
12.   Ibid., p. 151.
13.   Ann Ball, *Modern Saints*, pp. 226-27.
14.   The position of "soul friend" in Ireland predated the arrival of Christianity. Each Celtic king had a soul friend (*anmchara*) who counseled him; this was the druid whose flow of incantations guided him in guiding the king. After the arrival of Patrick and Columba, Christian clerics supplanted the druids. The description of the Christian spiritual director as soul friend evolved from the Celtic Church. Cf. Kenneth Leech, *Soul Friend*, pp. 49-50.
15.   Butler, vol. III, p. 686.
16.   Delaney, p. 46.
17.   Ibid., p. 120.
18.   Ibid., p. 92.

19 Clare to Agnes of Prague, *The Liturgy of the Hours*, vol. IV, pp. 1311-12.

20 Colman Majchrzak, *A Brief History of Bonaventurism*, p. 5.

21 Laurence Costelloe, *Saint Bonaventure*, p. 93.

22 *The Book of Saints*, p. 456.

23 Delaney, p. 420.

24 Ibid., p. 420.

25 Private letter of Jose Antonio Ubillus Lamadrid, C.M., from Lima, Peru; October 16, 1990; to the author.

26 Clifford Steven, *The One Year Book of Saints*, p. 315.

27 Delaney, p. 477.

28 Steven, p. 315.

29 Butler, vol. III, pp. 593-94.

30 Delaney, p. 451.

31 Basil Cole, "Mary and Joseph: Their love for each other," p. 14.

32 *Catherine of Siena as Seen in her Letters*, pp. 326-27.

33 Butler, vol. IV, p. 125.

34 Delaney, p. 114.

35 *The Book of Saints*, p. 330.

CHAPTER 7

TEACHER-STUDENT SAINTS

Teacher-Student

1. James of Nisibis and Ephraem of Syria
2. Macrina the Elder and Basil the Great
3. Macrina the Younger taught Gregory of Nyssa and Peter of Sebastea
4. Philastrius and Gaudentius
5. Ambrose and Augustine
6. Gregory Nazianzen the Younger taught Jerome and Paulinus of Antioch
7. Augustine taught Quodvultdeus and Alipius
8. Illtud taught Samson, Gildas and Leonorius
9. Tathai and Cadoc
10. Germanus of Autun and Droctoveus
11. Finnian of Clonard taught the twelve apostles of Ireland
12. Mobhi and Columba
13. Colman of Dromore and Mochae taught Finnian of Strangford
14. Ita and Brendan the Navigator
15. Brendan the Navigator and Colman of Cloyne
16. Comgall and Columban
17. Avitus of Clermont and Gregory of Tours
18. Isidore of Seville and Ildephonsus
19. Anseric of Soissons and Drausius of Soissons

163

20. Honorius and Boniface taught Wilfrid of Northumbria
21. Hilda taught Wilfrid of York, John of Beverley and Elfleda
22. Egbert and Alcuin
23. Wilfrid taught Willibrord, Wigbert and Egbert
24. Venerable Bede and Alcuin
25. Alcuin and Adalhard
26. Alcuin and Gregory of Utrecht taught Ludger
27. Theodard of Maestricht and Lambert of Maestricht
28. Boniface and Lull
29. Wolfgang of Wurzburg and Henry II
30. Gerard Sagrado and Adalbert of Prague taught Bl, Emeric
31. Adalbert of Madgeburg and Adalbert of Prague
32. Cunegund and Emma
33. Bl. Herman the Cripple and Bl. Benno of Osnabruck
34. Bruno of Rheims and Pope Bl. Urban II
35. Bl. Jutta and Hildegard of Germany
36. Albert the Great taught Thomas Aquinas and Bl. Ambrose Sansedoni
37. Mechtilde of Helfta and Gertrude the Great
38. Bernardino of Siena taught John of Capistrano and John of the Marches
39. Bl. Peter Favre and Alphonsus Rodriguez
40. Turibius of Mogrobejo taught Rose of Lima, Martin de Porres and John Massias
41. John Bosco taught Dominic Savio, Bl. Michael Rua, Bl. Louis Guanella and Bl. Louis Orioni

Classmates

42. Heraclas and Plutarch
43. Gregory Thaumaturgus and Athenodorus
44. Basil the Great and Gregory Nazianzen the Younger

45. Bl. Peregrine and Bl. Rizzerio
46. Thomas Aquinas and Bonaventure
47. Thomas Aquinas and Bl. Ambrose Sansedoni
48. John of Capistrano and John of the Marches
49. Francis Xavier and Peter Favre

Sowing the Seeds of Faith: Teacher and Student Saints

Teachers represent a most noble profession. Every culture esteems its teachers. Teachers receive, develop and hand on the culture's accumulated knowledge. These educators draw forth and develop in others new insights and approaches to the existing body of knowledge. A teacher's impact and importance can never be measured. To teach is to touch a life forever. "A teacher affects eternity; he can never tell where his influence stops."[1]

According to the Scriptures God constantly teaches people. God teaches the patriarchs, priests, prophets, and psalmists, who in turn teach the people for whom they hold responsibility. God is repeatedly besought: "Teach me your paths" (Ps 25:4). "Teach me your statutes" (Ps 119:26). "Teach me your way" (Ps 86:11). "Teach me to do your will" (Ps 143:10). Jesus is hailed as teacher by the scribes and Pharisees, disciples and apostles, and anonymous persons in the crowd. Jesus calls himself teacher. No title is used more often than teacher to describe Jesus.[2] He teaches by word and deed in formal and informal settings. Scholars claim that the scriptural instructions most likely spoken by Jesus were the kingdom sayings, the proverbial sayings, the parabolic sayings and the Our Father.[3] Jesus' whole life was an education and revelation for those seeking to learn the will of God and the meaning of human life. Jesus summed up his students' responses in the parable of the sower and the seed (Mt 13:4-23).

Many saints benefited from saintly companions in the classroom. Many represent the relationship of either teacher and student or classmates. The opportunity to learn is a blessing in itself. The opportunity to learn either from or with a saint made these persons a mutual blessing to one another.

Particular examples

1. AMBROSE AND AUGUSTINE

By his preaching Ambrose (340-97) attracted the ever-searching Augustine (354-430). Augustine approached Ambrose in order to be instructed in the faith.

Ambrose was a well-established political leader before he became a religious leader. His father had been praetorian prefect of Gaul. As a lawyer, Ambrose served as governor of the area surrounding Milan. In 374 when the bishop of Milan died, Ambrose sought to quell the near riot between the rival Arian and Catholic factions. So well did he succeed in pacifying the crowd, that the opposing parties acclaimed him as their candidate for bishop. He was a catechumen, not even baptized. He refused the position foisted on him by the populace, but the emperor soon confirmed the election. By the end of that same year Ambrose was baptized, ordained a priest and made a bishop.

Ambrose entered wholeheartedly into his new position. He gave away all his possessions and committed himself to an austere lifestyle. He studied intensely the Bible and Christian writers of theology. He defended the Church against internal theological and external political and military opponents. "[Ambrose] was considered by his contemporaries as the exemplar par excellence of what a bishop should be: holy, learned, courageous, patient, and immovable when necessary for the faith."[4]

In 384 Augustine moved to Milan to accept the position of the university's chair of rhetoric. For the purpose of hearing good rhetoric he attended the cathedral services. He was affected not only by the power of Ambrose's rhetoric but also by the content of his presentations. Augustine was baptized into the Christian faith at the Easter Vigil in 387. Later that same year he went back home to North Africa. The relationship of Ambrose and Augustine remained at the level of teacher-student. They were never close friends.

> St. Augustine learned all of this, humanly speaking, from his spiritual father, St. Ambrose. His preaching and his catechetical instructions at Milan revealed this intelligible world of Christianity to the mind of Augustine: the reality and the concept of sacred history, and the luminous inner conviction, indeed one of divine faith itself, that the canonical Scriptures are the very word of God incarnate in human speech. Above all, however, he learned that the Catholic Church, now extended over the whole earth, is "crowned with divine authority." It teaches these truths and presents the Sacred Scripture as the authorized representative and spokesman of God on earth. St. Augustine learned all these things, as all adult converts at that time learned them, in the teaching which the Church carried on in the catechumenate. St. Augustine's brief reference to his own baptismal instruction makes the point explicitly. He returned from Cassiciacum to Milan for the course of instructions, to consider "the depths of your counsel concerning the salvation of mankind."[5]

2. ITA OF KILLEEDY AND BRENDAN THE NAVIGATOR

Ita (d. c. 570) had a chance to marry, but chose instead to live the life of a virgin. She moved from Waterford to Limerick and there founded a convent of women for the ministry of the education of young boys. Brendan the Navigator (c. 484- c. 577) studied with Ita for five years. One of the stained glass windows in St. Brendan's Cathedral in Loughrea pictures Ita gently instructing young Brendan. Along with Brigid, Ita is considered one of the two most famous women saints of Ireland. The story is told that Brendan once inquired of his teacher what three things God most loved and most abhorred among his creatures. Ita replied:

> True faith in God with a pure heart, a simple life with a religious spirit, openhandedness inspired by charity — these three things God specially loves. A face which scowls upon all mankind, obstinacy in wrong-doing, and an overweening confidence in the power of money — these are three things that are hateful in God's sight.[6]

Marvellous miracles and visions are attributed to Ita. One tradition relates that the infant Jesus appeared to her. She composed poems which she sang as lullabies to the infant whom she affectionately called her Jesukin:

> Jesukin
> Lives my little cell within;
> What were wealth of cleric high —
> All is lie but Jesukin.
>
> Nursling nurtured, as 'tis right —
> Harbours here no servile sprite —
> Jesú of the skies, who art
> Next my heart thro' every night!
>
> Jesukin, my good for aye,
> Calling and will not have nay,
> King of all things, ever true,
> He shall rue who will away.
>
> Jesú, more than angels aid,
> Fosterling nor formed to fade,

Nursed by me in desert wild,
Jesú, child of Judah's Maid.

Son of Kings and kingly kin,
To my land may enter in;
Guest of none I hope to be,
Save of Thee, my Jesukin!

Unto heaven's High King confest
Sing a chorus, maidens blest!
He is o'er us, though within
Jesukin is on my breast![7]

Brendan at age six advanced from Ita's school to the monastic school of the abbot Jarlath. From there he was ordained by the same bishop who had baptized him as an infant. He founded many monasteries, including in 559 the famous Clonfert, which attracted during his leadership 3,000 monks. Brendan was a sea-faring missionary who traveled to many parts of Ireland, England, Scotland and, many would argue, even to North America. Brendan's account of his epic voyage, *Navagatio Sancti Brendani Abbatis*, was translated into Latin, French, English, German, Flemish, Spanish and Italian. Within five hundred years of his death, and even until now, this book can be found in all the great libraries of Europe. As a matter of fact, "In 1976-77 Tim Severin, an expert on navigation, following the instructions in the *Navagatio*, built a hide-covered curragh and then sailed it from Ireland to Newfoundland via Iceland and Greenland, demonstrating the accuracy of its directions and descriptions of the places Brendan mentioned in his epic."[8]

3. ALBERT THE GREAT AND THOMAS AQUINAS

Albert the Great (c. 1206-80) taught the great Thomas Aquinas (c. 1225-74). The two first met in the classroom at the University of Paris in 1247. The next year they traveled to Cologne, where they shared the teacher-student experience for another two years. At Paris the genius of the undergraduate Thomas had not yet been recognized. At Cologne, however, this graduate student had for the first time both the opportunity and the responsibility to participate in the university's disputations. Here Thomas' extraordinary ability became appreciated by Albert and others:

> Round about the same time, a classmate observed: "This Neapolitan Thomas is frightfully clever! Today he went over the lecture with me so thoroughly that I understood it better from him than I did from the Master." One of the students discovered some notes Thomas had taken on a difficult question that Albert had been disputing, and he took the notes to show Albert. Albert, as a result, decided to give Thomas what was evidently his first experience of taking an active part in a disputation. The student master was told to put a tricky question to Thomas in preparation for the disputation. Thomas tried to get out of it, in all humility, but was not allowed to escape; so he betook himself to prayer. When the time came, he responded to Albert's questions so authoritatively that Albert commented that he appeared to have taken the place of the Master rather than of a student, "determining" the question rather than "responding." After trying in vain to out-argue Thomas, Albert declared, "We call him the dumb ox, but one day he will emit such a bellowing in his teaching that it will be heard throughout the world."[9]

Thomas surprised his family by joining the fledgling Dominican community. His noble family, which was related to the Holy Roman Emperor and the King of France, expected him to join the prestigious Benedictines rather than the recently founded mendicant Dominicans. Thomas had been attending the Benedictine school at Monte

Cassino since he was five years old. When Thomas joined the Dominicans in 1244, after completing his studies at the University of Naples, his family within a few weeks kidnaped and imprisoned him in their castle for fifteen months so that he might come to his senses. Allegedly, some of his brothers sent a prostitute to Thomas' cell to dissuade him from his choice. The rotund Thomas unhesitatingly chased the woman from his cell. With much reluctance, the family accepted his choice of religious community. He went to Paris, where as a young student he suffered ridicule because of his great size; he was nicknamed "the dumb ox." When given a chance to demonstrate his ability, however, Thomas' greatness was quickly appreciated. Albert the Great recognized and helped to develop his student's God-given ability.

4. John Bosco and Dominic Savio

Dominic Savio (1842-57) was twelve years old when he became a student of John Bosco (1815-88) at St. Francis de Sales oratory in Turin. Dominic's parish priest had recommended that the youth participate in Bosco's program for training youths to care for neglected boys.

Dominic was a sensitive and somber youth. Providentially he was instructed by the wise and cheerful John Bosco. Bosco insisted that Dominic lead a balanced life. The teacher urged that the student not only pray hard but also work and play hard. Don Bosco taught Dominic that God is pleased by all our activities as long as they are done for His glory.

At the oratory Dominic organized a group of boys called the Company of the Immaculate Conception to promote religious devotions and to do practical chores. Don Bosco had to moderate Dominic's fervor: "Religion must be about us like the air we breathe; but we must not weary the boys with too many devotions and observances."[10] He added: "The penance God wants is obedience. There is plenty to put up with cheerfully — heat, cold, sickness, the tiresome ways of other people. There is quite enough mortification for boys in school life itself."[11] Don Bosco taught Dominic how he should view the boys:

> Let us regard those boys over whom we have some authority as our own sons. Let us place ourselves in their service. Let us be ashamed to assume an attitude of superiority. Let us not rule over them except for the purpose of serving them better . . . In serious matters it is better to beg God humbly than to send forth a flood of words that will only offend the listeners and have no effect on those who are guilty.[12]

Don Bosco had to moderate Dominic regarding his own bodily mortifications. One cold night Don Bosco discovered Dominic lying in bed with one sheet on and the other sheets lying beside him. Don Bosco excoriated Dominic: "Don't be so crazy. You'll get pneumonia." The ever serious Dominic replied, "Why should I? Our Lord didn't get pneumonia in the stable at Bethlehem."[13]

Teacher and student got along very well. They were good for each other. They both did every good thing they could for the love of God and the boys whom they served. Don Bosco wrote an account of his experiences and exchanges with young Dominic, carefully including nothing that he himself could not account for. Numerous supernatural enlightenments and moments of enrapt prayer were experienced by Dominic. One story that Don Bosco relates is that Dominic was missing from the day's normal activities for six hours. Don Bosco discovered Dominic by the lectern in the chapel, standing in a cramped posture, enrapt in prayer. When Don Bosco engaged him in conversation, Dominic claimed that he did not know that Mass was already over. Dominic explained these prolonged periods of intense prayer as "my distractions."[14]

General Observations

Numerous teacher-student relationships are found among the saints. The influence of a teacher upon a student, and vice versa, is difficult to measure; the opportunity for positive influence, however, is difficult to deny. The relationship in the learning process can be profound. The context is a classroom. The tools are paper, pen and books. The medium is the exchange of ideas. A relationship of mutual respect evolves as two people unite in dialogue. Different from all other relationships mentioned in this book, the starting point of the teacher-student relationship is rooted at the intellectual level. An affective relationship might emerge in time but the unique origin of the teacher-student relationship rests in the interpersonal intellectual life.

Some teachers affected their students so much that the students chose to follow in the footsteps of the instructor. James of Nisibis and his student Ephraem of Syria both attended the Council of Nicea in 325 and became renowned opponents of Arianism. Ephraem succeeded James as head of the theological school that he had founded. In fifth-century Ireland, Illtud taught Samson at Llanilltud Fawr Monastery in Glamorgan before both served as co-missionaries. At Flanders in the seventh century Theodard and Lambert were not only teacher and student but also co-missionaries and co-martyrs. Bernardino of Siena taught the classmates John of Capistrano and John of the Marches. Later these three Franciscans served together as missionaries. As already mentioned, John Bosco inspired his student Dominic Savio to join Bosco's apostolic community.

Many teachers were succeeded in their episcopal sees by former students. Philastrius, bishop of Brescia, was succeeded by Gaudentius; Anseric, bishop of Soissons, by Drausius; and Theodard of Maestricht, by Lambert.

Boniface taught the deacon Lull at Fulda, ordained him to the priesthood, and consecrated him eventually as his successor as bishop of Mainz.

Other saintly bishops taught future bishops of other dioceses. Avitus, bishop of Clermont, taught Gregory, the bishop of Tours; and Isidore of Seville taught Ildephonsus, the archbishop of Toledo.

Women, too, grace the field of teacher-student saints. Ita, one of the three most famous saints of Ireland (along with Brigid and Patrick), taught Brendan the Navigator in her convent school. Mechtilde of Helfta taught Gertrude the Great, and the two jointly published books about their mystical experiences.

Some saints are recognized for their extraordinary scholarship in presenting the teachings of the Church. Among the Doctors of the Church are included many pairs of teachers and students: Ambrose and Augustine, Gregory Nazianzen and Jerome, Isidore of Seville and Ildephonsus (considered a Doctor by the Church in Spain), Albert the Great and Thomas Aquinas. Two saints who were classmates, teaching colleagues and fellow Doctors of the Church are Bonaventure and Thomas Aquinas. Another saintly Doctor who was taught by a saint is Ephraem of Syria. The two women Doctors of the Church, Catherine of Siena and Teresa of Avila, did not have saintly teachers but did have saintly spiritual directors. Two teachers in this category were renowned by contemporary scholars for their virtually encyclopedic knowledge: Isidore of Seville and Bl. Herman the Cripple.

Some students were no youngsters when they began their studies. Augustine of Hippo was thirty; Jerome, thirty-eight; and Colman of Cloyne, fifty years old.

The classroom context of most teacher-student relationships, unlike most relationships between family members and friends, is brief. Augustine studied in Milan under Ambrose for only three years. Jerome studied at Constantinople under Gregory Nazianzen for about two years. Don Bosco taught Dominic Savio at Turin for only three years. Despite the short duration of teacher and student relationships, some lifelong friendships did evolve. Examples include the bonds between Albert the Great and Thomas Aquinas, Mechtilde and Gertrude the Great, and Bernardino of Siena and John of Capistrano. Some classmates, too, became lifelong friends, namely, Augustine and Alipius, as well as Basil the Great and Gregory Nazianzen.

Numerous saints were classmates. The brothers Heraclas and Plutarch were catechumens together at Alexandria. The brothers Gregory Thaumaturgus and Athenodorus interrupted legal studies at Beirut for theological studies at Caesarea. Basil the Great and Gregory Nazianzen studied at the rhetorical schools in Caesarea and Athens. Thomas Aquinas and Bonaventure studied together at the University of Paris and received their doctorates in theology at the same ceremony. Thomas had studied philosophy with Bl. Andrew Sansedoni at Cologne under Albert the Great. Bl. Peregrine and Bl. Rizzerio were classmates at the University of Bologna when both were inspired by the preaching of Francis of Assisi. Immediately, they decided to dedicate their lives to his vision and mission. Two former lawyers, John of Capistrano and John of the Marches, studied theology under Bernardino of Siena at Fiesole. Francis Xavier and Peter Favre were classmates and roommates at the University of Barbe, where they met Ignatius Loyola, an older student by fifteen years.

Classmates can have great impact on each other. Thomas Aquinas was marvelling at Bonaventure's great learning. The Dominican asked the Franciscan which books in particular had helped him to acquire so much wisdom. Bonaventure responded by simply looking up at the crucifix, pointing to it and saying: "It is from this wellspring of light and love that I have drawn whatever is to be found in my lectures or writings."[15] Another story is told that these two friends were given the same assignment by the pope: to compose a hymn on the Eucharist for the feast of Corpus Christi. Bonaventure happened to see the *O Sacrum Convivium* which Thomas was preparing. Bonaventure then went home and simply threw into the fireplace his own composition, so exquisite was the work of his classmate.

Application Of The Theme

Common Vision: Pass it on! Faith-filled teachers did just that for faith-ready students. In an atmosphere of intellectual openness and inquisitiveness teachers and students saw the faith in a new light. Study aided them to see with the eyes of faith insights which they never saw before.

Common Way: Docility and dialogue characterized the method of education for these saints. Students were docile; they were open-minded, teachable and receptive. Teachers invited dialogue; they believed that education was a two-way street in which teachers and students learned by speaking and listening to each other. Docility and dialogue required a holy humility.

Common Bond With Each Other: Years-long educational activity left a life-long influence. The exchange of profound ideas made a profound impact. Good people were helped to become better. Teachers informed and formed their students, as subtly as artists shape their subjects. These teachers and students enlightened and inspired one another.

Common Bond With God: God was the source of truth which the saints sought, taught and learned. The idea of truth was not an end in itself, but a means to an end. The ultimate truth was to know and love God.

APPENDIX: TEACHER AND STUDENT SAINTS

TEACHERS - STUDENTS

James of Nisibis (d. 338) taught **Ephraem of Syria** (c. 306-c. 373) and both later attended the Council of Nicea in 325 where they avidly opposed Arianism. In Nisibis James is remembered as the see's first bishop, builder of its great basilica and probably founder of its famous theological school. "He is named in the canon of the Syrian and Maronite Mass, and in the festal litany of the Chaldean."[16] Ephraem attended the theological school in his native Nisibis and succeeded James as head of the school. When the Persians captured the city in 363, Ephraem fled to a cave near Edessa, where he became a deacon and a monk, preaching and writing extensively. "Ephraem wrote voluminously in Syriac on exegetical, dogmatic and ascetical themes, drawing heavily on Scriptural sources. . . . He was responsible in large measure for introducing hymns in public worship and used them effectively in religious instruction."[17] He is remembered especially for his Marian writings and hymns. When a terrible famine raged in Mesopotamia a few years before his death, Ephraem organized a program of relief for the sick and hungry. In 1920 he was declared a Doctor of the Church, the only Syrian to be thus honored.

Macrina the Elder (c. 270-340) taught her grandson **Basil the Great** (329-79). Basil was among the oldest of ten children. The grandmother educated him at home before he left to continue studies at Constantinople and Athens.

Macrina the Younger (c. 330-79) taught her younger brothers **Gregory of Nyssa** (c. 330-95) and **Peter of Sebastea** (c. 340-91). When her fiancé died, she decided to dedicate her life to God. When her father died, she and her mother formed a religious community on one of the family's estates.

Gaudentius (d. c. 410) studied under **Philastrius** (d. 387) before entering the monastery at Caesarea in Cappadocia. Eventually the student succeeded his teacher as bishop of

Brescia. Gaudentius had other saintly contacts too; he was ordained bishop by Ambrose, and corresponded regularly with John Chrysostom. Gaudentius and two other bishops were sent by the pope to the East to defend Chrysostom and his work. Near Thrace the papal party of three bishops was captured. All were imprisoned and offered a bribe to witness against Chrysostom. They refused. Gaudentius writes of Philastrius that he was generous towards the poor and renowned for his gentleness. Philastrius' famous book against the Arians, *Catalogue of Heresies*, remains extant.

Ambrose (340-97) instructed **Augustine** (354-430) in his conversion to the Christian faith. Their relationship is described in this chapter.

Both **Jerome** (342-420) and **Paulinus of Antioch** (c. 354-431) studied the Scriptures for approximately two years (380-82) under **Gregory Nazianzen** at Constantinople. Jerome often mentions in his works the "satisfaction and gratitude, the honor and happiness of having had so great a master in expounding the divine writings."[18] When Gregory left Constantinople, so did Jerome.

Augustine (354-430) taught and befriended **Quodvultdeus** (d. c. 450), who later became bishop of Carthage. Quodvultdeus was exiled by the king of the Vandals after Carthage was captured in 439. The expatriated bishop died in Naples.[19]

Another student of Augustine (354-430) was his life-long friend and confidant, **Alipius** (c. 360-430). They were born in the town of Tagaste in North Africa just six years apart. Augustine instructed Alipius in grammar at Tagaste and in rhetoric at Carthage. There Augustine influenced his student to become a Manichean like himself. Alipius' father became furious and forbade his son to associate again with Augustine. This sanction, however, did not last. The two met again in Rome where Alipius had gone to study law and Augustine to teach rhetoric. Their friendship was renewed. They moved to Milan for better career opportunities. There their names were inscribed on the same list of catechumens and there they were baptized together by Ambrose at the Easter Vigil in 387. Soon the two returned to Tagaste, where they remained for three years. Then the young priest Augustine was ordained the bishop of Hippo; and within three more years, the recent convert and young priest Alipius was ordained bishop of Tagaste.

At Llanilltud Fawr monastery in Glamorgan "whence issued most of the Welsh saints of that period,"[20] the scholarly **Illtud** (450-535) instructed **Samson** (485-565), **Gildas** (c. 500- c. 570) and **Leonorius** (d. c. 570) in the Scriptures and philosophy. Whereas the authenticity of many details of their lives are questioned, the facts of their existence, ordinations, writings and relationships are generally accepted. The scholarly Illtud and his wife agreed to separate so that both might live monastic lives. He then founded and became the first abbot of the famous Llanilltud monastery. His three famous students became not only monks and abbots like their teacher but also missionaries. Samson "is indeed one of the greatest missionaries Britain has ever produced, and certainly the greatest of his century."[21] He established many churches and monasteries in Ireland, Brittany and Normandy. Gildas lived for a while as an ascetic at Llanilltud before traveling to Ireland as a missionary and then to Brittany, where he spent his last years as a hermit again. Leonorius, a king's son, returned to his brother's kingdom in Brittany, where he founded a monastery and worked for the spread of the faith.

The Irish priest **Tathai** (6th century) instructed **Cadoc** (d. 575) at the teacher's famous school at Llandathan where students came from all over the British isles, preferring Llandathan to all other schools. Cadoc studied with Tathai for twelve years.

Germanus of Autun (c. 496-576), the abbot of St. Symphronian abbey, instructed **Droctoveus** (d. c. 580). When Germanus was appointed the bishop of Paris in 555, he recommended that Droctoveus succeed him as abbot. As bishop, Germanus won fame for his charity, convert-making, and constant reprimands against the immorality of the royal court. "St. Germanus is one of those bishops to whom history has given the title, 'father of the poor.'"[22] When Germanus decided to establish a monastery attached to the cathedral church, he invited Droctoveus to be its first abbot. After Germanus' death, this famous Parisian monastery was re-named Saint Germain.

The sixth century Irish Church claims many teacher-student saints. The "Teacher of Irish Saints" is the title given to **Finnian of Clonard** (c. 470-549). Finnian corresponded with the saintly Gildas of Llanilltud (c. 500-70) and visited the saintly Cadoc of Llancafarn (d. c. 575). Finnian in turn instructed the so-called **twelve apostles of Ireland**. The twelve include among others the great Columba, Mobhi, and Brendan the Navigator. **Columba** (c. 521-97) continued his studies at Glasnevin under **Mobhi** (d. c. 545). Columba with twelve relatives later founded at Iona one of the greatest monasteries of all Christendom. The monks of Iona influenced all of Western Europe for centuries until the Rule of St. Benedict became virtually universal. Columba influenced two famous Irishmen: Colman of Lindisfarne, who became bishop and abbot of two monasteries; and his nephew Colman of Lann Elo, who served as abbot at one monastery, and then founded and served as abbot at a second monastery, before becoming a bishop.

Finnian of Strangford (d. c. 579) studied under **Colman of Dromore** (6th century) and at Mahee Island under **Mochae** (6th century). At Whitern, Finnian himself became a monk. From there he went to Rome, where he was ordained. Upon returning to Ulster, he founded many monasteries. He and Columba became embroiled in an unfortunate dispute when Columba copied without permission Finnian's copy of Jerome's psalter, which was the first and only of its kind in Ireland. The king settled in favor of Finnian, thereby requiring Columba to turn over to Finnian the second copy. Colman built a monastery at Dromore in County Down. He became the first bishop of that see.

Ita (d. c. 570) instructed **Brendan the Navigator** (c.

484- c. 577) at her convent school at Killeedy, Limerick. These two are described in the text of this chapter.

Brendan taught and baptized **Colman of Cloyne** (530-606), who was then fifty years old. Colman had been the royal poet at Cashel. Soon after his baptism, he was ordained to the priesthood and the episcopacy. Colman was the first bishop of Cloyne.

The severe ascetic **Comgall** (c. 517-603) taught the great missionary monk **Columban** (c. 540-615) whose monasteries flourished throughout France, Germany, Switzerland and Italy. Columban aroused the ire of the Frankish bishops because he employed in his monasteries the familiar Celtic liturgical practices rather than those of Rome. He also denied the Frankish bishops any jurisdiction over his monasteries.

Avitus (d. c. 600), the abbot at Perche, France, instructed and ordained the esteemed historian **Gregory of Tours** (540-94). Avitus was bishop of Clermont. Gregory was bishop of Tours, which position he held for over twenty years.

In Spain **Isidore of Seville** (c. 560-636) taught **Ildephonsus** (607-67). Isidore was "an encyclopedic writer on theology, scripture, biography, history, geography, astronomy and grammar."[23] As archbishop, he renewed and reorganized the Spanish Church. His student Ildephonsus became a monk, abbot and archbishop of Toledo. Both bishops brought development and unity to the Mozarabic liturgical rites.

Anseric of Soissons (6th century) instructed **Drausius of Soissons** (d. c. 674). Both in turn became the bishop of Soissons. Drausius built a monastery, a convent and two churches. He succeeded in enlisting even the help of a local tyrant in building the convent. Drausius is "admired for his austerities, preaching, and wise administration of his see."[24]

Hilda (614-80) was asked by Aidan (d. 651) to return from her sister's monastery to renew a lax monastery in Northumberland. She and her pupils became famous. Five of them became bishops, including **Wilfrid of York** (d. c. 744) and **John of Beverley** (d. 721). Another pupil, **Elfleda** (d. 714), succeeded Hilda as prioress of the double monastery. Hilda convened the council of Whitby to resolve the dispute between the Celtic and Roman liturgical calendars and rites. She preferred to continue using the Celtic way. She yielded, however, when the council decided in favor of the Roman way.

     Wilfrid of Northumbria (634-709) studied in Ireland under **Honorius** (d. 653) and then traveled to Rome with Benet Biscop to study under **Boniface** (c. 680-754), who was secretary to the pope. Wilfrid later returned to England, where he taught **Willibrord** (c. 658-739), **Wigbert** (d. c. 738) and **Egbert** (c. 639-729).

     Egbert spent his life as a monk at Landisfarne in England, at Rathmelsigi in Ireland and at Iona off the coast of Scotland. He successfully encouraged the Celtic monks to yield to the Roman liturgical calendar and ritual. He taught **Bl. Alcuin** (c. 735-804). **Venerable Bede** (c. 672-735) also taught **Alcuin**. They met at the cathedral school in York, where the student succeeded his teacher as head of the school. Both produced numerous treatises on the scriptures, theology and history. Bede concentrated his efforts on England, rarely leaving the monastery which he entered as a three-year-old. Bede began the practice of dating events *anno Domini*, i.e., the year of the Lord. He is the only English Doctor of the Church. His title "venerable" was applied to him by the Council of Aachen a century after his death.

     Charlemagne invited Alcuin to the continent to become head of the school at Aachen. Alcuin made this academy famous for learning. He transformed the Frankish world. "He was the moving force and spirit in the Carolingian renaissance and made the Frankish court the center of European culture and scholarship."[25] He established a system of elementary education to confront universal illiteracy. He was a deacon and may have been ordained a priest near the end of his life. Alcuin was never formally beatified but he is commonly referred to as "blessed."

Alcuin taught **Adalhard** (753-827), who was a grandson of Charles Martel, nephew of Pepin and cousin of Charlemagne. Adalhard became a tutor and advisor at the royal court. Twice he was exiled for suspected roles in palace political machinations. He possessed a great love for the sick and poor.

The abbot **Gregory of Utrecht** (c. 703-76) and Alcuin taught **Ludger** (d. 809). Gregory, who was a disciple of Boniface and successor to bishops Willibrod and Eoban, administered the diocese for twenty-two years, yet he was never ordained bishop until his deathbed. Ludger came at a young age to Gregory's abbey school. When Ludger was a deacon, Gregory released him from the monastery and studies in order that he might do missionary work in England. There Ludger spent another three and one-half years studying, this time under Alcuin at York. Ludger then went to Friesland, where he labored for the next thirty years as a missionary among the Germanic peoples. He refused Charlemagne's offer to be bishop at Trier. Eleven years later he relinquished and became the first bishop of Munster. It is said of Ludger that "his gentleness did more to attract the Saxons to Christ than all the armies of Charlemagne."[26]

In Flanders **Theodard of Maestricht** (d. c. 668) educated **Lambert of Maestricht** (c. 635-c. 705) and both gained fame as missionaries who won numerous converts from pagan beliefs and behaviors. When Theodard was killed, Lambert succeeded him as bishop of Maestricht. Lambert too was murdered. Theodard was murdered near Speyer, Germany while on a journey to protest to the king that nobles had been confiscating Church lands. Lambert was killed in Liege, where he criticized the king's successor, Pepin of Herstal, for his adulterous relationship with the queen's sister. Allegedly the murderer was the brother of Pepin's mistress.

Boniface (c. 680-754) was born in Devonshire, England, studied in monastery schools and was ordained a priest in 715. He enjoyed success as a preacher and teacher but he dreamed of being a missionary in Friesland. Eventually the pope called him to Rome, ordained him bishop, and missioned him to evangelize the Germanic peoples. "He [Boniface] won instant success with a huge gathering of pagans at Geismar by demolishing the Oak of Thor, an object of pagan worship, without harm to himself."[27] He built monasteries, established episcopal sees and restored the churches which Charles Martel had plundered. He resigned his see in 754 to devote his remaining years to the reconversion of the Frieslanders who had lapsed into pagan ways after the death of Willibrord. That same year of his resignation, however, Boniface and a group of followers were murdered by a band of pagans. Boniface is well heralded as the "Apostle of Germany." **Lull**, a fellow Briton and budding missionary, came as an already educated deacon to Boniface. Boniface continued Lull's education at Fulda. Upon completion of studies, the teacher ordained his student a priest and later the coadjutor bishop. Lull succeeded Boniface as bishop of Mainz. "He [Lull] was a founder of monasteries and a patron of the arts and of learning."[28]

Wolfgang of Wurzburg (c. 930-94) began his career as a teacher in the cathedral school of Trier and concluded his career as a tutor for **Henry II** (972-1024), the future emperor of the Holy Roman Empire. The teacher later entered the Benedictines, was ordained priest and later bishop. He associated with the ruling families. His student Henry became emperor in 1002. Henry strove to unite Germany. He conducted many wars to solidify his political position and established many sees and churches to achieve his cultural position. He successfully created political and ecclesiastical organization for the Empire and supported the Cluniac reforms even when local bishops opposed them.[29]

Bl. Emeric (1007-31), the son of King Stephen of Hungary, was educated by two saintly Benedictines: **Gerard Sagrado** (d. 1046), the "Apostle of Hungary," and **Adalbert of Prague** (956-97), the "Apostle of the Slavs." Adalbert of

Prague had been educated by **Adalbert of Madgeburg** (d. 981). Both Adalberts were missionary archbishops.

Cunegund (d. 1033) raised **Emma** (d. c. 1045) at the emperor's palace. Emma was a relative of Cunegund's husband, Henry II. Both women gave generously to the poor and encouraged their husbands to build churches and monasteries. Cunegund, after her husband died, and Emma, after her two children died, entered convents.

Bl. Herman the Cripple (1013-54) taught **Bl. Benno of Osnabruck** (d. 1088) at Reichenau abbey in Swabia. Herman was born terribly deformed and was physically almost helpless. At age seven he was placed in Reichenau abbey and spent the remainder of his life there. He was learned in many fields and was known to scholars all over Europe. Herman composed the hymn *"Salve Regina."* Benno was so expert in architecture that he saved the cathedral at Speyer from collapse and became the emperor's official architect. He was named bishop of Osnabruck. On several occasions he served as the emperor's envoy to the pope. While generally supportive of papal positions, Benno supported the Synod of Worms' deposition against the pope. Soon he and other bishops found themselves traveling to the papal residence at Canossa to beg the pope's pardon. The emperor himself later made the same journey.

Bruno (1030-1101) studied at the cathedral school in Rheims and later at the same school taught biblical exegesis to the future pope, **Blessed Urban II** (c. 1042-99). Both pursued for a while the Benedictine way of life, but both left: Bruno followed the advice of the holy bishop Hugh of Grenoble, to co-found the Carthusians and Urban, to serve as pope.

Bl. Jutta (d. 1136) was a hermitess around whom other women formed a religious community. The parents of **Hildegard** (1098-1179) brought her as an eight-year-old sickly child to the convent of Jutta. Jutta raised and educated Hildegard. The student succeeded the teacher as prioress of the convent. Hildegard's visions and revelations were investigated and approved by Pope Bl. Eugene III (d. 1153) and Bernard of Clairvaux (1090-1153).

The relationship between **Albert the Great** (c. 1206-80) and **Thomas Aquinas** (c. 1225-74) is described in this chapter.

Another student of Albert was **Bl. Andrew Sansedoni** (1220-86). Andrew and Thomas Aquinas are treated in the appendix under the section on classmates.

Mechtilde of Helfta (1241-98), of the noble von Hackeborn family, tutored **Gertrude the Great** (c. 1256-c. 1302) in their Benedictine convent. Both women became mystics, authors and best friends. Neither was formally canonized, but Pope Clement XII directed that Gertrude's feast be celebrated by the universal Church and allowed that the feast of Mechtilde be celebrated in Benedictine convents. More of their relationship is described in this book's first chapter: "The Benefit of Saintly Companions."

Bernardino of Siena (1380-1444) rejuvenated and reformed the Franciscan community. During his twelve-year term as vicar general, the community grew from 300 members to over 4,000. He "was really its second founder."[30] In his earlier days as an instructor Bernardino taught the classmates **John of Capistrano** (1386-1456) and **John of the Marches** (1394-1476), who had been law students together. Bernardino's two famous students later served with their teacher as missionaries in Italy, Germany, Hungary and Poland.

Bl. Peter Favre (1506-46) was a family friend who prepared the young **Alphonsus Rodriguez** (1533-1617) for his first Holy Communion. Alphonsus began school under the Jesuits but, when his father died, he returned home to run the family business. Alphonsus later married. At age fifty, after his wife and son had died, he applied to the Jesuits but was refused. He reapplied as a candidate for the lay brotherhood and was accepted. He served in the lowly position of porter at Montesion College at Majorca for twenty-four years.

There Peter Claver met Brother Alphonsus and was greatly influenced by him. Peter chose Alphonsus to be his spiritual director for the three years that Peter studied there.

Among the young people whom **Turibius Mogrobejo** (1538-1606) instructed and confirmed in the faith were **Rose of Lima** (1586-1617), **Martin de Porres** (1579-1639) and his fellow Dominican **John Massias** (1585-1645). Turibius was so respected as a lay law professor at the University of Salamanca, that Church officials appointed him chief judge of the Inquisition at Grenada. When the archbishopric of Lima became vacant, ecclesiastical and royal officials chose Turibius. He opposed the selection on the grounds of personal and professional inadequacy. Nonetheless, he was ordained and arrived at Lima, Peru in 1581. His archdiocese extended for more than 400 miles along the coast and hundreds of miles inland. The new archbishop traveled to every part of the see. He studied the Indian dialects so that he could communicate without the aid of an interpreter. He ate and slept in villages as he made continual rounds of his mission. He founded hospitals, schools, churches and the first seminary in the New World. He said Mass daily despite difficult circumstances. While the Indians loved him, many of the conquistadors despised him because he challenged their oppression of the poor. Many clergy did not like him because he criticized their lack of ecclesiastical discipline. The elderly bishop died far north of Lima; typically, he was on mission.

John Bosco (1815-88) taught many students who became renowned for holiness. His relationship with **Dominic Savio** (1842-57) is described in this chapter. Bosco taught also **Bl. Michael Rua** (1837-1910), who succeeded him as major superior of the new religious community; **Bl. Louis Guanella** (1842-1915), who founded Houses of Providence to care for the handicapped; and **Bl. Louis Orioni** (1872-1940), who founded the Works of Providence to care for young school-age boys.

CLASSMATES

Heraclas (c. 180-247) and his brother **Plutarch** (d. 202) interrupted their study of law at Alexandria in order to listen to Origen's lectures on theology. They became converts and the first two students at Origen's school of catechetics, which quickly became a lightning rod for persecutors of the faith. Heraclas escaped with his life and went on to become bishop of Alexandria, who eventually had to excommunicate Origen. Plutarch was captured and martyred, with Origen at his side encouraging him.

The brothers **Gregory Thaumaturgus** (c. 213-68) and **Athenodorus** (d. c. 269) were traveling from Neocaesarea through Caesarea on their way to continue law studies at Beirut. They met Origen in Caesarea and changed their itinerary, religion and career goals. Both men were elected bishops.

Basil the Great (329-79) and **Gregory Nazianzen** (c. 329-89) spent two years together in school at Caesarea, Cappadocia and another ten years together in school at Athens. At Athens another classmate was the future emperor Julian the Apostate, who was no saint. Basil and Gregory became lifelong companions. More is said about their relationship in the chapter on friends.

Bl. Peregrine (d. 1240) and **Bl. Rizzerio** (d. 1236) studied at the University of Bologna. After hearing Francis of Assisi preach, they felt moved to become Franciscans. Francis accepted them both. Peregrine made a pilgrimage to Palestine before spending the rest of his life as a lay brother at San Severino. Rizzerio was ordained a priest. He and Francis became close friends. He was present at the founder's death. Rizzerio later served as provincial in his native area of the Marches.

Thomas Aquinas (c. 1225-74) and **Bonaventure** (1221-74) attended the University of Paris as classmates and lecturers. Both received doctoral degrees in theology in 1257. They were active in the controversy between the secular priest-professors and the professors from the new mendicant orders. They were prolific authors and theologians; both have been named Doctors of the Church. Thomas was an extraordinary teacher and is counted amongst the greatest theologians of Christendom. Bonaventure was a great administrator, serving as minister general of the Friars Minor for seventeen years, later as cardinal archbishop, and an advisor to popes.

Another classmate of Thomas and fellow student of Albert at Cologne was the Dominican **Bl. Ambrose Sansedoni** (1220-86). Ambrose traveled throughout Germany, France, and Italy preaching and teaching. Wherever he went, avid listeners filled the churches and classrooms. He was invited to reconcile numerous disputes between civil factions and was invited by the pope to preach for the financial need and spiritual benefit of one of the Crusades. He was besought by his townspeople of Siena to ask the same pope to lift an interdict placed upon them. At home in the friary he performed menial tasks like every other friar.

John of Capistrano (1386-1456) and **John of the Marches** (1394-76) studied together under Bernardino of Siena (1380-1444). These two classmates tried unsuccessfully to unite the two Franciscan branches of the Conventual and Observant communities. Both men served the Church as ambassadors on papal missions and inquisitors against various heretical groups.

Bl. Peter Favre (1506-46) and **Francis Xavier** (1506-52) were roommates and classmates at St. Barbe College in Paris in 1525. These two became good friends and fellow Jesuits with Ignatius Loyola. Peter went to on to become a renowned teacher and preacher in Germany, France, Spain and Portugal. Francis became an extraordinary missionary to the Indies and Japan. He died only a short distance from China, which had been his destination.

Notes for Chapter 7

1   *Dictionary of Quotations*, 682.8.

2   John L. McKenzie, *Dictionary of the Bible*, p. 870.

3   Fran Ferder, *Words Made Flesh*, pp. 118-21.

4   Delaney, *Dictionary of Saints*, p. 49.

5   Eugene Kevane, *Augustine the Educator*, pp. 210-11.

6   *Butler's Lives of the Saints*, vol. I, p. 96.

7   Attributed to Saint Ita. Tr. by George Sigerson. *1000 Years of Irish Poetry*, pp. 19-20.

8   Delaney, p. 118.

9   *Albert and Thomas*, p. 209.

10   Butler, vol. I, p. 540.

11   Ibid.

12   *Office of Readings*, Jan. 31, pp. 1338-89.

13   Butler, vol. I, p. 540.

14   Ibid.

15   Laurence Costelloe, *Saint Bonaventure*, p. 93.

16   Butler, vol. III, p. 107.

17   Delaney, p. 198.

18   Butler, vol. III, p. 688.

19   Altaner, *Patrology*, p. 534.

20   *The Book of Saints*, p. 282.

21   Ibid., p. 496.

22   Ibid., p. 244.

23   Ibid., p. 286.

24   Delaney, p. 185.

25   Ibid., p. 39.

26   *The Book of Saints*, p. 352.

27   Delaney, p. 111.

28   *The Book of Saints*, p. 354.

29   Delaney, pp. 592-93.

30   Ibid., p. 103.

CHAPTER 8

MASTER AND DISCIPLE SAINTS

Master and many disciples

1. Jesus for Mary, the twelve apostles, Nicodemus and Joseph of Arimathea, Mary Magdalene, Mary Cleophas, Mary Salome, Joanna, Dismas the good thief, Balthasar, Caspar and Melchior

2. Paul for Ananias and Barnabas, Priscilla of Corinth and Aquila, Lydia, Gaius, Crispus, Jason, Philemon and Apphia, Onesimus, Phoebe, Dionysius the Areopagite and Damaris, Erastus, Mark and Luke, Silas, Timothy and Titus

3. Bernard of Clairvaux for Bl. Guy, Bl. Gerard, Bl. Nivard, Bl. Humbeline and Bl. Eugene III

4. Dominic de Guzman for Bl. Mannes, Hyacinth, Bl. Ceslau, Hedwig, Bl. Bartholomew of Braganza, Bl. Reginald of Saint-Giles, Bl. Isnardo of Chiampo, Bl. Jordan of Saxony, Bl. Nicholas Palea, Bl. Guala Romanoni, and Peter of Verona

5. Francis of Assisi for Clare of Assisi, Agnes of Assisi, Bl. Helen Enselmini, Bl. Giles of Assisi, Bl. Andrew Caccioli, Bl. John of Perugia, Bl. Guy Vignotelli, Bl. Luchesio and Bl. Bonnadonna, Elizabeth of Hungary, Elzear and Bl. Dephine, Bl. Peregrin of Falerine, Bl. Rizzerio of Muccia, Christopher of Romangnola, Bl. Andrew of Spello, Bl. Luke Belludi and Anthony of Padua

Master and disciple

6. Peter the Apostle for Priscilla, Pudens and Cornelius
7. John the Apostle for Polycarp and Ignatius of Antioch
8. Polycarp and Irenaeus
9. Maximinus of Trier and Paulinus of Trier
10. Antony of the Desert for Hilarion and Paul the Simple
11. Hilary of Poitiers and Martin of Tours
12. Martin of Tours and Brice
13. Antony of the Desert and Pambo
14. Pambo for Athanasius and Melania the Elder
15. John Chrysostom for Eutropius and Tigrius
16. John Chrysostom for Palladius and John Cassian
17. John Chrysostom and Olympias
18. Augustine of Hippo and Alipius
19. Zebinus and Maro
20. John the Dwarf and Arsenius
21. John Stylites and Simeon Stylites
22. Patrick of Ireland and Mochta
23. Mobhi and Columba
24. Gregory the Great and Augustine of Canterbury
25. Augustine of Canterbury and Ethelbert
26. John of York and Wilfrid the Younger
27. Nilus of Rome and Bartholomew of Rossano
28. Edmund Rich and Richard de Wyche
29. Peter Nolasco and Raymond Nonnatus
30. Bl. Peter Favre for Peter Canisius and Francis Borgia
31. Teresa of Avila and Bl. Anna Garcia
32. Philip Neri for John Leonardi, Joseph Calasanz and Camillus de Lellis
33. Alphonsus de Liguori and Gerard Majella
34. Bl. Dominic Barberi and John Henry Newman
35. Justin de Jacobis and Ghebre Michael
36. John Bosco and Bl. Michael Rua

Leading and Learning By Example:
Master and Disciple Saints

The master-disciple relationship occurs in many vocations, for example, the arts, literature, science, crafts, education and the spiritual life. Etymologically, the Latin word for master is *magister*, which means teacher; and the Latin word for disciple is *discipulus*, which means pupil. The master-disciple relationship differs from the usual teacher-student relationship. Disciples identify themselves exclusively with their masters, whereas students associate themselves first with a school and only second as part of a particular teacher's class. Disciples adhere not only to the instructions of their masters but also to his or her vision. Disciples follow masters not just for the completion of some course work but for a significant part or the whole of their lives. Disciples oftentimes leave their families, friends and familiar surroundings in order to dedicate themselves to their masters. A master-disciple intimacy results.

The Scriptures provide examples of master and disciple relationships. The Old Testament presents the pairs of Elijah and Elisha as well as Jeremiah and Baruch. The New Testament offers John the Baptist with his disciples, Jesus with his twelve apostles and seventy-two disciples, Peter with the disciple Mark, and Paul with the disciples Timothy and Titus.

Throughout virtually every century of the Church's history, an outstanding spiritual leader attracted without intention or effort numerous disciples. The master exuded a commanding charismatic presence. His or her manner and message appealed. The master received commitment from the disciple. The disciple received instruction and inspiration from the master. Master and disciple became bound to each other in their common commitment to God, God's people and God's mission.

Particular examples

1. POPE GREGORY THE GREAT AND AUGUSTINE OF CANTERBURY

Gregory the Great (c. 540-604) served as the political prefect and mayor of Rome before becoming a monk, papal deacon, and pope. As pope, he commissioned Augustine (d. 604) and forty other monks to leave the tranquility of their Roman monastery, which Gregory had recently founded, in order to travel to England to evangelize the Anglo-Saxons.

Gregory resigned his political office in 574, converted his home in Rome into St. Andrew's monastery and developed on his Sicilian estates another six monasteries. Four years later he left his monastery to serve as papal deacon and eventually as papal nuncio. After eight years of papal service he resigned his position to pursue again the monastic life. In 589 he decided to evangelize England. He advanced just beyond the city's walls when word arrived that the pope was recalling him to Rome.

Within a few months after his return a plague descended upon Rome. Gregory organized the public response. After the pope caught the plague and died, Gregory was elected pope.

The significance of his achievements are unparalleled in papal history. He dissuaded the Lombards on various occasions from invading the city. He wrested religious authority from ambitious Byzantine patriarchs. He protected the Jews from discrimination and returned to them a synagogue which a converted Jew had confiscated and turned into a church. He revived religion in Rome by enforcing ecclesiastical discipline. He wrote treatises explaining and defending the faith. He composed hymns to mellifluously communicate the faith; Gregorian chant originated with his support. He sent Augustine to England, fulfilling the mission which he had begun and never completed. "Of all his religious work in the West that which lay closest to Gregory's heart was the conversion of England, and the success which crowned his efforts in that direction was to him . . . the greatest triumph of his life."[1]

Augustine succeeded Gregory as prior of the monastery. In 596 Gregory called upon his monastic successor to be his missionary successor. Augustine and forty monks set out on foot for England. In Provence, however, their confidence was shaken by rumors of the natural danger of the English Channel and the human dangers from the barbarous Anglo-Saxons. The monks persuaded Augustine that they should return to the safety of their monastery. Augustine wrote to Gregory of their decision. Gregory wrote back, refusing to accept their retreat and assuring them that the English would be receptive. The journey continued. Upon their arrival the king of Kent gave them a friendly reception as well as land for a church and a monastery at Canterbury. The king converted to Christianity in the following year. Augustine and company enjoyed much success in convert-making, which Augustine insisted was always to be done without coercion. Augustine established sees at London and Rochester. Gregory and Augustine are each known as "Apostle of the English."

The letter from Gregory to Augustine and his monks was preserved at Canterbury by Venerable Bede, who received a copy from Nothelm. Gregory identified himself with the English mission:

> Since it is better not to begin good works than to have second thoughts and withdraw from those that are begun, you must, my dearest sons, zealously complete the good work you have begun. Neither the toil of the journey, nor the tongues of evil speakers should deter you; therefore carry out with all instancy and fervour what you have begun by God's help, knowing that the

greater the labour, the greater the reward of eternal glory. Humbly obey therefore in all things Augustine the *praepositus*, whom moreover we have appointed to be your abbot, knowing that whatever at his command ye fulfill will be for the good of your own soul. May almighty God protect you by his grace and grant me to behold in the eternal country the fruit of your labour, for although I cannot labour with you, I do indeed desire to do so: may I share in the joy of your reward.[2]

2. BERNARD OF CLAIRVAUX AND COMPANIONS

Bernard of Clairvaux (1090-1153) served as master to many disciples. Shortly after his mother died, he decided to cease the frivolous ways of his youth and to dedicate himself to religious life. He persuaded thirty-one companions to go with him to Citeaux, where in 1098 the first Cistercian monastery had been founded for strict observance of the Benedictine rule. Among the disciples who became saints were three of his brothers, Bl. Guy (d. c. 1157), Bl. Gerard (d. 1138) and Bl. Nivard (c. 1100-1150), and Bernard's former novice and future pope, Bl. Eugene III (d. 1153). History records Bernard's personal conviction and ability to inspire and persuade others to join him in the Cistercian way:

He arose steadily fixed in the resolution of following the severe Cistercian life. His friends endeavoured to dissuade him from it; but he not only remained firm — he enlisted four of his brothers as well, and an uncle. Hugh of Mâcon (who afterward founded the monastery of Pontigny, and died bishop of Auxerre), an intimate friend, wept bitterly at the thought of separation, but by two interviews was induced to become his companion. Nor were these the only ones who, with apparently no previous thought of the religious life, suddenly decided to leave the world for the austere life of Cîteaux. Bernard induced in all thirty-one men to follow him — he who himself had been uncertain of his call only a few weeks before. It is a happening unparalleled in Christian history. Bernard's eloquent appeals were irresistible; mothers feared for their sons, wives for their husbands, lest they came under the sway of that compelling voice and look. They assembled at Châtillon, and on the day appointed for their meeting Bernard and his brothers went to Fontaines to take farewell of their father and beg his blessing. They left Nivard, the youngest brother, to be a comfort to him in his old age. Going out they saw him at play with other children, and Guy said to him, "Adieu, my little Nivard! You will have all the estates and lands to yourself." The boy answered, "What! you then take Heaven, and leave me only the earth. The division is too unequal." They went away; but soon after Nivard followed them.[3]

At Citeaux Bernard and company were met by Stephen Harding who with Robert Molesme and Alberic were struggling to make a success of their new creation. Bernard brought new hope to a fast fading dream. Bernard was brilliant, wise, charming, charismatic. Shortly after Bernard completed his novitiate, Stephen Harding missioned this monk of three years to start a new foundation. Bernard and twelve monks achieved their mission at Clairvaux in 1115. By the time he died in 1153, Bernard had founded an additional sixty-eight Cistercian monasteries.

Bernard counselled popes and kings. He mediated ecclesiastical and political disputes and healed a papal schism. He prevented a border war and intervened to eliminate pogroms in the Rhineland. He disputed philosophically with Abelard about rationalism, and theologically with the Cathari about Albigensianism. People constantly came to him for advice and sought his assistance in settling apparently irreconcilable differences. Respected by all parties, he became known as "the oracle of Christendom." He was a prolific author and famed preacher.

3. IGNATIUS LOYOLA, FRANCIS XAVIER AND BL. PETER FAVRE

Ignatius Loyola (1491-1556) founded the Society of Jesus in 1534. Francis Xavier (1506-52), Bl. Peter Favre (1506-46) and four other students accompanied Ignatius in this endeavor. In less than twenty years the community grew to 1,000 members who were ministering in eleven countries.

Ignatius underwent his conversion long before he founded the Jesuit community. As a twenty-two-year-old soldier, he received a leg wound during battle. While recuperating, he asked for romantic novels to read, but nothing was available except the life of Christ and biographies of the saints. Ignatius was so moved by what he read that he decided to dedicate his life to Christ. He literally hung up his sword at an altar and proceeded to make a lengthy retreat where he experienced visions and wrote the bulk of his *Spiritual Exercises*. He spent the next dozen years studying at Barcelona, Alcala, Salamanca and Paris for the purpose of preparing himself to minister the faith to others.

At Paris Ignatius met several faith-filled companions. He invited divinity students to make the spiritual exercises with him, which they did. Immediately after graduation with master's degrees, when Ignatius was forty-three years old, and both Francis and Peter were twenty-eight, the group took vows of chastity and poverty in service to Jesus and the Church. Peter Favre, the only priest in the group, celebrated Mass. Two years later they made another retreat, one year in length, after which the other six were ordained priests. The party hoped to journey to the Holy Land but a sea war between Venetians and Turks made the

pilgrimage impossible. Ignatius, Peter and another member traveled instead to Rome, where they offered the
society's services to the pope. The Society of Jesus received
papal approbation in 1540.

Peter Favre was one of the original members of
Ignatius' prayer group and the Society of Jesus. Peter
gained renown as a teacher, preacher and papal representative. His preaching attracted to the community two other
saints: Peter Canisius and Francis Borgia. Peter's part in
the foundation of the community is reflected in the following:

> On August 15, 1534, the seven men climbed to
> Montmartre, the mountain where according to tradi-
> tion the martyrdom of St. Denis and his companions
> had taken place. . . . Favre was the only priest in the
> group, having been recently ordained (on May 30).
> He celebrated the Mass. At the moment of Commun-
> ion, each pronounced his vows — so carefully studied
> and perfected. Favre gave the Eucharist to his six
> companions. As they left the chapel, pure joy inun-
> dated the hearts of these men: the joy of having given
> a purpose to their lives for all time; the joy of belong-
> ing unreservedly to Christ; the joy of participating
> henceforth in the great work of redemption, without
> limits, without boundaries, without reserve; finally,
> the joy of a fraternal community of faith, hope and
> charity. They spent the rest of the day in prayer and
> in "spiritual colloquies" in the deserted countryside.[4]

Francis Xavier and another Jesuit were commissioned
in 1541 as the order's first missionaries. Ignatius wrote to
Francis:

> You must bear in mind that our Lord did not call you
> to enter His society, in order that you might lead the
> life of a hermit and seek your own satisfaction, of how
> elevated and pure so ever a nature. Your vocation
> compels you to seek to promote the salvation of

others, in order thus to imitate the Son of God, Who left the bosom of His Father in order that He might redeem our souls, that He might give them food, and peace, and life by means of His own weariness, sufferings, and death. Therefore, I exhort and command you to follow so great an Example, so illustrious a Leader, to quit Onate in order to visit and seek out many persons who are desirous of serving God, and of modeling their households according to the counsel you may give them. You ought to feel persuaded that these journeys will be anything but pleasing to your natural man. And I have reason to believe that their result cannot fail to be satisfactory.[5]

Francis and his Jesuit companion reached Goa in 1542. Preaching, teaching, ministering the corporal works of mercy, and convert-making filled their days. From Goa they continued on to India, Sri Lanka, Malacca, Mortai and Japan. Francis headed on alone for China but died just six miles short of the coast of the mainland. "Indeed, Francis Xavier is perhaps the greatest individual missionary the Church has produced since St. Paul."[6] Forty years after his ministry in Japan the Church had mushroomed to 400,000 members![7] Between 1542-44 Francis Xavier wrote about the conditions under which he labored:

We have visited the villages of the new converts who accepted the Christian religion a few years ago. No Portuguese live here — the country is so utterly barren and poor. The native Christians have no priests. They know only that they are Christians. There is nobody to say Mass for them; nobody to teach them the Creed, the Our Father, the Hail Mary and the Commandments of God's Law.

I have not stopped since the day I arrived. I conscientiously made the rounds of the villages. I bathed in the sacred waters all the children who had not yet been baptized. This means that I have purified a very large number of children so young that, as the saying goes, they could not tell their right hand from their left. The older children would not let me say my Office or eat or sleep until I taught them one prayer or another. Then I began to understand: "The kingdom of heaven belongs to such as these."

I could not refuse so devout a request without failing in devotion myself. I taught them, first the confession of faith in the Father, the Son and the Holy Spirit; then the Apostles' Creed, the Our Father and Hail Mary. I noticed among them persons of great intelligence. If only someone could educate them in the Christian way of life, I have no doubt that they would make excellent Christians.

Many, many people hereabouts are not becoming Christians for one reason only: there is nobody to make them Christians. Again and again I have thought of going round the universities of Europe, especially Paris, and everywhere crying out like a madman, riveting the attention of those with more learning than charity: "What a tragedy: how many souls are being shut out of heaven and falling into hell, thanks to you!"

I wish they would work as hard at this as they do at their books, and so settle their account with God for their learning and the talents entrusted to them.

This thought would certainly stir most of them to meditate on spiritual realities, to listen actively to what God is saying to them. They would forget their own desires, their human affairs, and give themselves over entirely to God's will and his choice. They would cry out with all their heart: Lord, I am here! What do you want me to do? Send me anywhere you like — even to India![8]

4. Justin de Jacobis and Ghebre Michael

Justin de Jacobis (1800-60) possessed a humility and sincerity that endeared him to virtually all whom he met. As a young priest in Naples, many said about him: "Everybody loved him."[9] In 1839 when the Vatican re-opened the mission in Ethiopia which had been closed for over 200 years after violent mutual persecutions between the Roman Catholic and the Ethiopian Church, Justin was assigned as the apostolic vicar. His approach was to listen and learn from the people. "For two years Father de Jacobis set himself to learn about the country, its people and its languages, and to break down prejudice by kindness and quiet humility."[10]

The civil and religious leaders of the Ethiopian Church enlisted his assistance. When a delegation was being formed to approach the Coptic patriarch in Constantinople for the purpose of filling the twelve-year-long vacancy in the primatial see of the Ethiopian Church, Justin, an educated European priest, was invited to join the entourage to lend greater dignity to their group. He hesitated because of the long-standing friction between the Ethiopian Church and Catholics. He did not want to interfere. He wanted only to assist the Ethiopians. He suggested that the group travel beyond Constantinople to Rome to further justify his presence. Besides Justin, the delegation would consist of a lay minister of state, a secretary, and the monk Ghebre Michael (1791-1855), who was renowned for holiness, scholarship and integrity.

At Constantinople the patriarch railed against the presence of the Catholic priest. The patriarch rejected every suggestion of the delegation. He appointed as bishop a brash and ignorant man younger than the canonical age permitted. Defeated, discouraged, and in disagreement with the patriarch's advice not to visit the pope, the contingent continued their journey to Rome. The pope received them warmly. They celebrated Mass together and conversed afterwards. Throughout the journey Justin had been his usual humble, gentle self. His Ethiopian companions, who had not met him prior to this journey, grew to admire him. As a matter of fact, Justin impressed them more favorably than had their Coptic patriarch.

On the return trip from Rome to Ethiopia, Ghebre Michael indicated to Justin that he was considering conversion to Catholicism. He did so in 1844. The two then began a college seminary to foster native vocations. Vocations and the Catholic faith flourished so that a bishop was needed to shepherd the mission. When the bishop arrived, so did persecution. Justin, Ghebre and other Catholics sought refuge on the island of Massawa. Here Justin was secretly ordained bishop. The first priest whom he ordained was Ghebre, at age sixty, in 1851.

The persecutions continued intermittently. In 1855 both Justin and Ghebre were captured. Justin was imprisoned for several months before intervention by the British led to his release. Ghebre was condemned to death but his sentence was commuted to life imprisonment. For three months this sixty-four-year-old man was dragged in chains behind the king's traveling entourage. He died a martyr along the highway. Ironically the disciple was beatified some few years before the master; Ghebre in 1926 and Justin in 1939. They were canonized together in 1975. Excerpts from Vincentian documents describe the temperaments of the two men:

> In his years in the monastery he [Ghebre Michael] had found much that was not to his liking, reflecting a general fall-off in standards in Ethiopian monasticism. His personal inclination was to do further research into the history and ideals of monasticism, and because of his interest in that direction he was officially commissioned to undertake this work. This involved travelling around the country consulting

manuscripts in the libraries of different monasteries; and while staying in each monastery he would gather a group of pupils around him whom he would teach. By about 1838 he had completed what he had set out to do but in the course of his researches he had come to realize that there were underlying problems which were theological rather than just matters of monastic ideals or discipline. He felt that he would not find answers to these problems in Ethiopia and he made up his mind to make a pilgrimage to Jerusalem; he planned to go alone but for various reasons he ended up as part of the delegation to Cairo, which was to proceed to the Holy Lands afterwards. He had no previous knowledge of Justin and his initial attitude was one of suspicion because of the mere fact that Justin was a Catholic priest; this gradually changed to an attitude of admiration as he came to appreciate the depth of Justin's holiness reflected in his way of life and in his attitude to persons and situations.[11]

Mgr. De Jacobis seems specially made for living with the Abyssinians. Good, charming, kind, mortified, patient he differs in no way from the least of the priests whom he imitates in food, clothing and everything lawful in their lifestyle. He goes barefoot, and for clothing wears only a pair of shorts, a tunic of coarse cloth and a little cloth cap on his head. His bed is the hide of a cow and his "horse" is a walking-stick five or six feet long; if on his journeys he is sometimes followed by a pack-horse it is not for his own use but for those who are with him and who seem in his eyes to have more need for it. This simple, frugal life, so hard for a European used to different things, has earned general esteem for him. He is called a saint. And if God has merciful plans for Abyssinia, Mgr. De Jacobis seems to me the best person for carrying them out.[12]

General Observations

A master can attract a huge number of disciples. Jesus was an itinerant preacher who in less than three years and in a distance less than 100 miles between the Sea of Galilee and the city of Jerusalem attracted several thousands of hearers. Many followed as disciples, even though many others found his teachings too hard to accept. Paul traveled in excess of 4,000 miles during a ministry which lasted from 43-67 A.D. He won disciples virtually wherever he went. Bernard of Clairvaux brought to the monastic life at Cluny thirty-one men besides himself. In the next thirty-eight years he founded sixty-eight monasteries in addition to Clairvaux. In the Middle Ages Francis of Assisi and Dominic won many disciples, who became saints themselves.[13] Francis' community was approved by Rome in 1211 and Dominic's in 1216. By 1325 both communities had grown phenomenally: the Franciscans numbered 35,000 men and the Dominicans, 12,000.[14] Francis' appeal to candidates continues to this day: "Though never ordained, Francis' impact on religious life since his times has been enormous. Probably no saint has affected so many in so many different ways as this gentle saint of Assisi."[15] Ignatius of Loyola founded the Jesuits in 1540 and by 1600 membership had burgeoned to 8,519; and that figure virtually doubled to 16,000 in the next 50 years.[16] Vincent de Paul founded the Vincentians in 1625 and his community of men grew to 2,000 members before the turn of the century.[17] Some readers may wonder about the numbers of women religious. Generally, women's communities outnumber men's ten to one, and the number of members, three or four to one. The project of calculating and analyzing the growth of all the communities of women religious has been too vast for any researcher thus far.

The master-disciple relationship involves a call and response. While John the Baptist originally pointed out

Jesus to Andrew and John, Jesus directly told them: "Come and see" (Jn 1:39). In another pericope the brothers Andrew and Peter as well as the brothers John and James the Elder were fishing. Jesus directly called them: "Come after me and I will make you fishers of men" (Mt 4:18-22). Another day in Galilee Jesus came across Philip. Jesus simply said: "Follow me" (Jn 1:44). Not only did Philip respond but he also brought Nathaniel to Jesus, of whom Jesus commented, "Before Philip called you, I saw you under the fig tree" (Jn 1:48). Matthew was busy collecting taxes when Jesus invited him: "Follow me" (Mt 9:9). In each of these cases the disciples responded affirmatively.

Not in all cases, however, was the response positive. Jesus called the rich young man, but he went away sad because of his unwillingness to give up all that he had (Lk 18:18-25). Another potential disciple wished to go and bury his father first. Jesus responded: "Follow me, and let the dead bury their dead" (Mt 8:21-22). After his conversion Paul preached to the Gentiles, whom he invited to step forward to commit themselves to the Christian way. Sometimes very few people stepped forward. In Corinth only two persons committed themselves. In Athens, after Paul's famous speech about the Unknown God, only two others joined him. Those who did commit themselves to his message offered him hospitality, traveled with him on his journeys, and even accompanied him in prison. Other masters throughout the centuries witnessed a similar variety of responses to their calls for discipleship.

Masters and disciples sometimes had fallings-out. Jesus was betrayed by Judas, was denied by Peter, and was doubted by Thomas. Paul was abandoned on his first missionary journey by John Mark. Alipius' father did not like Augustine and insisted that his son end his friendship with his boyhood buddy, which separation lasted for about a dozen years. Martin of Tours, with the boorish Brice, suffered many offenses but was always willing to forgive his uncouth companion. Francis of Assisi was threatened with expulsion from the community he had founded because the majority thought he insisted on too strict a practice of poverty. Dominic struggled with his community over the same matter. Vincent de Paul was criticized by his community members because he took over thirty years to compose a brief statement of the Rules and Constitutions. In addition, Vincent continued sending missionaries to Madagascar even though successive waves of missionaries were being slaughtered by the local population there.

These great masters could not do every good thing themselves. They needed others. They were not reluctant to involve others. The masters wanted their disciples not only to keep the faith but also to spread it. Jesus sent his disciples with the following commission: "Go, therefore, and make disciples of all the nations. Baptize them in the name of the Father, and of the Son, and of the Holy Spirit" (Mt 28:19). Polycarp sent Irenaeus to Gaul. Pope Gregory sent Augustine to Canterbury. There, Augustine converted King Ethelbert, who in turn peacefully encouraged his subjects to convert. Founders of all communities sent forth their members with this same evangelical mandate.

Many times the disciples themselves eventually became masters to a new round of disciples. All of Jesus' apostles were traditionally believed to have become local leaders of the dispersed Church. Jesus' beloved apostle John inspired Polycarp, who inspired Irenaeus. Francis' disciple Clare encouraged her sister Agnes and Clare's friend Agnes of Prague who both became abbesses in their own convents.

Some of these disciples began their work for the Lord at very young ages. Simeon Stylites began his column-sitting at age seven. Alipius began his friendship with Augustine during their boyhood years. Bernard of Clairvaux at age twenty-two brought himself and others to Cluny. At age twenty, Anne Garcia began her discipleship under Teresa of Avila.

Some disciples succeeded their masters in responsibilities. Maximus and Paulinus were successive bishops of Trier. Hilary of Potiers, then Martin of Tours and finally Brice were successive bishops in Gaul. Dominic was followed as superior of his order by Bl. Jordan of Saxony and Jordan, by Raymond of Peñafort; Peter Nolasco by Raymond Nonnatus as head of the Mercedarians; Alphonsus Liguori as general superior of the Redemptorists by Gerard Majella; and John Bosco as general superior of the Salesians by Michael Rua.

The conversions experienced by these saints were occasioned oftentimes by reflection upon the tragedies of war and death. Unkind reality virtually forced them rather than gently invited them to turn to God. Nicodemus and Dismas, the good thief, amended their lives after witnessing the suffering and death of Jesus. Bernard of Clairvaux lost his mother when he was seventeen years old; and only after his sister Humbeline roused him from depression, did he begin to look for new meaning in life. When Francis Borgia lost his wife, whom he had married at nineteen and with whom he had raised eight children, "he decided to pursue the religious life which had beckoned him all his life."[18] Nilus lived a rather dissolute life until age thirty when the woman with whom he lived and their son died. Camillus de Lellis was a former soldier with a crippled leg and an addiction of gambling. He entered the Capuchins, who refused to advance him beyond the novitiate. Philip Neri, however, took him under his wing, challenged him and encouraged him. Camillus responded in heroic fashion. Ghebre Michael converted from the national Ethiopian Church after being treated badly by the Coptic patriarch and being treated well by the Catholic priest Justin de Jacobis. Clare of Assisi and her sister Agnes responded to the Holy Week sermons preached by Francis.

Peter Canisius and Francis Borgia independently heard the homilies of Peter Favre and then joined the Jesuits.

Application Of The Theme:

Common Vision: Masters enlightened the minds and inspired the hearts of disciples, who yearned to experience life with Jesus Christ. Masters revealed the core of their being-with-the-Lord. This self-revelation affected disciples in the core of their being-for-the-Lord. Jesus Christ was at the center of self-image and action for masters and disciples.

Common Way: Masters modeled and disciples followed a prescribed way. Prayer, fasting, almsgiving, community living and community service marked the usual means along the way. Union with Jesus identified the end. Masters and disciples became changed in mind, heart, lifestyle and life-goals.

Common Bond With Each Other: Masters and disciples oftentimes lived and witnessed together. They shared deeply with each other at a level that they shared with few other people. They grew together as they drew closer together. They developed a mutual respect, appreciation and quality of communication.

Common Bond With God: They drew close to God. God was at the center of their being. All they did was evaluated and integrated according to its effect on their relationship with God. Masters and disciples by the grace of God became like the Lord they sought to imitate.

APPENDIX: MASTER AND DISCIPLE SAINTS

MASTER AND MANY DISCIPLES

Jesus (4 B.C.-30 A.D.) was master to many disciples. His mother **Mary** (1st century) is the first and most perfect disciple. She heard the word of God and kept it. By the time Jesus entered public ministry, the Gospels say nothing about his foster-father **Joseph** (1st century).

Other disciples include the apostles: **Peter** (d. c. 64) and his brother **Andrew** (1st century); **James the Elder** (d. 42) and **John** (c. 6-c. 104), the sons of Zebedee; **Philip** (1st century), **Bartholomew** (1st century), **Matthew** (1st century), **Thomas** (1st century), **James the Younger** (d. 62), the son of Alphaeus, **Jude Thaddeus** (1st century), **Simon the Zealot** (1st century) and **Matthias** (1st century), who replaced the traitorous Judas Iscariot.

Andrew, Simon Peter, and Philip hailed from Bethsaida. Andrew, John the beloved apostle and Philip were disciples of the Baptist prior to becoming disciples of the Lord. Philip "always takes the fifth place in the catalogue of the apostles, and is mentioned three times as a confidant of our Lord in St. John's Gospel."[19] Bartholomew, who is also called Nathaniel in St. John's Gospel, was called to the Lord by Philip. Matthew, author of the first Gospel, was called Levi before he left his position as tax collector to follow the Lord. Thomas is remembered for his doubts regarding the resurrection of the Lord, but he also made a strong profession of faith and expressed courage in readiness to die with Jesus. James the Younger, the son of Alphaeus, was the first bishop of Jerusalem and the author of the canonical letter which bears his name. Simon the Zealot is also known as the Canaanean. Matthias was chosen by lot to replace Judas Iscariot; Matthias was a disciple of the Lord since his baptism and witnessed the resurrection.

Nicodemus (1st century) and **Joseph of Arimathea** (1st century) assisted in the burial of the Lord. Nicodemus provided "a mixture of myrrh and aloes which weighed about a hundred pounds" (Jn 19:39). Joseph sought and received permission from Pilate to remove the dead body for proper burial. None of the Gospels mention Nicodemus as a disciple. His actions and words, however, indicate discipleship. He seems to have been a member of the Sanhedrin. He reminded the Pharisees and scribes that the Law required that an accused person get a formal hearing before receiving judgment. All four Gospels mention Joseph as a disciple who feared repercussions from the Jewish authorities.

Present at the crucifixion were **the four Mary's: Jesus' mother, Mary Magdalene, Mary Cleophas and Mary Salome**. Jesus' mother was commented on above. The three remaining Mary's discovered the empty tomb on Easter Sunday. Mary Magdalene's reputation suffers guilt by association. The story of the penitent woman immediately precedes the story of Mary Magdalene who had seven demons cast from her by Jesus. Traditionally, it has been presumed that the anonymous woman was Mary Magdalene. Contemporary scholars inform us that no basis exists for that identification. Similarly, no basis exists for Mary Magdalene's identification with the sister of Martha and Lazarus. All that we definitely know is that Mary Magdalene followed Jesus during his ministry, stood at the foot of the cross, and was the first person to whom Jesus appeared after his resurrection. Mary Cleophas was the wife of Cleophas and the mother of the apostle James the Younger. Mary Salome was the wife of Zebedee and mother of the apostles James the Elder and John. **Joanna** (1st century) was wife of the chief steward of King Herod. She accompanied the Mary's who discovered the empty tomb. **Dismas** (1st century) is the name given to the good thief who was crucified with and believed in Christ.

Tradition provides the names of **Balthasar, Caspar** and **Melchior** as the Three Wise Men (1st century). Matthew relates that these astrologers from the East inquired: "Where is the newborn king of the Jews?" King Herod requested that the three return with information "so that I may go and offer him homage too." The Magi ignored Herod's request. Contemporary scholars suggest that the astrologers came from the Persian Empire.

Paul (d. c. 65) attracted many disciples. His first defenders were **Ananias** (1st century) and **Barnabas** (1st century). Ananias responded to the Lord's call to seek out Paul. Ananias restored Paul's eyesight and baptized him. After his conversion Paul retired to the Arabian desert for three years, then visited Jerusalem, where he met little acceptance. He returned to his native city of Tarsus for a few more years. Barnabas rescued Paul from oblivion and brought him to Antioch as a teacher in the Church. The two traveled to Jerusalem with the Church's donation. Barnabas integrated Paul into the community at Antioch.

Paul accepted the hospitality of his converts. **Priscilla** (1st century) and **Aquila** (1st century) hosted Paul in Corinth and Ephesus, and allowed Peter to use their home as headquarters in Rome. **Lydia** (1st century), the purple-dye dealer, was Paul's hostess and first convert in Philippi. At Corinth Paul baptized only two persons: **Gaius** (1st century), Paul's host, and **Crispus** (1st century), president of the synagogue. At Thessalonica, Paul's host **Jason** (1st century) later became bishop in Paul's native Tarsus.

Philemon (1st century) and his wife **Apphia** (1st century), who were later martyred, followed Paul as did their former slave **Onesimus** (1st century). The deaconess **Phoebe** (1st century), from Cenchreae near Corinth, reputedly delivered Paul's letter to the community at Rome. In Athens, after Paul's famous sermon about the Unknown God, only **Dionysius the Areopagite** (1st century) and the woman **Damaris** (1st century) stepped forward for baptism. In Corinth the treasurer of the city, **Erastus** (1st century), left the city and his position in order to serve as companion to Paul and Timothy on their journey to Macedonia.

Two of Paul's disciples were among the four evangelists: **Mark** (d. c. 74) and **Luke** (1st century). John Mark served as one of Paul's companions on the first missionary journey but left part way through the trip. Years later, he returned to Paul's good graces in Rome. He was also a disciple of Peter. Peter called him "my son, Mark" (1 P 5:13). **Silas** (1st century) replaced John Mark for Paul's second and third journeys and helped to deliver to Antioch the decisions of the Council of Jerusalem. Luke seems to have been a physician. He traveled with Paul on his missionary journeys and accompanied him during his first and second imprisonments in Rome. Paul's letters to **Timothy** (d. c. 97) and **Titus** (1st century) reveal the deep affection he felt for them and the faith they shared. Paul addresses Timothy: "my child whom I love" (2 Tm 1:2). He calls Titus: "my own true child in our common faith" (Tt 1:4).

The story of **Bernard of Clairvaux** is described in this chapter.

Dominic (1170-1221) inspired and received into his order many disciples later famous for their sanctity. **Hyacinth** (1185-1257) and his brother **Bl. Ceslau** (d. 1242) were apostles to Poland. **Hedwig** (c. 1174-1243) and her husband built numerous monasteries and hospitals in Silesia. **Bl. Bartholomew of Braganza** (c. 1200-71) founded in 1233 a military order for the maintenance of public order and twenty years later he was ordained bishop of Nimesia in Cyprus. **Bl. Reginald of Saint-Giles** (1183-1220), one of Dominic's ablest disciples, helped to establish the new order in Bologna and Paris. In 1219, Dominic gave the habit to **Bl. Isnardo of Chiampo** (d. 1244), who led an extremely ascetical life but, nevertheless, was very stout. Physical exertion of any kind was difficult for him. His persuasiveness and learning, which he manifested in his preaching, enabled him to convert many persons. He suffered in that "he was extremely fat and people used to ridicule him about it when he was preaching."[20] **Bl. Nicholas Palea** (1197-1255) opened two Dominican houses and served two non-consecutive terms as provincial of the Dominicans in Rome. **Bl. Guala Romanoni** (c. 1177-1244) became the first prior at Brescia and Bologna and served as bishop of Brescia until

1242, when he retired because of civil unrest. **Bl. Jordan of Saxony** (d. 1237) met Dominic, joined the community, was elected provincial the next year and master-general the following year. He succeeded Dominic and greatly expanded the mission areas of the community. He preached extensively to college students.

Peter of Verona (1205-52) was born to Catharist parents, who educated him in Catholic schools and then the University of Bologna. Here Peter became attracted to the teachings of Dominic. Peter joined the order and was assigned as inquisitor in the north of Italy. His preaching attracted many followers but also some Catharist enemies, who killed him in a surprise attack.

In the Middle Ages **Francis of Assisi** (c. 1181-1226) inspired many disciples on the road to sainthood. *The Franciscan Book of Saints* lists for the thirteenth century over sixty saintly sons and daughters of "Il Poverello". Francis inspired **Clare** (1194-1253) by a Lenten sermon and she ran away from home at age eighteen to join him. Two weeks later her fifteen-year-old sister **Agnes** (1197-1253) also ran away to follow Francis. The father sent strong armed men to retrieve his daughters. Needless to say, they did not succeed. Three years later Clare was appointed superior of the women's convent at San Damiano. Thus began Francis' and Clare's work of the Poor Clares. Clare served as superior of the community for the next forty years. Agnes was with Clare at the foundation of San Damiano, then served as abbess in another convent, eventually establishing three more. She attended Clare at her deathbed and followed her older sister in death, three months later.

In 1221 Francis received **Anthony of Padua** (1195-1231), who transferred to the Franciscan community after his ordination in the Canons Regular of St. Augustine. Anthony went briefly to Morocco to preach among the Moors, but sickness forced his return. His excellent preaching attracted large crowds. In 1226 he settled in Padua and devoted himself to preaching, having secured from his community and the pope release from other responsibilities. His preaching was the primary cause for the moral and theological reform of the city. In 1231 he died at the age of thirty-six, exhausted and ill. "He was undoubtedly one of the greatest preachers of all times."[21]

A wealthy neighbor of Anthony admired him and his founder. He sought to join the community. Francis received **Bl. Luke Belludi** (1200-c. 1285). Luke eventually became provincial of the order, nursed Anthony on his deathbed and built a basilica to house Anthony's remains and to perpetuate the fruitful mission of Anthony.

The following disciples received their habits from Francis. **Bl. Helen Enselmini** (c. 1208-42) of Padua became famous as the recipient of many visions. **Bl. Giles of Assisi** (d. 1262) accompanied Francis on evangelical expeditions around Assisi and later ventured out on pilgrimages to Compostela, Rome, the Holy Land and Tunis. **Bl. Andrew Caccioli** (d. 1254) was sent to the mission area of Lombardy. **Bl. John of Perugia** (d. 1231) was sent to preach to the Moors in Spain, where he was beheaded. The emir eventually converted to Christianity and donated his house, where the execution had taken place, to become a friary. **Bl. Guy Vignotelli** (c. 1185-1245) left all to follow Francis after having heard him preach at Cortona, where he built a hermit's cell on a bridge. He was later ordained but continued to live a hermit's life. All of these disciples were renowned for prayer, poverty, the performance of miracles, charity and holiness of life.

People from all walks of life wanted to become a saint after the example of Francis. He formed the Third Order to enable lay persons to follow his way but without religious vows. The pope officially approved the Third Order in 1221. **Bl. Luchesio** (d. 1260) and his wife, **Bl. Bonnadonna** (d. 1260) were the first Third Order Franciscans. Queen **Elizabeth of Hungary** (1207-31) followed soon behind them. **Elzear** (1285-1323) and his wife **Bl. Delphine** (1283-1360) are believed traditionally to be Third Order members.

Two students, **Bl. Peregrin of Falerine** (d. 1240) and **Bl. Rizzerio of Muccia** (d. 1236), heard Francis preach at Bologna. They were so moved that they left all and joined the saint's community. Two parish priests, **Bl. Christopher of Romangnola** (1172-1272) and **Bl. Andrew of Spello** (d. 1254) heard Francis preach and asked to join the group.

MASTER AND DISCIPLE

Peter (d. c. 64), the head of the twelve apostles, used the home of **Priscilla** (d. c. 98) as his headquarters in Rome. Under her home are the catacombs which bear her name and are visited even today by pilgrims. She was probably the mother of the senator **Pudens** (1st century). Peter baptized the centurion **Cornelius** and his whole household.

Among the many disciples of **John the Evangelist** were **Polycarp of Smyrna** (c. 69-c. 155) and **Ignatius of Antioch** (d. c. 107). John converted Polycarp and ordained him bishop around the year 96. Polycarp worked diligently against the heresies of Valentinianism and Marcionism. When he was eighty-six years old, he was arrested and martyred during the persecution of Marcus Aurelius. "Polycarp was probably the leading Christian in Roman Asia in the second century and an important link between the apostolic age and the great Christian writers of the late second century."[22] Ignatius was the bishop of Antioch. He was arrested during the persecution of Emperor Trajan. His sea trip to Rome took him along the coast of Asia Minor and Greece. Along the way he dictated seven letters which have great doctrinal importance.

Polycarp inspired his disciple **Irenaeus** (c. 125-203). Gregory of Tours tells us that Polycarp sent Irenaeus as a missionary to Gaul, where he became bishop of Lyons and evangelized the locals and wrote against the heretical Gnostics. "His treatise against the Gnostics is witness to the apostolic tradition and in it, at this early date, is a testimony to the primacy of the Pope."[23]

Maximinus (d. c. 347) and **Paulinus** (d. 358), master and disciple, were successive bishops of Trier. Both men avidly supported Athanasius against Arianism. Paulinus was exiled to Phrygia by the Arian emperor and died there three years later.

Antony of the Desert (251-356) had many disciples, one of whom was **Hilarion** (c. 291-c. 371). Hilarion's pagan parents sent him to study at Alexandria, where he was baptized at age fifteen. He took Antony as his life's model. Hilarion lived in the desert with Antony for two months. The disciple found too many distractions in the desert, however, with so many people visiting Antony for physical and spiritual healing. Hilarion sought greater solitude, and so withdrew to Majuma in the Gaza desert near Egypt.

Another disciple of Antony was **Paul the Simple** (d. c. 339). Paul's wife was unfaithful and so at age sixty, Paul finally left her and joined Antony in the desert. Initially, Antony hesitated to accept Paul because of the recruit's advanced age. Antony gave Paul an arduous test of asceticism to measure his ability and interest. Paul passed with flying colors. In time, Antony described Paul as the ideal monk.

Hilary of Poitiers (d. c. 368) inspired discipleship in **Martin of Tours** (c. 316-97), who subsequently raised and inspired **Brice** (d. 444). All three became bishops in Gaul. Hilary became a convert as an adult. He was married when he was elected bishop of Poitiers about 350. The Arian controversy was raging. Hilary opposed the Arian emperor and was exiled to Phrygia. "He was so successful in refuting Arianism at a council of Eastern bishops at Seleucia in 359 and in encouraging the clergy to resist the heresy that the Arians requested the emperor to send him back to Gaul."[24] Hilary is a Doctor of the Church.

Martin of Tours grew up in Pannonia (in what is now Hungary) and became a soldier like his father. When he was about twenty-one years of age, a famous incident occurred: Martin cut his cloak in two to share with a beggar. That night he experienced a vision of Christ wearing Martin's half cloak. Martin converted to Christianity, laid down his weapons and lived as a pilgrim and recluse for three years. When Hilary returned to Poitiers, Martin joined him. Other hermits then joined Martin to form the first monastic community in Gaul. Martin was named bishop of Tours. He won converts and averted bloodshed between warring theological and political factions.

Brice (d. 444) was raised by Martin of Tours. Brice's manner, however, was far different from Martin's. Brice was vain, ambitious and allegedly licentious. Martin remained patient with him; others did not. Brice was driven from his see by his Christian followers. After seven years' repentance Brice returned and ruled from that time on with great humility and charity.

Pambo (d. c. 390) founded the Nitrian Desert monasteries in Egypt. He had been a youthful disciple of **Antony**. In his adult years Pambo attracted many wisdom seekers, among whom were the Alexandrian opponent of Arianism, **Athanasius** (c. 297-393), and **Melania the Elder** (c. 342-c. 410), who assisted Pambo as he lay dying and who paid his funeral expenses.

Pambo was renowned for his austerities: "assiduous manual labor, usually in the making of mats from palm-leaf strips, long fasts, and other severe physical mortifications, and prayer uninterrupted over long periods of time; his personal appearance was so majestic as to divert attention from the rags with which he was clothed."[25] He practiced unusual brevity in his speech. The story is told that his teacher assigned him Psalm 38 for his first reading lesson. Pambo heard the first line, "I said, I will take heed to my ways that I sin not with my tongue." Pambo interrupted the teacher and declared: "That will do for today." He then went off to reflect on the lesson and returned six months later for the next lesson! Another story is told that Melania once gave him a generous gift of silver. He received the gift, explained that it would be used for the needs of all the monasteries, but he spoke no word of thanks. She commented: "There is three hundred pounds of silver, my father." Pambo responded, "He to whom you have offered this gift has no need for you to tell Him its value."[26] Once after he received a gift of some money, he was invited by the donor to count it. Pambo replied, "God does not ask how much, but how."[27]

John Chrysostom (c. 347-407) is esteemed for his prophetic and eloquent preaching.[28] The empress ordered his exile (wherein he eventually died) for criticizing her dissolute life. His disciples **Eutropius** (d. 404) and **Tigrius** (d. 406) were arrested on the false charge of having set fire to the cathedral and Senate building in protest of John's exile. Both men were tortured. Eutropius died. Tigrius survived and was exiled to Mesopotamia, where he died two years later. John's disciple **Palladius** (365-431), whom he had ordained bishop of Helenopolis, went to Rome to seek appeals for Chrysostom's release from the emperor and pope. When Palladius faced the Byzantine emperor, he was punished with exile. Another disciple and intercessor was **John Cassian** (c. 360-c. 433), who lived as a monk at Bethlehem and Egypt before meeting Chrysostom at Constantinople around 400. Five years later, when Chrysostom had been deposed as patriarch, Cassian too traveled to Rome to plead on his master's behalf. The pope and western emperor demanded Chrysostom's release but the ambassadorial party was ambushed and imprisoned. Cassian is considered a saint in the East but has never been canonized in the West.[29] Throughout his exile Chrysostom corresponded with his disciple and friend **Olympias** (c. 361-c. 408).

Alipius (c. 360-430) was a lifelong disciple of **Augustine** (354-430). They were boyhood friends from Tagaste, North Africa. Alipius studied Manicheanism under Augustine and joined his tutor in that sect. Alipius' father forbade him to associate further with Augustine. Alipius went to Rome to study law. When Augustine appeared there, Alipius rejoined him. Together they went to Milan and there converted to Christianity in 387. The next year they returned to

Tagaste to live a community life established by Augustine based on prayer and penance. In 391 they were ordained priests at Hippo. Within a few years Alipius became bishop of Tagaste and Augustine became bishop of Hippo.

The Maronite rite receives its name from the Bait-Marun monastery which was built on the banks of the Orontes River around the relics of the hermit **Maro** (d. 433). Maro, a Syrian ascetical wise man, followed the example of his master **Zebinus** (5th century). Master and disciple were renowned for their austerities and prayerfulness, passing the night while standing although sometimes resorting to lean on a cane. Pilgrims sought out both men as spiritual guides. Zebinus tried to avoid visitors. Maro welcomed them and invited visitors to stand the night with him. Chrysostom corresponded with Maro.

Arsenius (c. 355-450) was recommended by Pope Damasus to serve as tutor for the children of the imperial family at the court in Constantinople. After a decade-long period in the employment of the emperor, Arsenius opted for the austerities of the desert. He traveled to Skete, where **John the Dwarf** (5th century) instructed him in the regimen of the hermits.

Simeon Stylites the Younger (c. 517-92) became a stylite, that is, a column-sitter, at age seven under the tutelage of **John Stylites** (6th century). Simeon lived on a pillar for the next sixty-eight years. At age twenty he moved to a more remote spot to escape admiring crowds. At age thirty he founded a monastery. At thirty-three he was ordained a priest while he remained on his pillar; the two bishops climbed a ladder for the laying on of hands. When Simeon celebrated Mass, recipients of communion would climb the ladder. John moderated Simeon's unusual austerity of fasting and prayer, but after the master's death the disciple survived on just a few kinds of fruits and vegetables. From his pillar he preached, advised and worked miracles to which many witnesses attested.[30]

The last living disciple of **Patrick of Ireland** (c. 389-

461) was **Mochta**. For thirty years Patrick evangelized the Emerald Isle. His fame spread to Britain, where Mochta was born to Christian parents. They brought the youth to Patrick for instruction in the faith. Mochta learned well. He traveled to Rome, where Pope Leo the Great ordained him bishop. He returned to Ireland, where Patrick appointed him bishop of Louth monastery.

The great **Columba** (c. 521-97) attended Glasnevin monastery as a disciple of **Mobhi** (d. 545), one of the twelve apostles of Ireland. Customarily, young clergy lived for a time with older outstanding clergy. Mobhi trained four of Ireland's outstanding saints, one of whom was Columba.[31] Columba, however, ran into a few difficulties: he copied without permission Finnian's sole copy of Jerome's Psalter and instigated a riot which resulted in the deaths of 3,000 persons, for which he was blamed and publicly censured. He fled Ireland in shame on a self-imposed life-long exile. He landed at the Scottish isle of Iona, where he began with twenty repentant relatives "a monastery that grew into the greatest monastery in Christendom."[32] Iona's influence for education, evangelization and holiness impacted all of Scotland and northern England. Among other accomplishments, Columba made it public policy that women be excluded henceforth from military service.

Augustine of Canterbury and **Gregory the Great** are described in this chapter.

Augustine of Canterbury (d. 604) persuaded **Ethelbert**, the king of Kent (560-616), to convert to Christianity. Thousands of his subjects freely followed this first Christian king of the English. "He [Ethelbert] granted religious freedom to his subjects, believing conversion by conviction was the only true conversion."[33] The king encouraged neighboring kings to follow suit. Ethelbert ruled justly for fifty-six years.

John of York (8th century) and **Wilfrid the Younger** (d. c. 744) were successive bishops. Both bishops retired early, says Alcuin, so that they could be unencumbered by administrative responsibilities and free for spiritual pursuits.

Two Calabrians of Greek origin who followed the Greek rite were **Nilus of Rome** (c. 910-1004) and his disciple **Bartholomew of Rossano** (d. 1065). Nilus lived a morally unrestrained life until his young wife and child died. He wanted to change his ways and so entered the monastery. Invaders forced the monks to flee from Calabria. They escaped to Frascati near Rome, where Nilus instructed Bartholomew to found Grottaferrata monastery.

Edmund Rich (c. 1180-1240) and **Richard de Wyche** (1197-1253) followed similar paths to sanctity. Both master and disciple studied at Oxford and Paris, received doctorates in theology, became priest-chancellor of Oxford university and bishops of the Church, Edmund at Canterbury and Richard at Chichester. Richard was chancellor to Edmund. Both encountered challenges to ecclesiastical authority from the king. Both resisted the king's infringements and threatened excommunication.

Raymond Nonnatus (c. 1204-40) was a disciple of **Peter Nolasco** (c. 1189-1258). Traditionally they are regarded as the co-founders of the Mercedarians.

Bl. Peter Favre (1506-46), who roomed with Francis Xavier at St. Barbe College in Paris, and together joined the Society of Jesus, attracted two famous disciples: **Peter Canisius** (1521-97) and **Francis Borgia** (1510-72). Both men joined the Jesuits after hearing Peter Favre preach. Peter had attempted to work for unity with Protestant reformers but he soon realized that the Church itself first needed reform. He preached throughout Germany, France, Spain and Portugal. He was chosen to be the pope's personal theologian at the Council of Trent. Unfortunately Peter died in Rome while preparing for the council.

Peter Canisius was missioned by Ignatius to teach at the first Jesuit school at Messina. Peter taught and administered at other universities, too, before devoting himself to itinerant preaching. He crossed the whole of Germany. After

Boniface, Peter Canisius is regarded as the "second apostle of Germany." He attended two sessions of the Council of Trent. A prolific writer, he is a Doctor of the Church.

Francis Borgia served for ten years as a lay advisor to Emperor Charles V before being promoted to other royal positions. Two years after his wife died, he arranged for the care of their eight children and entered the Jesuit community. His preaching throughout Spain and Portugal attracted large crowds. He was given significant responsibilities within the Jesuit community and in 1565 was elected superior general of all Jesuits. He established universities and opened missions including those in America. He so revitalized the Jesuits that he is often referred to as the second founder of the Society of Jesus.

Teresa of Avila (1515-82) enjoyed the constant companionship and secretarial service of **Bl. Anna Garcia** (1549-1626) for the last six years of the foundress' life. Anna had been a shepherdess until age twenty when she joined the Carmelites. After the death of Teresa, she was sent to many cities to establish Carmelite convents.

At the beginning of the Catholic Reformation **Philip Neri** (1515-95) lived in Rome, where a general malaise and atmosphere of corruption hung like a pall over the city. Philip responded by establishing the Oratorian Order to assist pilgrims with prayer and counseling. He attracted numerous converts to the Church and priests to his burgeoning community. This apostle of Rome "was consulted by rich and poor, powerful and helpless for his spiritual wisdom and his ability to look into men's minds."[34] **John Leonardi** (c. 1550-1609) and **Camillus de Lellis** (1550-1614) were two of his disciples.

John Leonardi took seriously the call to reform proclaimed by Philip Neri and the Council of Trent. John gathered a group of laymen to minister in prisons and hospitals. He wanted to found a new congregation of secular priests but he encountered stiff opposition. Philip Neri continuously encouraged John in the process of founding this new community. In 1595 his congregation of Clerks Regular of the Mother of God was approved by the pope. John is regarded as one of the founders of the College for the Propagation of the Faith.

Camillus de Lellis turned with the help of Philip Neri from public sinner to publicly acclaimed saint. He was a soldier addicted to gambling. He cured his habit by devoting himself to the care of the sick. Philip was his confessor and encouraged him to seek ordination and to found his own congregation, the Ministers of the Sick. In 1591 the pope recognized the new religious order. Camillus and his community members labored throughout Italy, Hungary and Croatia.

Alphonsus de Liguori (1696-1787) received **Gerard Majella** (1726-55) into the Redemptorist religious community which Alphonsus had just founded. Alphonsus dedicated his life to preaching, reforming the clergy, and evangelizing the rural poor. Gerard Majella followed his master's footsteps in community and in holiness. A lay brother, Gerard worked as a tailor and an infirmarian. He was blessed with spiritual gifts and served as spiritual advisor to countless visitors.

Bl. Dominic Barberi of the Mother of God (1792-1849) brought into the Catholic Church many members of the Oxford movement in England. His most prominent convert was **John Henry Newman** (1801-90), the future Cardinal Newman. Dominic was ordained a priest in 1818 for the Passionist Community. He was sent in 1841 to England as head of the Passionist mission where he was renowned for asceticism and scholarship. John Henry Newman has not yet been canonized but is regarded as the outstanding English churchman of his century.

Justin de Jacobis (1800-60) converted **Ghebre Michael** (1791-1855) to the Church. The example of the Roman Catholic priest inspired the Ethiopian monk to become a disciple and convert. They are described in this chapter.

Bl. Michael Rua (1837-1910) was an early disciple of **John Bosco** (1815-88). Michael joined the Institute and succeeded John as general of the community. "Nearly three hundred new Salesian houses were opened under his leadership."[35]

Notes for Chapter 8

[1]   *Butler's Lives of the Saints*, vol. I, p. 570.

[2]   Margaret Deanesly, *Augustine of Canterbury*, pp. 26-27.

[3]   Butler, vol. III, pp. 360-61. Eventually Bernard's father and sister joined him at Clairvaux.

[4]   Andre Ravier, *Ignatius of Loyola and the Founding of the Society of Jesus*, pp. 72-73.

[5]   *Letters from the Saints*, Claude Williamson, ed., pp. 80-81.

[6]   *The Book of Saints*, p. 227.

[7]   Ibid.

[8]   From the letters to Ignatius from Francis Xavier, *The Liturgy of the Hours*, vol. I, pp. 1210-11.

[9]   Butler, vol. III, p. 231.

[10] Ibid.

[11] Thomas Davitt, *Justin de Jacobis, CM*, p. 28.

[12] Ibid., pp. 27-28, 55.

[13] The Franciscans claim over 60 beati and sancti in the 13th century, among whom are Clare, Agnes, Anthony of Padua and Bl. Giles of Assisi. The Dominicans similarly claim many holy members, most famously, Bl. Ceslau and Bl. Jordan of Saxony.

[14] Hostie, *The Life and Death of Religious Orders*, appendix p. viii.

[15] Delaney, *Dictionary of Saints*, p. 235.

[16] Hostie, appendix p. viii.

[17] Ibid., p. xi.

[18] Delaney, p. 114.

[19] *The Book of Saints*, p. 455.

[20] Ibid., p. 286.

[21] Delaney, p. 63.

[22] Ibid., p. 475.

[23] Ibid, p. 301.

24   Ibid., p. 285.

25   Butler, vol. III, p. 137.

26   Ibid.

27   Ibid.

28   Cf. *The Radical Tradition: Revolutionary Saints in the Battle for Justice and Human Rights.*

29   Delaney, p. 318.

30   Butler, vol. III, p. 479.

31   D'Arcy, *The Saints of Ireland*, p. 31.

32   Delaney, p. 155.

33   Ibid., p. 201.

34   Ibid., p. 420.

35   *The Book of Saints*, p. 401.

CHAPTER 9

SAINTLY CO-FOUNDERS

Men's Communities

1. Amatus and Romaricus (Abbey of Remiremont)
2. Bartholomew of Rossano and Nilus of Rome (Grottaferrata Monastery)
3. John and Euthymius of Bithynia (Iviron Monastery)
4. Anthony Pechersky and Theodosius Pechersky (Kiev Monastery)
5. Robert of Molesmes, Stephen Harding and Alberic (Cistercians)
6. Felix of Valois and John of Matha (Trinitarians)
7. Raymond of Peñafort and Peter Nolasco (Mercedarians)
8. The Seven Founders (Servites)
9. Anthony Zaccaria, Ven. Bartholomew Ferrari and Ven. James Morigia (Barnabites)

Women's Communities

10. Salaberga and Waldebert (convent at Laon)
11. Clare of Assisi and Francis of Assisi (Poor Clares)
12. Jane de Chantal and Francis de Sales (Visitation Sisters)
13. Bl. Alix le Clerc and Peter Fourier (Congregation of Augustinian Canonesses of Our Lady)

14. Louise de Marillac and Vincent de Paul (Daughters of Charity)
15. Bl. Marie Louise Trichet and Louis Marie Grignion de Montfort (Daughters of Wisdom)
16. Vincentia Gerosa and Bartolomea Capitanio (Sisters of Charity of Lovere)
17. Elizabeth Bichier and Andrew Fournet (Daughters of the Cross)
18. Bl. Mary de Matthias and Ven. John Merlini (Sisters of the Adorers of the Sacred Heart)
19. John Bosco and Mary Mazzarello (Daughters of Our Lady Help of Christians)

Communities for The Lord: Co-Founder Saints

Many persons jointly undertake projects: for example, business ventures, social movements, and political revolutions. Delicate is the balance that makes for success. External and/or internal forces can make or break the project. The quality of the leaders of the project is crucial. They share vision, strategies and risks. They require of one another dedication and cooperation.

The Scriptures present a record of many people who collaborated on religious projects. In post-exilic Israel, Ezra and Nehemiah co-founded a revival community which provided hope to a spiritually depressed nation. Later, the Maccabee family joined together in religious and political opposition to Hellenizing influences. In the New Testament Jesus entrusted to Peter and Paul the task of developing the Church.

Throughout the Church's history, holy men and women have founded thousands of religious communities. Some of them made their foundations jointly; they are co-founders. They shared a common vision and developed a common way to incorporate that vision.

Instinctively, he (the founder) perceives how desirable it would be to express his ideas to others who would give him the same Gospel answer. As the disciple's search deepens, so does his desire for communication and communion. As a result, any chance encounter can move him toward an exchange of thought. If the two are capable of listening and of being open, the exchange may be prolonged into sharing, then later, putting what they have in common. They become magnetized through their common quest, astonished at the coincidence of their understanding of the Gospel and at their insights concerning the Person of Christ.[1]

Surprise at the unforeseen encounter or the certitude of their parallel direction brought about exchanges. Exchanges gave way to sharing. Links of friendship instigated prolonged contacts. This is how they decided, without yet knowing too well the why or how, either to maintain frequent contact or to stay together. Unconsciously, they were drawn together by a common quest. Up to this time, they had been only individuals influenced by hopes as strong as they were vague. Henceforward, they would form a company.[2]

Particular Examples

1. ANTHONY ZACCARIA, VEN. BARTHOLOMEW FERRARI AND VEN. JAMES MORIGIA

The Barnabite community of priests and brothers, more formally known as the Clerks Regular of St. Paul, was founded by Anthony Zaccaria (1502-39), Ven. Bartholomew Ferrari (1499-1544) and Ven. James Morigia (1497-1546). Their mission was "to regenerate and revive the love of divine worship, and a properly Christian way of life by frequent preaching and faithful ministering of the sacraments."[3] These men wished to reform ecclesiastical and clerical life. Anthony had been a practicing physician who felt called not only to heal bodies but also souls. He moved to Milan where he dedicated himself to the corporal and spiritual works of mercy, joining other men and women in Church service.

An excerpt follows from a sermon preached by Anthony Zaccaria to members of his society:

> We are fools for Christ's sake: our holy guide and most revered patron was speaking about himself and the rest of the apostles, and about the other people who profess the Christian and apostolic way of life. But there is no reason, dear brothers, that we should be surprised or afraid; for the disciple is not superior to his teacher, nor the slave to his master. We should love and feel compassion for those who oppose us, rather than abhor and despise them, since they harm themselves and do us good, and adorn us with crowns of everlasting glory while they incite God's anger against themselves. And even more than this, we should pray for them and not be overcome by evil, but overcome evil by goodness. We should heap good works like red-hot coals of burning love upon their heads as our Apostle urges us to do, so that when they become aware of our tolerance and gentleness they may undergo a change of heart and be prompted to turn in love to God.
>
> In his mercy God has chosen us, unworthy as we are, out of the world, to serve him and thus to advance in goodness and to bear the greatest possible fruit of love in patience. We should take encouragement not only from the hope of sharing in the glory of God's children, but also from the hardships we undergo.
>
> Consider your calling, dearest brothers; if we wish to think carefully about it we shall see readily enough that its basis demands that we who have set out to follow, admittedly from afar, the footsteps of the holy apostles and the other soldiers of Christ, should not be unwilling to share in their sufferings as well. We

should keep running steadily in the race we have started, not losing sight of Jesus, who leads us in our faith and brings it to perfection. And so since we have chosen such a great Apostle as our guide and father and claim to follow him, we should try to put his teaching and example into practice in our lives. Such a leader should not be served by faint-hearted troops, nor should such a parent find his sons unworthy of him.

2. VINCENT DE PAUL AND LOUISE DE MARILLAC

Vincent de Paul (1580-1660) founded the Congregation of the Mission in 1625 as a community of priests and brothers who, in imitation of Jesus, would preach the Gospel to the poor. He noticed that the poor's hunger for spiritual food would be better met if their hunger for material food were likewise assuaged. So with Louise de Marillac (1591-1660) he co-founded the Daughters of Charity in 1633. These saints dedicated themselves to a practical love for God and the poor. Vincent was fond of saying to his confreres: "Let us love God, my brothers, let us love God, but let it be with the strength of our arms and the sweat of our brow."[4] He instructed his community members that it is necessary at times to leave chapel in order to respond to the cries of the poor, to "leave God for God."

Louise came to Vincent for spiritual advice. Her life had been full of suffering: she was an illegitimate child who never experienced full acceptance in the family; she married but was widowed twelve years later; she suffered from a scrupulous conscience. Vincent advised her to lose herself in the service of others and so she and other wealthy women founded the Ladies of Charity to undertake the practical service of feeding the hungry and caring for the sick. Louise and a few others wished to form a religious community to dedicate their lives to prayer and service. In

time Louise became an outstanding care-giver, administrator and saint. Shortly after her death, which occurred
six months before his own, Vincent de Paul reflected about
her with her sisters:

> Meditating before God a little while ago, I said: "Lord,
> it is your will that we should talk about your servant,"
> for she is the work of his hands; and I wondered:
> "What did you see during the thirty-eight years that
> you have known her? What did you see in her?" Some
> little flicker of imperfection came to mind, but mortal
> sins, Oh, never! The slightest stirring of the desires of
> the flesh was intolerable to her. She was a pure soul in
> everything, pure in her youth, in her marriage, in her
> widowhood.
>
> She would scrutinize herself in order to tell her sins
> and all her imaginations. She would make her confes-
> sion with great clarity. Never have I had anyone
> accuse himself with such precision. And she would cry
> so much that it was quite a job to quiet her down.
>
> Indeed, you should realize that your mother had great
> depth and a sound inner life which so regulated her
> thoughts and her will that she applied them only to
> serve God and to love him.[5]

Vincent and Louise wanted the members of their
community to be freed of the traditional religious enclo-
sure. They wanted the sisters to enjoy a physical presence
with the poor and to render them practical service and
included their vision of mission in the rules of the Daughters of Charity; the sisters would have:

> for a monastery, the houses of the sick;
> for a cell, a rented room;
> for a chapel, the parish church;
> for a cloister, the streets of the city and the
> wards of hospitals;
> for an enclosure, obedience;
> for the grating, the fear of God;
> for a veil, holy modesty.[6]

3. LOUIS MARIE GRIGNION DE MONTFORT AND BL. MARIE LOUISE TRICHET

Louis Marie Grignion de Montfort (1673-1716) and Bl. Marie Louise Trichet (1684-1759), poor priest and upper middle class young lady, fire-brand preacher and demure pray-er, founded the Daughters of Wisdom in 1702 at Poitiers. They shared a faith-motivated love for the poor. He worked in the local hospital as chaplain and invited her to be a housekeeper there, although the hospital authorities wished to give her other responsibilities. Her desire, however, was to be among the poor who called her "Good Mother Jesus."[7] Louis did not stay long at Poitiers. He was asked to leave the hospital because his unauthorized reorganization of the staff caused much unrest. He was next asked to leave the city altogether because his preaching stirred up the poor. Marie Louise felt abandoned. He urged her to stay at the hospital. She did. She kept faith in God's love for her and the poor. She followed the charism of Louis which urged her to keep seeking Jesus Wisdom.

Two weeks before he died, Louis Marie wrote to Marie Louise to encourage her. She and the sisters wanted to continue their work of education of children but they kept running into obstacles: their neighbors did not want them to reside in their home; Louis was on mission and away more than he was with them, and morale was low. The foundation seemed on the verge of collapse. Nothing seemed to be going right. Marie Louise saved this last letter from her co-founder as inspiration for the community about their motivation and mission:

> My dear Daughter in Jesus Christ,
> May Jesus and his Cross reign forever!
>
> I worship the justice and love with which divine Wisdom is treating his little flock, allowing you to live in cramped quarters here on earth so that later you

may find spacious dwellings in his divine heart which was pierced for you to enter. How pleasant and safe is this sacred refuge for a soul truly possessing Wisdom! Such a soul came forth with the blood and water which flowed when the lance pierced the divine heart, and it is here that it finds a refuge when persecuted by its enemies. Here it can remain hidden with Jesus Christ in God, more victorious than any hero, crowned with more laurels than any king, shining with greater splendor than the sun and raised higher than the very heavens.

If you truly seek to be a disciple of divine Wisdom and one chosen among so many, then this unkind treatment you are suffering, the contempt, the poverty, the restrictions, all these should be pleasing to you since they are the price you have to pay to obtain Wisdom and true freedom and become partakers of the divinity of the heart of Jesus crucified.

If I were to look at these setbacks from a human standpoint, I would be tempted, like the foolish people of this corrupt world, to complain and be anxious and worried, but that is not how I look at things. Let me tell you that I expect more serious setbacks, more painful ones to test your faith and confidence. We will then found our community of the Daughters of Wisdom, not on quicksands of gold and silver which the devil is always using to adorn his house, nor indeed on the strength and influence of any human being, for no matter how holy and powerful man may be he will always be no more than a wisp of straw. We want to found our Congregation on the Wisdom of the Cross of Calvary. This adorable Cross has been stained with the blood of a God and chosen by Jesus to be the spouse of his heart, his heart's only desire and inspiration, the only object worth his toil, his only arm in combat, his only crown of glory, his only guide in his judgments. It is hard to understand that this great Cross was lost, scorned and hidden in the earth for more than four hundred years.

My dear daughters, apply this to the state in which you find yourselves. I think of you always, especially during holy Mass. I will never forget you, provided you love the precious Cross. I am united with you in bearing the cross as long as you follow the holy will of God and not your own. In this holy will I am all yours. . . .[8]

4. John Bosco and Mary Mazzarello

John Bosco (1815-88) and Mary Mazzarello (1837-81) co-founded in 1872 the Daughters of Our Lady Help of Christians, who are more often called the Salesian Sisters. The community grew out of a Marian sodality which Mary's pastor had founded on the advice of Don Bosco and which she had joined as a charter member at the age of seventeen. The sodality provided for young girls what Don Bosco provided for young boys: an open and loving atmosphere in which learning and play took place. As Mary said: "Laugh and play and dash about as much as you like but be ever so careful not to do or say anything that would be displeasing to God."[9] The sodality was very successful in achieving its mission.

Don Bosco suggested that the women form a religious community. Mary, a virtually unlettered seamstress, was chosen by Don Bosco to be the leader among the ten other women. In the next nine years, under Mary's guidance the community opened sixteen convents throughout Italy, France and Argentina. In the next sixty years, over eight hundred convents were opened worldwide. Mary died with Don Bosco holding her hand. The co-founders are buried side by side in Turin. The following quotation is taken from among Mary's letters to John Bosco.[10] There are no extant letters from John to Mary; she discarded them all. Her sense of humility outweighed her sense of history.

Mornese, December 24, 1877

Viva Gesú Bambino!
Reverend and dear Father:

Allow me to unite my own greetings, which even though poorly expressed, are no less sincere and heartfelt, with the many others that you are receiving during these days. I hope that with the Lord's help, you may make saints of all the Daughters of Mary Help of Christians, both present and future, and after sanctifying several thousand of us, you may guide us to paradise above. Of course, you will have to work hard at it, but our good Jesus will comfort and strengthen you. Everyday I pray for you to receive this grace. On this night and tomorrow too, I am going to beg Him so much that He will have to listen to me and bless you, dear Father, granting you all the help you need.

On my part, I promise you that, with the help of our good Jesus, I will do all I possibly can to help you and to lighten your burden. Oh Reverend Father, do not spare me in any way. Do with me as you wish, correct me without any hesitation and just treat me as a father would treat his eldest daughter. What I recommend to you above all else is that you pray for me. I need it so much! . . . If I can always give good example to my Sisters, everything will go well. If I can love Jesus with all my heart, I shall know how to make others love Him too. Therefore, pray hard to the Child Jesus for me, especially on this blessed night; tell Him some of those little words with which you always obtain every grace.

I would have so many other things to tell you, but what can I do? My heart is full, but my hands do not know how to write them. In your great kindness, interpret them all, and accept my greetings. Please give me your fatherly blessing, as I respectfully kiss your consecrated hand, assuring you that I am, Reverend, Father,

Your most humble daughter in Jesus Christ.
(poor) Sister Mary Mazzarello

General Observations

Religious communities have arisen throughout Church history. The goal remains the same: to provide persons a context of prayer and community in which each member commits himself or herself to live out the evangelical counsels of chastity, poverty and obedience. The motivation remains the same: love of God and neighbor. The particular means vary according to the current social need, contemporary spirituality and particular community charism. Four distinct forms of religious life can be identified throughout Church history: monasticism, mendicant orders, apostolic societies and teaching congregations.

Co-founders are discovered within each of these four forms. Monasticism is represented by Amatus and Romaric of the Remiremont Monastery; the Carthusians founded by Bruno of Rheims and Hugh of Grenoble; the Cistercians Robert of Molesmes, Alberic and Stephen Harding; the re-foundation of the Cistercians by Bernard of Clairvaux and his sainted brothers; and the re-foundation of the Carmelites by Teresa of Avila and John of the Cross. The mendicant orders are represented by the Poor Clares, founded by Clare and Francis. Examples of the apostolic societies are the Barnabites, who were founded by Anthony Zaccaria, Ven. Bartolomeo Ferrari, and Ven. James Morigia; the Daughters of Charity who were jointly founded by Louise de Marillac and Vincent de Paul; and the Visitation Sisters who were founded by Jane de Chantal and Francis de Sales. One teaching congregation is the Daughters of Wisdom co-founded by Louis Marie Grignion de Montfort and Marie Louise Trichet.

Religious communities are numerous. The author of the world-renowned *The Life and Death of Religious Orders* notes that "in the eighteenth and nineteenth centuries, I found out that there were about 276 orders or congregations of male religious that had been in existence for one hundred years or more and some 2,000 congregations of women religious."[11] This large number of communities refers to existing communities. Most communities do not last; "this [extinction] happened, for example, to 76% of all men's religious orders founded before 1500, and to 64% of those founded between 1500 and before 1800."[12]

Co-founders had to be uniquely idealistic and realistic persons. As idealists, they looked at the present state of affairs and wished for the elusive more. They could never be satisfied with a business-as-usual stance. They envisioned what could be and how it could be achieved. They were challenging and creative. As realists, they rooted themselves in the present and worked to create the future. They took on the responsibility for leading and providing for their followers. Co-founders were simultaneously animators and administrators.

Co-founders required much courage. They forsook the comfort of existing companions and careers, leaving behind the known for the unknown. Vincent de Paul transferred from the diocesan priesthood in order to found his religious community. Robert of Molesmes transferred from the Benedictines to found the Cistercians; one year later he was ordered by the pope to return to his original community. Bruno of Rheims gave up his university career; Anthony Zaccaria, his medical practice; and Andrew Fournet, his legal studies. Francis of Assisi, Ven. Giacomo Morigia and Bl. Alix Le Clerc abandoned frivolous lifestyles. Two seventeenth-century widows, Jane de Chantal and Louise de Marillac, made arrangements for the raising of their children and then founded religious communities. Romaric and Clare of Assisi abandoned their lives of nobility in exchange for lives of poverty, chastity and obedience.

Some co-founders reformed existing communities. They acknowledged but would not accept the existing laxity and mediocrity. They recognized that, although the institutional structure may have evidenced worldly success, the internal spirit had evaporated. Collapse was inevitable if not imminent. These re-founders restored the primitive spirit and in doing so rescued their communities from inevitable eventual extinction.

Application Of The Theme

Common Vision: Co-founders shared an insight. They tried to look at the world with the eyes of Jesus Christ. Their vision was blessed. They saw what their contemporaries could not see. They envisioned that they could constructively confront the outstanding Christian needs of their moment in history. Co-founders were Spirit-filled.

Common Way: Co-founders needed a way to implement their vision. They needed to concretize their insight into reality. They took a step. One step led to another. Their vision and way unfolded as they walked together. Spirit-filled, they were Spirit-led. They humbly allowed the mystery of God to originate and expand their religious communities.

Common Bond With Each Other: Co-founders constantly interacted with each other. New communities met new needs with a new fervor. Charter community members lived a vibrant community life. Spirit, not structure, reigned at this time. Inspiration, not institutionalism, guided their steps. Prayer, not pragmatism, dictated their direction.

Common Bond With God: This founding time of almost all communities was a graced moment. God called and community members responded with unparalleled blessings. Saints and *beati* abounded because grace abounded. At virtually no other time in a community's entire history will so many holy people be found.

APPENDIX: CO-FOUNDER SAINTS

MEN'S COMMUNITIES

The Benedictine hermit **Amatus** (d. c. 630) converted the Merovingian nobleman **Romaric** (d. 653). In 620 they co-founded the double monastery of the Abbey of Remiremont on Romaric's estate. Amatus was named the first abbot and served in that capacity for three years before retiring to the solitary life. Romaric succeeded as abbot and presided for thirty years. Hundreds of monks came to their monastery. Romaric was converted at the royal court. While dining at table, Romaric asked the question, "What must I do to gain eternal life?" Amatus pointed to a silver dish as symbolic of all prized possessions. He said, "Go sell what you have, give it to the poor, and you shall have treasure in heaven. And come, follow me."[13] Romaric took the words to heart.

Bartholomew of Rossano (d. 1065) was a disciple of **Nilus of Rome** (c. 910-1004). Nilus led a rather dissolute life until the age of thirty when his wife and their child died. Nilus then entered the monastery. Nilus and Bartholomew were the founders of Grottaferrata monastery at Frascati near Rome. Both composed Greek hymns. Both persuaded Pope Benedict IX to do penance and try to improve his moral and spiritual life. Bartholomew made the monastery a famous center of learning.

John (d. c. 1002) and his son **Euthymius** (d. 1028) left Georgia to live as monks on Mount Olympus. Later they co-founded the Iviron Monastery.

Anthony Pechersky (983-1073) and **Theodosius Pechersky** (d. 1074), who are not blood relatives, are considered in the Ukrainian Church as co-founders of Russian monasticism.[14] Anthony received Theodosius into the heremetical life in the caves near Kiev. Anthony guided Theodosius and others in a life full of extreme austerities. After Anthony left the cave community to lead a solitary life, the monks elected Theodosius as his successor. He immediately transformed the monastic community into the spiritual, moral, educational, social and cultural center of the local Christian community of Kiev.

Robert of Molesmes (c. 1024-1110) left the Benedictine Order because he felt so frustrated trying to reform the order from within. In 1098 Robert, the prior; **Alberic** (d. 1109), the subprior; **Stephen Harding** (d. 1134); and eighteen other monks co-founded at Citeaux a new order called the Cistercians. Their austerities soon attracted many candidates. Within one year, however, the pope, Blessed Urban II ordered Robert to return to his original monastery at Molesmes, where this time his reform movement succeeded. Robert was succeeded as abbot by Alberic, who was succeeded by Stephen. The latter introduced severe austerities that reduced the monastery's income and discouraged new candidates. A mysterious malady killed many of the monks, and it seemed for a short while that the young community might die.

Felix of Valois (1126-1212) and his disciple **John of Matha** (1160-1213) founded the Trinitarians in 1198 with the mission of ransoming Christians who had been captured by the Moors. Felix, with certain followers, established his headquarters in Paris and Cerfroid. John and his disciples centered their activities in Spain and Barbary. By 1240 the Trinitarians had burgeoned to some 600 monasteries. Much uncertainty surrounds the history of these two men and the founding of their order. The Trinitarians claim that the two founders were canonized in 1262 but that "the bull (of canonization) is nowhere extant."[15] Their cult was recognized in 1666, but since 1969 it has been restricted to particular calendars.

The traditionally held, although not necessarily historically accurate, story of the foundation of the Mercedarians reports that about the year 1218 **Peter Nolasco** (c. 1189-1258) and **Raymond of Peñafort** (1175-1275) reorganized in Spain a lay confraternity whose mission was to ransom Christian captives from the Moors. Much of Spain in the thirteenth century lay under the rule of the Moors. The revitalized lay community developed into the Order of Our Lady of Ransom, which is known popularly as the Order of the Mercedarians. Peter is said to have personally ransomed several hundred captives. Raymond served as Peter's spiritual director, invested him in the habit of the Order, and established him as the first Master General of the Order.

Raymond Nonnatus (c. 1204-40) succeeded Peter as the chief ransomer of Christians taken captive by the Moors. Many times Raymond offered himself as hostage in exchange for captives. He worked mainly in Barcelona but at times traveled to Algeria to complete his mission. He converted several Muslims and, for that, was condemned to death. He was tortured and imprisoned. Eventually, he was ransomed by Peter Nolasco. Raymond was appointed cardinal by the Pope but died not far from Barcelona as he was beginning his trip to Rome. He received his name *non natus*, meaning not born, because he had to be delivered by caesarean operation when his mother died in childbirth.

In 1240 seven prominent merchants of Florence banded together as the Servants of Mary, or **Servites**. They preferred to withdraw from the city's political strife and theological controversies in order to dedicate their lives to God and the Blessed Mother of God. Their daily life consisted of prayer, penance and practical service. They retreated to Monte Senario where, under the direction of **Peter of Verona** (1205-52), they adopted a religious habit and a religious rule. The men's names are **Bonfiglio Monaldo**, **Bonaiunta Manetto**, **Manetto Antellese**, **Amadeo Amedei**, **Ugiccione Uguccioni**, **Sosteneo Sostenei** and **Alessio Falconieri**.

The Barnabite community, or more formally, the Clerks Regular of St. Paul, was founded by **Anthony Zaccaria** (1502-39), **Venerable Bartholomew Ferrari** (1499-1544), and **Venerable James Morigia** (1497-1546). The founding of the Barnabite community is described in this chapter.

WOMEN'S COMMUNITIES

Salaberga (7th century) and **Waldebert** (d. c. 665) co-founded the double (male-and-female) monastery at Laon around the year 650. Waldebert was the second successor to Columban as abbot of Luxeuil where he served for forty years. He introduced the Rule of Benedict, freed the monastery from episcopal control, and won numerous benefactions for the monastery. Salaberga was married twice. Her second husband and she agreed to separate to enter the monastic life. She entered one convent, and then on the advice of Waldebert, began the monastery at Laon.

On Palm Sunday in 1212 **Clare of Assisi** (1194-1253) was so moved by a sermon preached by **Francis of Assisi** (c. 1181-1226) that she ran away from home to join him in total dedication to God. Clare was eighteen years old. Two weeks later her sister Agnes, who was fifteen years old, followed Clare. Because Francis as yet had no convent for women, he hid Clare with the Benedictines. Her family was incensed. Nothing, however, could dissuade her. In 1215 Francis gave Clare the church of San Damiano, where she and other women could live the Franciscan life. Clare was joined shortly by her mother, a second sister, three members of an outstanding local family and many others. Francis appointed Clare the superior and she served in this capacity for forty years. Thus began the Poor Clares, sister community of the Franciscans. Clare was consulted by popes, cardinals and bishops. "She was indeed as much instrumental in the rapid spreading of the Franciscan movement as St. Francis himself."[16]

Francis de Sales (1567-1622) assisted **Jane de Chantal** (1572-1641) in founding the Visitation Sisters. Jane was a young widow of three years with four young children when she first heard Francis preach a series of Lenten sermons in the cathedral of her brother, the archbishop of Bourges. She persuaded Francis to be her spiritual director. She wanted to enter the Carmelite Order, but he dissuaded her from that and instead persuaded her to found a society of women who would serve not behind the grill of the cloister but rather in the streets of the city. Six years after their initial meeting in 1604, she provided for her children, put her affairs in order, and with three other women founded at Annecy the Congregation of the Visitation. These two best friends were buried near each other at Annecy. In response to Jane's constant exhortations and encouragement, Francis wrote for her and the community his *Treatise on the Love of God*. These co-founders introduced a new emphasis into the Christian and religious life: *douceur*, i.e., everything was to be done with the gentleness of Jesus.

Peter Fourier (1565-1640) was assigned in 1598 as parish priest to the long neglected village of Mattaincourt in Lorraine, France. For thirty years he labored indefatigably in this stronghold of Calvinism. Responding to the gamut of people's needs, he converted the village into a model parish. Here he attracted and invited **Bl. Alix le Clerq** (1576-1622) to forego her frivolous ways and dedicate her life to God. Together they founded the Congregation of Canonesses of Saint Augustine. Its mission was the education of young girls. He tried unsuccessfully to found a men's corresponding community.

Louise de Marillac (1591-1660) and **Vincent de Paul** (1580-1660), who co-founded the Daughters of Charity, are described in this chapter.

Louis Marie Grignion de Montfort (1673-1716) and **Bl. Marie Louise Trichet** (1684-1759), who co-founded the Daughters of Wisdom, are described in this chapter.

About 1824 **Bartolomea Capitanio** (1807-33) and **Vincentia Gerosa** (1784-1847) founded an institute for the education and health of poor youths. These two women had already independently organized works of charity. Bartolomea had formed a sodality for educating young people. Vincentia had dedicated herself to the care of the sick. These two women then joined forces and named their institute the Sisters of Charity of Lovere. Vincentia carried on the mission of the institute after Bartolomea died at age twenty-six.

Andrew Hubert Fournet (1752-1834) and **Elizabeth Bichier** (1773-1838) in 1816 founded the Daughters of the Cross, dedicated to the education of children and to the practical assistance of the aged and infirm. Andrew grew up seeking the good life promised by a career in law. He resisted the vocation to priestly service which his mother had encouraged for many years. Then on a visit to his holy priest-uncle he was inspired to abandon the ways of a young bon vivant to pursue the priesthood. Andrew gave up his comfortable lifestyle and dedicated himself to simple living. Elizabeth grew up during the French Revolution. That experience developed within her both character and faith because she protected her deceased father's property against confiscation by the National Assembly and promoted the faith against atheism and the constitutional priests of the revolution. She lived with the Carmelite nuns and the sisters of the Society of Providence before co-founding the Daughters of the Cross. In less than a quarter of a century the community, which she helped to establish, grew to over sixty houses throughout France.

Shortly after her seventeenth birthday **Blessed Mary de Matthias** (1805-66) listened to a parish mission preached by Caspar del Bufalo. She sensed "a definite call to some special work for the good of souls."[17] Within a short while she met **Venerable John Merlini** (1795-1873), a disciple of Caspar and his successor as head of the Missioners of the Precious Blood. Mary and John became fast friends. He served as her director and advisor until her death forty years later. Together they founded the Sisters Adorers of the Precious Blood. Disciples soon joined her. Her religious houses and works multiplied. She focused her efforts on providing schools for younger children and spiritual programs for older girls and women.

John Bosco (1815-88) and **Mary Mazzarello** (1837-81), who co-founded the Daughters of Our Lady Help of Christians, known more popularly as the Salesian Sisters, are described in this chapter.

Notes for Chapter 9

1   Raymond Hostie, *The Life and Death of Religious Orders*, p. 263.

2   Ibid., pp. 254-55.

3   *Butler's Lives of the Saints*, vol. III, p. 20.

4   Robert Maloney, *The Way of Vincent de Paul*, p. 152.

5   St. Vincent de Paul, *Conferences of St. Vincent de Paul to the Daughters of Charity*, vol. IV, pp. 118-19.

6   Ibid., p. 264.

7   *Marie Louise Trichet: The Folly of Love*, p. 2.

8   St. Louis Marie de Montfort, *God Alone: The Collected Writings of St. Louis Marie de Montfort*, Letter #34, pp. 38-39.

9   Butler, vol. II, p. 314.

10   St. Mary Mazzarello, *The Letters of Saint Mary Mazzarello*, Letter # 9, p. 22.

11   Hostie, p. iii.

12   Fitz and Cada, "The Recovery of Religious Life," pp. 705-6.

13   Butler, vol. III, p. 550.

14   Julian J. Katrij, *A Byzantine Rite Liturgical Year*, p. 398.

15   Butler, vol. IV, p. 393.

16   *The Book of Saints*, p. 126.

17   Butler, vol. III, p. 368.

CHAPTER 10

SAINTLY CO-WORKERS

Administrators

1. Pope Cornelius and Cyprian
2. Pope Sixtus II and deacon Lawrence of Rome
3. Gregory of Nyssa and Cyril of Jerusalem
4. Augustine and Alipius
5. Pope Celestine I with Germanus of Auxerre, Augustine and Palladius
6. Prosper of Aquitaine with Augustine, John Cassian, Pope Celestine I and Pope Leo the Great
7. Pope Leo the Great and defenders of the faith
8. Queen Regent Bathildis and Eligius
9. Holy Roman Emperor Henry II and Godehard
10. Pope Gregory the Great and Hugh of Grenoble
11. Aelred of Rievaulx and David I of Scotland
12. Colette and John of Capistrano

Innovators

13. Empress Helen and Macarius
14. John Stylites and Simeon Stylites
15. Bruno of Rheims and Hugh of Grenoble
16. Celsus of Armagh and Malachy
17. Juliana Falconieri and Philip Benizi
18. Vincent de Paul and Louise de Marillac
19. Madeleine Sophie Barat and Philippine Duchesne

Public Servants

20. Cosmas and Damian
21. Bridget of Sweden and Catherine of Sweden
22. Bl. Damien the Leper and Mother Marianne Cope*

Scholars

23. Ven. Bede and Nothelm
24. Mechtilde and Gertrude of Helfta

Religious

25. Jerome and Paula
26. Melania the Younger and Pinian
27. Adelaide with abbots Majolus and Odilo
28. Clare of Assisi and Bl. Agnes of Prague

Missionaries

29. Maximinus of Trier, Athanasius of Alexandria and Paul of Constantinople
30. Paulinus of Trier and Athanasius
31. Germanus of Auxerre and Lupus of Troyes
32. Germanus of Auxerre and Patrick of Ireland
33. Pope Gregory the Great and Augustine of Canterbury with Peter, Lawrence, Justus, Mellitus, Paulinus of York and Ethelbert
34. Columban with Deicolus and Gall of Switzerland
35. Aidan and King Oswald of Northumbria

---

* Damien the Leper will be declared Blessed in June 1995. The *positio* to advance the cause for canonization of Mother Marianne Cope was accepted in Spring, 1993.

36. Theodore of Canterbury with Vitalian, Adrian, Chad, Wilfrid and Trumwin
37. Boniface with Gregory II, Willibrord, Sturmi, Zachary, Eoban, Winebald, Willibald, Walberga, Lull, Tetta, Thecla and Lioba
38. Cyril and Methodius
39. Bernard of Clairvaux with Bl. Guy, Bl. Gerard, Bl. Nivard, Bl. Humbeline, Malachy, Bl. Eugene III, Hildegard and Robert of Newminster
40. Turibius of Mongrovejo and Francis Solano
41. Lawrence of Brindisi and Bl. Benedict of Urbino

Laborers in the Vineyard: Co-Worker Saints

Work is oftentimes a social activity, done for and with others. Through work we make and re-make the world in which we live. Through work we express ourselves and fashion ourselves. Sociologists inform us that the vast majority of persons enjoy their work and co-workers. Philosophers tell us that being and working are essentially related. Theologians describe work done for the Lord as ministry. Secular and sacred work differ in motivation and compensation.

The Scriptures provide numerous examples of people working together for the glory of God and the service of the community.

The Israelite community was formed by the grace of God and the joint instrumentality of Moses, Aaron and Miriam. The post-exilic Jews were re-formed as a people by the combined efforts of Ezra the priest and Nehemiah the governor. Jesus founded the Church and the Kingdom of God on earth and planned for its continuation through the twelve apostles and countless disciples. He sent them forth two by two (Lk 10:1-12). Paul the apostle took along partners on each of his three missionary journeys.

Many saints collaborated in religious ministry. Some saints met in ministry and became friends. Other saints were family members and friends who joined together for ministry. Space allows us to mention only a few representative saints from among the many hundreds whom we could have included in this category.

Particular examples

1. CYPRIAN AND POPE CORNELIUS

Cyprian (c. 200-58), the bishop of Carthage in North Africa, and Cornelius (d. 253), the pope of the universal Church, faced the challenge of dealing pastorally with Christians who had lapsed by not acknowledging their faith during the Roman persecution. A few years later both men faced persecution themselves. They acknowledged the faith and were martyred, Cyprian near Carthage and Cornelius near Rome.

Cyprian, a well-educated rhetorician, converted to Christianity just a dozen years before he died. But what a significant dozen years! "Cyprian wrote numerous theological treatises on the Church, ministry, the Bible, virginity, and the *lapsi*, and is considered a pioneer of Latin Christian literature."[1] Within a period of two years Cyprian was converted, was ordained a priest, then a bishop, and immediately became embroiled in the controversy of the *lapsi*, i.e., those Christians who under pressure had denied their faith to remain alive. The *lapsi*, a local resident priest decided, could be restored to full Church membership without undergoing any penalty. Bishop Cyprian disagreed. Cyprian convoked an African regional council to deal with the issue. The council resolved that the *lapsi* must perform some penance. The excessively lenient priest and his leading supporters were excommunicated. In the meantime, Pope Cornelius was dealing with the opposite problem in Rome: with persons who were not too lax but too strict, who wanted to refuse re-admission to the Church to any baptized persons who had denied their faith in Jesus. Pope Cornelius rejected both extremes. He walked the thin line between the laxists and rigorists. Cornelius and Cyprian suffered much criticism among Church members for their balanced but unpopular points of view.

Long standing written and pictorial tradition has memorialized the joint efforts of Cornelius and Cyprian. Both men are named together in the First Eucharistic Prayer. The feasts of both men are joined together in the universal liturgical calendar.

Shortly before they died as martyrs, Cyprian sent Cornelius an encouraging and complimentary letter for the witness which the pope was giving to the whole Church:

> Cyprian sends greetings to his brother Cornelius. My very dear brother, we have heard of the glorious witness given by your courageous faith. On learning of the honor you had won by your witness, we were filled with such joy that we felt ourselves sharers and companions in your praiseworthy achievements. After all, we have the same Church, the same mind, the unbroken harmony. Why then should a priest not take pride in the praise given to a fellow priest as though it were given to him? What brotherhood fails to rejoice in the happiness of its brothers wherever they are?
>
> Words cannot express how great was the exultation and delight here when we heard of your good fortune and brave deeds: how you stood out as leader of your brothers in their declaration of faith, while the leader's confession was enhanced as they declared their faith. You led the way to glory, but you gained many companions in that glory, being foremost in your readiness to bear witness on behalf of all, you prevailed on your people to become a single witness. We cannot decide which we ought to praise, your own ready and unshaken faith or the love of your brothers

who would not leave you. While the courage of the bishop who thus led the way had been demonstrated, at the same time the unity of the brotherhood who followed has been manifested. Since you have one heart and one voice, it is the Roman Church as a whole that has thus borne witness.

Dearest brother, bright and shining is the faith which the blessed Apostle praised in your community. He foresaw in the spirit the praise your courage deserves and the strength that could not be broken; he was heralding the future when he testified to your achievements; his praise of the fathers was a challenge to the sons. Your unity, your strength have become shining examples of these virtues to the rest of the brethren.

Divine providence has now prepared us. God's merciful design has warned us that the day of our own struggle, our own contest, is at hand. By that shared love which binds us closely together, we are doing all we can to exhort our congregation, to give ourselves unceasingly to fastings, vigils and prayers in common. These are the heavenly weapons which give us the strength to stand firm and endure; they are the spiritual defenses, the God-given armaments that protect us.

Let us then remember one another, united in mind and heart. Let us pray without ceasing, you for us, we for you; by the love we share we shall thus relieve the strain of these great trials.[2]

2. POPE GREGORY VII AND HUGH OF GRENOBLE

The Church reformers, Gregory VII (born Hildebrand) (c. 1021-85) and Hugh (1052-1132), faced herculean internal and external challenges to the Church. Both preferred, however, the quiet of the monastery of Cluny and retreated there for a while as a respite from their pastoral responsibilities.

Hugh was well-born and highly respected. Even though

he was not a cleric, he was appointed a canon of the cathedral church. While attending a regional Church council at which the problem of a vacant see was on the agenda, he was elected its bishop. The presiding papal legate conferred on him all orders including the priesthood and then sent Hugh to Rome for episcopal ordination by the pope. Afterwards Hugh went to his see, where a great shock awaited him. "The greatest sins were committed without shame; simony and usury were rampant; the clergy openly flouted the obligation to celibacy; the people were uninstructed; laymen had seized Church property and the see was almost penniless."[3] For two years he labored zealously but unsuccessfully to correct the situation. Discouraged, he abandoned his see in favor of Cluny, where Odilo was abbot and Hugh was the prior. He was there a short time when Pope Gregory VII, who had been a monk at Cluny, encouraged the bishop to return to his diocese.

Hildebrand had been called from his diocese by his former teacher, John Gratian, now Pope Gregory VI. The new pope wanted his former student to serve as papal secretary. When his mentor died, Hildebrand immediately left Rome and returned to Cluny. He was there two years when another pope called him back to Rome to serve as papal treasurer. After that pope died, the next six popes asked Gregory to remain as advisor and administrator. He negotiated political alliances and treaties, decided theological disputes, confronted problems, and never "looked the other way."

Hildebrand himself was then elected pope as Gregory VII. "He immediately set to work to reform a very corrupt and decadent Church."[4] Like Hugh, Gregory faced the situations of usury, clerical simony and concubinage. Lay investiture was the bane of his reign. It required that he twice excommunicate Emperor Henry IV and his hand-chosen anti-pope. Gregory had to take refuge in Castel

Sant' Angelo when Henry attacked the city. Gregory had
to flee from there in turn when the Normans raided that
citadel under the guise of rescuing the pope. Gregory's
reforms upset many people including corrupt political and
religious leaders and even many common folk who had
learned to be comfortable with decadent ways under loose
Church discipline. Gregory's reforms eventually took root
and gave foundation to the process of revitalization of the
Church.

In a letter to Hugh, Gregory gives us a sense of the pain
that the pope himself experienced. He suffered from
feelings of inadequacy combined with the nearly overwhelming burden of the papal office. The work of the Lord
can be both exacting and exhausting, as Gregory testified:

> Gregory, the bishop, servant of the servants of God, to
> Hugh, abbot of Cluny, health and apostolic benedic-
> tion.
>
> Were it possible, I wish you could know all the trouble
> that besets me, all the labour that mounts up day by
> day to weary me out and deeply distress me. Then
> your brotherly sympathy would incline you towards
> me in proportion to the tribulations of my heart, and
> your own heart would pour forth a flood of tears to beg
> Him, by whom all things are made and who rules all
> things, to stretch forth His hand to me in my misery,
> and with His wonted loving kindness set this wretched
> being free. Often indeed have I implored Him that
> even as He Himself has imposed the burden, so He
> would either take me from this life, or use me for the
> profit of our holy mother the Church. So far, however,
> neither has He rescued me from great afflictions, nor
> has my life proved useful, as I hoped it would, for the
> service of the Church with whose chains He has bound
> me.
>
> Hence it comes about that between the grief which on
> the one hand assails me daily anew, and on the other
> the hope too long deferred, tossed at every turn by a

thousand tempests, I endure a life which is a continual death. And still I wait for Him who has bound me with His fetters, brought me back to Rome against my will, and once there has encompassed me with difficulties beyond number. Again and again I implore of Him: Make haste, do not delay; come speedily, do not linger, and deliver me, for the love of Blessed Mary and St. Peter. But because praise has no value, nor hallowed prayer any speedy efficacy in the mouth of a sinner, I pray, beg, and beseech you with all assiduity to request those whose merit of life gains them a hearing, to plead to God for me with the same love and charity with which they ought to love the mother of us all.[5]

3. MADELEINE SOPHIE BARAT AND PHILIPPINE DUCHESNE

After the decade-long turmoil of the French Revolution and its subsequent Reign of Terror, the pope and Napoleon signed the 1801 Concordat which did not restore confiscated Church property but did restore peace and prestige by recognizing Catholicism as "the religion of the great majority of French people."[6] In this context two outstanding women joined forces to promote religion, both its revival in France and its propagation in the United States.

Madeleine Sophie Barat (1779-1865) and three other women were received in 1800 by an ex-Jesuit priest who hoped to found a woman's counterpart to his then-suppressed order. These women were to instruct young girls. Within two years the group of four had grown to twenty-three. Madeleine was elected their superior, a position which she held for the next sixty-three years. During her lifetime she delicately directed the foundation and expansion of the community. She dealt head-on with the usual political, economic and interpersonal challenges that confront any founder and new organization. She successfully established over one hundred convents in twelve countries located in Europe, North America and Africa.

Madeleine found a great companion in the person of Rose Philippine Duchesne (1769-1852). Philippine asked Madeline if she and a few companions from the disbanded Visitation Sisters might join Madeleine's four-year-old community. Philippine, who was ten years older than Madeleine, gladly placed herself as a novice under the direction of the younger woman. Philippine was quite conscious of her faults: her impetuosity, stubbornness, and lack of sophistication. She knew that her social manner and penitential practices annoyed people around her. Madeleine was graced socially and spiritually. All who met her, loved her. And she loved God and all persons in need. The two women, so different in background, were similar in vision. They understood and encouraged each other. Everything these co-workers did, individually, interpersonally and institutionally, was done for the glory of God and the good of the mission. Madeleine wrote to Philippine about her delight in the vision they shared:

> I have had two letters from you, my dear daughter, which I loved reading because in them you promise that once and for all you are resolved to love our Lord and to correct your faults of character in order to please him and draw souls to him. We have a double purpose in our efforts: our own perfection and the salvation of souls. We must be saints. If you only realized how ardently I desire this for you, I believe you would make the necessary efforts. But if you grasped how much more our Lord desires it — then you would indeed be faithful to his call.[7]

While Madeleine remained in France as the animator and administrator of the new community, Philippine was granted her heart's desire of serving as a missionary among the pioneers in the United States of America. Philippine and four sister companions arrived at St. Charles, Missouri near St. Louis. "They started the first free school west of the Mississippi."[8] Their mission flourished all along the Mississippi where they opened six new houses in the next eight years. Philippine resigned twenty-two years later as the administrative head of the American branch of the Sacred Heart Sisters. This seventy-one-year-old woman, however, was not inclined to remain idle. Instead she answered the plea of the famous Fr. De Smet and traveled to Sugar Creek, Kansas where she opened a school for the Pottawatomie tribe. She died eleven years later at St. Charles.

4. BL. DAMIEN THE LEPER AND MOTHER MARIANNE COPE

Joseph De Veuster, known in religion and society as Father Damien the Leper (1840-89), came from his native Belgium to Honolulu in 1864. He served there nine years before volunteering for the Hawaiian island of Molokai to care for the victims of Hansen's disease, which is commonly known as leprosy. He labored there the rest of his life, which was shortened by this dreaded disease. In serving the lepers, he was frequently at odds with the authorities of his own religious community, the local government, and his chief adversary, a local priest. "Officially, Damien was the pastor of the Catholics in the colony, but actually he served as the lepers' physician, counsellor, house-builder, sheriff, grave-digger, and undertaker."[9]

Mother Marianne Cope (1838-1918), baptized Barbara, was born in Germany and was raised in Utica, in upstate New York. As provincial of the Franciscan Sisters of Syracuse, she and other American provincials received in the mail a request from the government of Hawaii to send trained personnel to care for the lepers. Mother Marianne, a former administrator of Syracuse's first hospital, St. Joseph's, led six sisters to Honolulu. "They were the first members of a religious community founded in the United States to work in the foreign missions."[10] Hawaii, at that time, was not part of the United States. The date was 1883.

Damien and Marianne were present together for the first time in 1884 at the dedication of a chapel at a Honolulu hospital for lepers. No communication between them at that time is recorded. The following year, however, Damien's leprosy was confirmed. Hospital records state that "she herself provided care and shelter for the outcast sick priest when he was an unwelcome visitor to Honolulu."[11] During these visits Damien pleaded with Marianne to come to Molokai to provide a nurse's care for all the lepers who had no nurses at all, and especially for the women lepers and the children of leprous parents:

> Mother Marianne listened. She had planned from the beginning to extend the Franciscan mission to Molokai. Governmental authorities would not allow the move. They wanted her to continue being in charge of the hospital for leprosy patients in Honolulu. Also there was fear what might happen to the sisters. It was a well-known fact that it was not safe at Molokai for any woman. The government wanted males to do the nursing at Molokai. No males, however, stepped forward, neither from civilian nor religious life.[12]

When a minor political revolution occurred in Honolulu in 1887, new leaders came into power. They immediately passed and enforced a law which required that all lepers be deported and confined at Molokai. These same officials, however, offered no support to the leper colony. They literally did not want to see the problem. Government administrators made no provisions for these patients' arrival, room and board, medical care and physical safety. The mistreatment of women and children was notorious. Damien and Marianne created a system to identify and protect the children coming from her hospital to his island.

Damien would meet the boats at the shore. Marianne's children would hold tightly to a note which introduced them to him. A typical note would read:

> My dear Reverend Father,
>
> May I recommend to your special care some of our good girls and boys — Kealoha is a remarkable good child. We have instructed her to go at once to you. Her brother Kuhililou, although not a Catholic, is an excellent good boy. He has been my office boy, and has been faithful and good. I trust he will continue so. Our hearts are sore to have so many of our patients torn from us. We love them, and do not like to see them go. Hoping you are improving and recommending myself and the sisters to your good prayers, I remain in Jesus' Sacred Heart, very respectfully yours.
>
> Sister Marianne[13]

Father Damien kept appealing to authorities to allow the sisters to come to Molokai, especially since no one else wanted to come. He repeatedly quoted from one of Marianne's letters to demonstrate the willingness of the sisters. "Our hearts are bleeding to see them [the patients] shipped off. If it were the will of God, how much we would like to accompany them — but our future looks dark."[14] Even a petition from hundreds of the lepers pleading for the sisters was ignored. Finally, a wealthy donor insisted that something be done for the welfare of the unescorted women patients. He paid for the construction of a hospital at Molokai. Again, no one else stepped forward to staff the hospital except the sisters!

Finally, Mother Marianne moved to Molokai on November 14, 1888. Five months later, on April 15, Damien died. Marianne personally nursed him. She prepared his body and soul for death and outfitted his coffin. Damien died in peace, since Marianne had promised to continue the work he had begun. She spent the next thirty years on Molokai. Neither she nor any of her sisters ever contracted the disease.

General Observations

Work provided the common ground for saintly co-workers. Their common project of serving God and neighbor brought these selfless servants together. Action-oriented by nature, these saints wanted to do something good for God by doing something good for God's people.

Their ministries covered the spectrum of Church apostolates. Popes Sixtus II and Cornelius died in defense of the faith, and Popes Leo the Great and Gregory the Great labored to propagate the faith. Hermit-monks, like the centenarian Antony, assisted bishop Athanasius at Alexandria to defend the Church against Arianism and, in the desert, to hide Athanasius during some of the bishop's five exiles. Sixth-century Celtic missionary monks like Columban and Comgall, and twelfth-century itinerant friars like Francis and Dominic jointly evangelized western Europe. Scholars like Bonaventure and Thomas Aquinas, both as classmates and teachers, advanced the understanding and articulation of the faith.

Saintly co-workers covered the full range of relationships. Spouses like Melania and Pinian, Henry II and Cunegund, Stephen and Gisella, Louis of Thuringia and Elizabeth of Hungary expanded Church institutions. Parents like Paula of Bethlehem, Joan of Aza and Bridget of Sweden raised their children with experience in prayer and service. Brothers like Cosmas and Damian, and Cyril and Methodius, and sisters like Clare and Agnes, and Cuthburga and Quenburga evangelized by words and deeds. Relatives like Barnabas and John Mark, Boniface and Lioba, and Alexis and Julianna Falconieri shared Church vision and Church mission. Friends like Basil and Gregory, and Augustine and Alipius became co-workers; some co-workers like Francis de Sales and Jane de Chantal, and Margaret Mary Alacoque and Claude la Colombiere became best friends. Teachers and students learned together, like

Mechtilde and Gertrude the Great, as well as John Bosco and Dominic Savio. Masters and disciples spread the good news together like the hosts of followers of Paul, Dominic and Francis. Co-founders together developed their communities like Francis and Clare, Francis de Sales and Jane de Chantal, and Vincent de Paul and Louise de Marillac. Co-martyrs worked and then died together as in the cases of the companions of Ignatius of Antioch, Paul Miki of Japan and Charles Lwanga of Uganda.

Strains in the working relationship sometimes arose. Paul and Barnabas split up over Paul's manner of treating young John Mark. Best friends Basil and Gregory Nazianzen became estranged over Gregory's refusal to accept a difficult assignment from Basil, his metropolitan bishop. Gregory of Tours twice rebuked Brice for his vanity and laxity. Columba ignited a public dispute when he copied without permission Finnian's unique copy of Jerome's psalter. All these saints, however, after some time of alienation, became reconciled. Barnabas and John Mark returned to aid Paul during his house arrest in Rome. Gregory eventually went to the see assigned him, although he retired from it one year later. Gregory of Tours eventually chose Brice to succeed him as bishop. Columba handed over his misbegotten copy of the psalter. All these saints experienced hurt in their relationships, recognized the situation, and reconciled themselves to their co-workers.

Application Of The Theme

Common Vision: Many people sense when something needs to be done. A few are able to see what needs to be done. Visionary co-workers had an end in sight. They envisioned what was possible. They were practical dreamers, driven by the desire to achieve a certain good and to avoid a certain evil.

Common Way: A job needed to be done. Some co-workers stepped forward. Many more persons followed. They used their skills to do good for the benefit of others and the praise of God. They let their actions speak louder than their words, confronting the needs of their times with the abilities which God had given them.

Common Bond With Each Other: Their common project brought them together physically. Their common effort molded them together morally. Their relationship was both affective and effective. Their work was love made visible. Since happiness results from achieving good goals by good means, their work together made them happy together. They assisted and complemented each other. What was impossible for one, was made possible by two.

Common Bond With God: Happiness with God was the paramount goal of these co-workers. Happiness with God resulted when work was done with, through, and for God. While happiness on earth would always remain partial, happiness in heaven would be complete. Co-workers had faith that God would see to the continuation of their work when they were gone.

APPENDIX: CO-WORKER SAINTS

ADMINISTRATORS

Cornelius (d. 253) and **Cyprian** (c. 200-58) are described in this chapter.

Pope Sixtus II (d. 258) and six of his seven deacons were celebrating Mass when they were arrested during the persecution of Emperor Valerian. The seventh deacon, **Lawrence** (d. 258), escaped capture and, anticipating his own imminent death, sold the Church's treasures and gave the proceeds to the poor. He was brought to trial by the prefect and was commanded to present to the emperor the

Church's treasure about which rumors abounded. Lawrence requested a reprieve of three days to complete the task. He "then presented the blind, the crippled, the poor, the orphans and other unfortunates to the prefect and told him they were the Church's treasures."[15] The outraged prefect ordered Lawrence to be burned alive. With unusual equanimity, Lawrence jested with his persecutors as he lay on the red-hot iron griddle, saying that they could turn him over since he was sufficiently burned on the one side![16] "According to Prudentius, Lawrence's death and example led to the conversion of Rome and signaled the end of paganism in the city."[17]

Gregory of Nyssa (c. 330-c. 395) was sent to investigate the orthodoxy of **Cyril of Jerusalem** (c. 315-86). Cyril had been exiled three times because of his opposition to Arianism and each time was recalled by a change in the political administration of the city. Gregory was sent by a local Church council to investigate the orthodoxy of Cyril. "Gregory reported that the see of Jerusalem was morally corrupt, torn by factionalism and Arianism, but that its faith and that of Cyril were orthodox."[18] Both men attended together the ecumenical Council of Constantinople in 381.

Augustine (354-430) and **Alipius** (c. 360-430), lifelong friends, served as bishops for more than three decades in neighboring dioceses in North Africa.

Pope Celestine I (d. 432) supported **Germanus of Auxerre** in the struggle against Pelagianism and semi-Pelagianism. He began the Christianization of Ireland by sending **Palladius** (d. 432), who became the isle's first bishop, and immediate predecessor of Patrick (c. 389-c. 461). Celestine and **Augustine** corresponded and provided mutual support in the dispute that many of the African bishops directed against the authority of the Church at Rome.

Prosper of Aquitaine (c. 390-c. 465) corresponded with **Augustine**, disputed the semi-Pelagian position held by **John Cassian**, and visited **Pope Celestine** in Rome where he remained as secretary to **Pope Leo the Great** (d. 461).

Leo the Great succeeded one saint, **Celestine I**, as pope and corresponded with other saints in his day: **Cyril of**

Alexandria (c. 376-444), **Peter Chrysologus** (406-c. 450), **John Cassian** (c. 360-c. 433), **Flavian** (d. 449) and **Turibius of Spain** (d. c. 450). Twice he reprimanded **Hilary of Arles** for overstepping his competency and encroaching on papal authority. He wrote authoritatively against the heresies confronting the Church in his day: Eutychianism (denial of two natures in the one person of Christ), Manicheanism (denial of the inherent worth of the material world), Nestorianism (denial of the Logos as subject of Christ's humanity), Pelagianism (denial of the necessity of grace for human obedience to divine law) and Priscillianism (denial of human freedom which is independent of a determining fate). When the appointed Roman leaders abdicated their responsibility, he confronted both the ferocious Attila the Hun, whom he persuaded to spare Rome in exchange for the payment of annual tribute, and Genseric the Vandal, who had plundered Rome for two weeks.

Eligius (c. 590-660) acted as counselor to the queen regent **Bathildis** (d. 680) in Noyon, Flanders. Born to a metalsmith and apprenticed to a goldsmith, he "became a leading craftsman noted for his exquisite work."[19] He shared his wealth to ransom slaves and to establish churches, convents and monasteries. He became the king's and then the queen's counselor, winning many converts by his charity and buoyancy of spirit in the face of opposition. Bathildis (d. 680), married to a king, became mother to three other kings. As queen regent, she freed many captives and founded several monasteries.

Henry II (972-1024) and **Godehard** (962-1038) worked together for the propagation of the faith in Germany. Godehard so successfully reformed his local monastery that Henry appointed him bishop and reformer of all monasteries. "He (Godehard) built churches, schools, and a hospice, imposed strict discipline on the canons, encouraged education in his diocese, and ministered to the sick and the poor."[20] St. Gotthard's Pass is named after him.

Henry believed that a vibrant Church was necessary for a vibrant Empire. To the pleasure of Rome and the occasional dissatisfaction of local religious leaders, he was a staunch supporter of Church reform.

Gregory the Great (c. 1021-85) and **Hugh of Grenoble** (1024-1109) are described in this chapter.

Before **Aelred of Rievaulx** (1110-67) became a Cistercian monk, he served as master of the household in the court at the invitation of **David I of Scotland** (1084-1153). Everyone enjoyed Aelred's presence on account of his meekness and great learning. He, however, preferred monastic life to that of the court and so became a monk and eventually the abbot at Rievaulx.

Colette (1381-1447) and **John of Capistrano** (1386-1456) worked together for the renewal of the Poor Clares. She began her renewal movement as a lay tertiary, who eventually became a nun and founded seventeen Franciscan convents. He had been working for the renewal of the men's community when he met her. He advised and encouraged her and worked for reconciliation between not only Franciscan factions but also the pope and anti-pope, the papacy and heretics, and the papacy and governments.

Innovators

Helen (c. 250-c. 330), the wife of a Roman general who divorced her for political reasons, was the mother of Emperor Constantine. Constantine became a catechumen on his deathbed. She converted to Christianity in 313 with the promulgation of the Edict of Milan when she was sixty-three years of age. From that moment forward, she did all she could to promote the Christian religion. She built churches, supported monasteries and performed numerous acts of charity. As an octogenarian she traveled to the Holy Land. There with the help of **Macarius** (d. c. 335), bishop of Jerusalem, she sought to discover and properly display the holy places of Jesus' life. Tradition holds, on the evidence of sacred and secular scholars, that she indeed discovered the true cross of Jesus' crucifixion.

John Stylites (6th century) and **Simeon Stylites** (c.

517-92), master and disciple, witnessed to Christ by their preaching, prayer and asceticism.

Bruno (c. 1030-1101) fled Rheims where he had studied and taught theology and served as chancellor, rather than be named archbishop. He took up the life of a hermit under the famed reforming abbot Robert of Molesmes. Bruno and six other monks, however, left Robert, moved to Chartreuse near Grenoble, and founded the Carthusian Order. The local bishop, **Hugh of Grenoble** (1052-1132), assisted these monks. Hugh provided them with property and protection from curious neighbors. The monks built a common oratory and solitary cells and dedicated themselves to prayer, poverty and manual labor. The Carthusian Order "is the only old religious Order in the Church which never had any reform and has never stood in need of any."[21] Bl. Peter the Venerable, who served as abbot at Cluny twenty-five years after Bruno, describes the habits of the early Carthusians:

"They wear hair shirts next to their skin and fast almost perpetually; eat only bran-bread; never touch flesh, either sick or well; never buy fish, but eat it if given to them as an alms. . . . Their constant occupation is praying, reading and manual work, which consists chiefly in translating books. They celebrate Mass only on Sundays and festivals."[22]

Celsus of Armagh (1079-1129) and **Malachy** (1095-1148) brought stability to the local see by ending the custom of hereditary succession. Celsus was a layman who inherited the see and only then was ordained priest and bishop. He ruled well. On his deathbed he named Malachy as his successor based on reason of right living and not on the grounds of right lineage. Celsus' family, however, resisted the change; they supported Celsus' cousin as archbishop of Armagh. Malachy refused for three years to press the issue, until the papal legate insisted that he occupy the see. Malachy refused to enter the city for another two years, until the cousin died. Then the family chose Celsus' brother as successor. Finally Malachy entered the city and his supporters battled those of Celsus' family. Celsus' brother fled, reportedly with the Book of Armagh and the crozier, the two symbols of episcopal authority. Eventually Malachy recovered the symbols and asserted his authority. Never again was there hereditary succession in Ireland. Malachy was named papal legate to Ireland.

Philip Benizi (1233-85), the superior of the men's Servite community, helped **Juliana Falconieri** (1270-1341) to establish a women's Servite Third Order. He invested her in the habit of the Order. She lived at home until both of her parents died, and then moved to a community house of similar Third Order women who all practiced a life of prayer and works of mercy.

Vincent de Paul (1580-1660) and **Louise de Marillac** (1591-1660) labored for thirty-five years for the evangelization and liberation of the poor in France.

Madeleine Sophie Barat (1779-1865) and **Philippine Duchesne** (1769-1852) are treated in this chapter.

PUBLIC SERVANTS

Cosmas (d. 303) and **Damian** (d. 303) worked as brother physicians in Cilicia. **Bridget of Sweden** (1303-73) and her daughter **Catherine** (c. 1331-81), after both were widowed, spent twenty-five years together in the religious community founded by the mother and developed by the daughter.

Bl. Damien the Leper (1840-89) and **Marianne Cope** (1838-1918) are described in this chapter.

SCHOLARS

Venerable Bede (c. 672-735) credits **Nothelm** (d. c. 740) with providing much of the information which Bede incorporated into his *Ecclesiastical History*. Nothelm, before being appointed archbishop of Canterbury, had traveled to Rome to research the correspondence between Pope Gregory the Great and Augustine of Canterbury. Bede adds: "They [Nothelm and his abbot] also partly informed me by what

bishops and under what kings the provinces of the East and
West Saxons, as well as of the East Angles and the
Northumbrians, received the faith of Christ."[23] Bede, the
only Doctor of the English Church and one of the most
learned men of his time, embodies in his writings "a veritable
summary of the learning of his time."[24] Bede entered a
monastery school at age three, was ordained at age thirty,
and "except for a few brief visits elsewhere spent all his life
in the monastery, devoting himself to the study of Scripture
and to teaching and writing."[25]

Mechtilde of Helfta (1241-98) and **Gertrude** (c.
1256- c. 1302) were teacher and student, best friends and
collaborators. They produced books of popular prayers by
writing down each other's revelations. They collaborated on
Mechtilde's *Book of Special Graces* and Gertrude's *Book of
Extraordinary Grace*.

RELIGIOUS

Jerome (342-420) and **Paula** (347-404) worked together for forty years in Rome and Bethlehem, where they
eventually established four monasteries.

Melania the Younger (383-439) and her husband
Pinian (d. 432) spent their entire adult lives promoting
monasticism and aiding the poor throughout Italy, the Near
East and North Africa.

Adelaide (931-99) suffered terribly from the intrigues
of palace politics. Her first husband was probably poisoned
to death by ambitious opponents. She refused to marry the
son of her husband's nefarious successor and was imprisoned. When the German king, Otto the Great, defeated her
oppressors, she married him. They had five children. But
after her second husband's death, her only daughter-in-law
by her first marriage influenced Adelaide's oldest son and
later her grandson to expel her from the kingdom. Throughout all this strife Adelaide sought only peace with her
malefactors. She found guidance from the wise abbots of
Cluny, **Majolus** (906-94) and **Odilo** (962-1049). These two

men, who led the reform of Cluny for twenty-five and fifty years respectively, involved her in the program of monastic renewal and Church expansion. Odilo sold Church treasures during a famine to purchase food for the starving masses. Odilo instituted the practice of "Church sanctuary" as a safe haven from aggressors.

Clare of Assisi (1194-1253) and **Bl. Agnes of Prague** (1205-82) developed the new community of the Poor Clares.

MISSIONARIES

Maximinus of Trier (d. c. 347) provided refuge to **Athanasius of Alexandria** (c. 297-373) and **Paul of Constantinople** (d. c. 350) in their politico-religious exiles during the Arian controversy. **Paulinus of Trier** (d. 358), who was the episcopal successor to Maximinus, continued the diocese's material and theological support for Athanasius. This stance cost Paulinus his position and life. The heretical Arian emperor exiled him to Phrygia, where he died.

The two Gallic bishops **Germanus of Auxerre** (c. 378-448) and **Lupus of Troyes** (c. 383-478) traveled from their dioceses to Britain in order to confront the rampant heresy of Pelagianism. They converted many Britons and established schools to teach the Christian truths. Some of their success is no doubt related to the story popularly told of Germanus' military tactics. The Britons were numerically overwhelmed by Picts and Saxons. He led the frightened Britons high into a ravine and had them shout as loud as possible "Alleluia." The echoes reverberated throughout the mountainous region and frightened the Picts and Saxons, who fled. Germanus was hailed as a hero. Both bishops intervened diplomatically to save their local dioceses from military destruction, Germanus' by Roman leaders and barbarian forces and Lupus' by Attila the Hun. Both bishops had been married but after a few years left their wives to devote themselves completely to episcopal austerity and ministry.

Patrick of Ireland (c. 389-461) was ordained bishop by **Germanus of Auxerre**, where Patrick had been living for some fifteen years. Patrick succeeded **Palladius** who died less than one year after beginning the mission in Ireland.

Augustine of Canterbury (d. 604) was missioned to England by **Gregory the Great** along with forty other Benedictine monks, including **Peter of Canterbury** (d. 606) and **Lawrence of Canterbury** (d. 619). Augustine became the first archbishop of Canterbury and Lawrence, the second. Peter became the first abbot at Canterbury. The group left Rome in 596 but grew fainthearted along the way and urged Augustine to seek papal permission to abort the mission. Pope Gregory forbade them to do so and urged them forward. They landed on the island of Thanet in the next year. The king of Kent, **Ethelbert**, welcomed them and received baptism the next year. Thousands of his subjects followed his example. The king "granted religious freedom to his subjects, believing conversion by conviction was the only true conversion."[26] This first Christian king of the English ruled peacefully for fifty-six years. He donated land for the church and monastery at Canterbury. Augustine sent Peter and Lawrence to Rome to gather more missionaries. They returned with a large number including **Justus** (d. c. 627), **Mellitus** (d. 624) and **Paulinus of York** (c. 584-644). Augustine did not succeed in persuading the Celtic monks to adopt Roman customs in the liturgy, but rather only heightened their opposition to him.

Columban (c. 540-615), not to be confused with the seven Irishmen named Colman and four others named Columba, left his monastery at Bangor to minister as a missionary on the continent. He and his twelve apostles, two of whom were **Deicolus** (c. 530-c. 625) and his younger brother **Gall** (d. c. 635), established numerous monasteries in France, Germany, Switzerland and Italy. Deicolus stayed in Germany. Gall chose to remain in Switzerland, whose national patron he became. Columban kept traveling because he kept arousing people's ire: he refused to drop the Celtic liturgical customs in favor of Roman ways, and he challenged a political leader for keeping concubines and marrying none of them.

Aidan (d. 651) studied under **Senan** (d. 560), who also taught **Chad** (d. 672). Aidan joined the monks at Iona before traveling to Lindisfarne, in response to a request from **Oswald, king of Northumbria** (c. 604-42). Lindisfarne became known as the English Iona, whence secular and religious leaders propagated the faith.

Theodore of Canterbury (602-90) developed the missionary Church in England into a fully organized Church body. Having been sent to England by Gregory the Great's distant successor, **Vitalian** (d. 672), Theodore was selected after **Adrian** (d. 710) refused the see. African-born Adrian was already an abbot near Naples and preferred not to be archbishop, and so he agreed to assist Theodore. Once at Canterbury, the new archbishop appointed his traveling companion abbot of the local monastery. Theodore, the first metropolitan of England, called councils to settle doctrinal and disciplinary matters. He also reconciled the dispute between **Chad** (d. 672) and **Wilfrid** (634-709) as to which one was the rightful bishop of York. Theodore appointed **Trumwin** (d. c. 690) bishop of the southern Picts. As the Picts advanced militarily, so did the boundaries of the diocese. Bede commented that the Church in England had made greater progress under Theodore than it ever had before.

Boniface (c. 680-754) and many companions worked zealously for the evangelization of the Germanic peoples. Boniface yearned to exchange his monk's life in his native England for the missionary life in Germany. Pope **Gregory II** (d. 741) granted the request.

Boniface's travel was interrupted by Bishop **Willibrord** (c. 658-739) who asked Boniface to join the mission at Friesland, where he served for three years. Boniface became adept in dealing with the Carolingian and Merovingian leaders and in asserting the rights of the Church against the encroachments of the state.

In 722 bishop Boniface challenged the pagan priests at Geismar that he could destroy the Oak of Thor without the pagan gods destroying him. To the shock of the crowd

Boniface chopped down the oak but the pagan gods did not slay him. After that feat, success greeted everything he did. He opened male and female monasteries with attached schools. He established sees throughout Germany. He founded with **Sturmi** (d. 744) the Fulda monastery, which served as the center of learning and spirituality for northern Europe. Boniface became in quick succession the regional bishop, the metropolitan bishop, the papal legate to Germany, and archbishop of Mainz with the blessing of his close friend **Pope Zachary** (d. 752). At age seventy-three Boniface retired from his see to return to the Frieslanders whose faith was waning. The Irish missionary **Eoban** (d. 755) joined him. These two and fifty-one other companions were attacked and killed by pagan opponents. Boniface's contribution to the Church was enormous. "Among the apostles of all time he stands on a par with St. Paul and St. Francis Xavier."[27] A renowned historian, Christopher Dawson, notes that Boniface "had a deeper influence on the history of Europe than any Englishman who has ever lived."[28]

In order to comprehensively evangelize the Germanic peoples, Boniface appealed to his English countrymen. They came in droves. The brothers **Winebald** (d. 761) and **Willibald** (c. 700-86) became bishops and their sister **Walburga** (d. 779) became an abbess. Willibald served as bishop for forty-five years. Walburga served as abbess for a double male-female monastery for eighteen years. **Burchard** (d. 754) and **Wigbert** (d. c. 738), priest and monk respectively, became bishop and abbot. **Lull** (d. 786) came as a twenty-year-old deacon, whom Boniface taught, ordained a priest and later made his successor as bishop. From the famous Wimborne abbey came many outstanding women, namely, the above mentioned Walburga, the abbess **Tetta** (d. c. 772), who sent to Boniface numerous nuns including **Thecla,** the abbess of Kitzingen (d. c. 790), and **Lioba** (d. 780), a relative and best friend of Boniface.

Cyril (c. 825-69) and **Methodius** (c. 826-84) traveled from their native Thessalonika to convert the Slavonic Moravians.

Bernard of Clairvaux (1090-1153) and his brothers **Bl. Guy** (d. 12th century), **Bl. Gerard** (d. 1138) and **Bl. Nivard** (c. 1100-58), and their sister **Bl. Humbeline** (1092-1135) discovered sanctity in the Cistercian life, of which Bernard is regarded as the re-founder. **Malachy** (1095-1148) visited often and wanted to join the community but the pope would not permit him. Bernard investigated and then advised Pope **Bl. Eugene III** (d. 1153) to approve the visions of **Hildegard** (1098-1179). Bernard encouraged her, in the face of local opposition, to found her community at Rupertsberg. He cleared the rumors against and restored the good reputation of **Robert of Newminster** (d. 1159), who transferred from the Benedictine community to the Cistercians.

Turibius of Mongrovejo (1538-1605), archbishop of Lima, Peru, received into his diocese the fire-and-brimstone Franciscan preacher, **Francis Solano** (1549-1610). Francis ministered in Spain for twenty years before traveling to the New World, where he labored for his last twenty years. The ship on which he was traveling from Panama to Peru crashed into a sandbar and broke up. Francis alone opted not to enter the lifeboat but to remain behind with the chained black slaves who were hanging desperately onto the hull of the ship. Three days later all were rescued. Francis served in present-day Argentina and Paraguay before being assigned to Lima. Turibius and Francis loved and protected the Indians, learned their dialects and preached against injustice. Francis preached so powerfully that one day, by comparing Lima to Nineveh, a riot erupted which Turibius had to help calm.[29] Francis performed miracles and preached prophecies which became true; he became known as the "Wonder Worker of the New World."

Lawrence of Brindisi (1559-1619) and **Bl. Benedict of Urbino** (1560-1625) were Franciscans who were sent to Austria and Germany to preach and teach Catholic doctrine in defense against Lutheran advances. They gained much success for the Church and they opened numerous friaries for the Franciscans. Lawrence gained fame as an erudite author, negotiator for and among governments, and administrator of the highest offices among the Franciscans.

Notes for Chapter 10

1 Delaney, *Dictionary of Saints*, p. 167.
2 *The Liturgy of the Hours*, vol. IV, pp. 1406-08.
3 *Butler's Lives of the Saints*, vol. II, p. 4
4 Delaney, p. 266.
5 *Letters from the Saints* (1964), pp. 175-76.
6 Paul Johnson, *A History of Christianity*, p. 363.
7 Louise Callan, *Philippine Duchesne*, p. 107.
8 Delaney, p. 186.
9 Carson, "Damien, Father," p. 627.
10 Cullen, "The new American saints?", p. 10.
11 L.V. Jacks, *Mother Marianne of Molokai*, p. 4.
12 Private notes of Sister Mary Laurence Hanley, Director of the Cause of Mother Marianne. Notes were written July 6, 1993.
13 Letter from Mother Marianne at Branch Hospital to Father Damien at Molokai: September 26, 1887.
14 Letter from Father Damien at Molokai to Mr. R.W. Meyer, December 8, 1887.
15 Delaney, p. 349.
16 Ibid.
17 Ibid.
18 Ibid., p. 170.
19 Ibid., p. 194.
20 Ibid., p. 260.
21 Butler, vol. IV, p. 43.
22 Ibid., p. 42.
23 Ibid., p. 140.
24 Delaney, p. 94.
25 Ibid.
26 Ibid., p. 201.
27 *The Book of Saints*, p. 98.
28 Christopher Dawson, *The Making of Europe*, 1946, p. 166; as in Butler, vol. II, p. 480.
29 Butler, vol. III, p. 94.

CHAPTER 11

SAINTLY CO-MARTYRS

Martyrs of the Roman Empire

1. Ignatius of Antioch with Rufus and Zosimus at Rome
2. Justin Martyr and six companions at Carthage
3. Perpetua and Felicity with their instructor Saturus at Rome
4. Pope Pontian and anti-pope Hippolytus at Sardinia
5. Denis, Rusticus and Eleutherius at Paris
6. Timothy and his wife Maura in Upper Egypt
7. Maurice and the Theban Legion in Switzerland
8. Marcellus the centurion and Cassian the notary at Tangiers
9. Laurentia and Palatias, servant and mistress, at Fermo
10. Marcellinus and Peter, priest and exorcist, at Rome
11. Orentius and his six brothers at Antioch
12. Januarius, three deacons and two laymen at Naples
13. Vincent, Orontius and Victor
14. The Four Crowned Ones

Celtic Martyrs

15. Dymphna, Gerebern and two companions

Martyrs of Moorish Spain

16. Flora and Maria, and forty-six others

Martyrs of the English Reformation

17. John Fisher and Thomas More
18. Bl. John Beche and Bl. Margaret Pole
19. Forty English and Welsh Martyrs, including Robert Southwell and Edmund Campion

Martyrs of Ireland

20. Oliver Plunkett

Martyrs of India

21. Rudolph Aquaviva and four other Jesuits

Martyrs of Japan

22. Paul Miki and twenty-five companions
23. Bl. Alphonsus Navarette and Bl. Ferdinand Ayala and companions
24. Bl. Apollinaris Franco and companions

Martyrs of the New World

25. Martyrs of Paraguay
26. North American Martyrs

Martyrs of Vietnam

27. Andrew Dung-Lac and 116 companions

Martyrs of the French Revolution

28. Martyrs of Paris
29. Martyrs of Laval
30. Martyrs of Arras
31. Martyrs of Orange
32. Martyrs of Compiegne
33. Martyrs of Valenciennes

Martyrs of Korea

34. Andrew Kim Tae-gon and 102 companions

Martyrs of Uganda

35. Charles Lwanga and twenty-one companions

Martyrs of the Twentieth Century

36. Eastern Europe
37. China
38. Latin America
39. Africa

Together in Life and Death: Co-Martyr Saints

Martyrs believe so firmly in someone or something that they willingly die for the sake of that person or principle. The cause or conviction may be of a religious, political, economic or social nature. Many claim, with Arthur Schnitzler, that "martyrdom is proof of intensity and not of correctness."[1] For Christian martyrs, their goal and motivation is the same: "Those things I used to consider gain I have now reappraised as loss in the light of Jesus

Christ. For his sake I have forfeited everything . . . so that Christ may be my wealth" (Ph 3:7-9).

Religious martyrdom occurred throughout the Old and New Testaments.[2] Several Scriptural references attest to the martyrdom of the Israelite prophets.[3] John the Baptist, who bridges the testamental periods, died a martyr. Jesus was called by the early Church "the first martyr."[4] Ten of the twelve apostles were martyred.[5] The deacon Stephen was stoned to death as Saul watched (Ac 7:54-8:3). This same Saul, converted, became Paul and was decapitated for the faith.[6] The entrance antiphon for the feast of the first martyrs of the Church of Rome prays: "The saints are happy in heaven because they followed Christ. They rejoice with him forever because they shed their blood for love of him."[7] Jesus warned his followers to expect persecution for the faith (Lk 21:12-17).

Martyrs wished to imitate Christ in his suffering and death. St. Augustine emphasizes that "it is the reason why, not the suffering that constitutes the martyr."[8] The martyrs' actions confirmed their belief in Jesus' teachings and his promise of eternal life. And so through martyrdom, the faith continued to spread. Tertullian observed: "The blood of martyrs is the seed of Christians."[9] Edith Wharton once commented, "I don't believe in God but I do believe in his saints."[10] And so martyrdom both reflects a profound faith and propagates a similar faith.

Particular Examples:

1. IGNATIUS OF ANTIOCH AND COMPANIONS

Ignatius of Antioch (d. c. 107) and two other citizens of that city, Rufus (d. c. 107) and Zosimus (d. c. 107), were transported to Rome during the persecution of Emperor Trajan. There they were tried in court, condemned to death for their faith, and thrown to the beasts at the end of the seasonal games in the amphitheatre. During their journey from Antioch to Rome, Ignatius dictated seven letters of paramount doctrinal importance. Those seven letters present teachings on God, the Trinity, the Incarnation, Redemption, the Church, Eucharist and marriage. In one letter Ignatius urged the Christian communities which were located along the ship's coastal route in Asia Minor and Greece not to interfere with the purpose of his journey. He provides a moving statement of his readiness and desire for martyrdom:

> I am writing to all the churches to let it be known that I will gladly die for God if only you do not stand in my way. I plead with you: show me no untimely kindness. Let me be food for the wild beasts, for they are my way to God. I am God's wheat and shall be ground by their teeth so that I may become Christ's pure bread. Pray to Christ for me that the animals will be the means of making me a sacrificial victim for God.

> No earthly pleasures, no kingdoms of this world can benefit me in any way. I prefer death in Christ Jesus to power over the farthest limits of the earth. He who died in place of us is the one object of my quest. He who rose for our sakes is my one desire. The time for my birth is close at hand. Forgive me, my brothers. Do not stand in the way of my birth to real life; do not wish me stillborn. My desire is to belong to God. Do not then, hand me back to the world. Do not try to tempt me with material things. Let me attain pure light. Only on my arrival there can I be fully a human being. Give me the privilege of imitating the passion of my God. If you have him in your heart, you will understand what I wish. You will sympathize with me because you will know what urges me on.[11]

2. ROBERT SOUTHWELL AND COMPANIONS

Officially canonized among the Forty Martyrs of England and Wales and counted among the hundreds of Catholics murdered by the English is Robert Southwell (c. 1561-95). His Catholic father, who was included among the king's favorites and who had married the queen's governess, decided to conform to the machinations of the king. Young Robert, who had studied at Douai and Paris before entering the Jesuit seminary in Rome, decided otherwise. Ordained at twenty-three years of age, he returned two years later to England to minister to Catholics. He was numbered among the native-born and foreign-trained clergy whom Elizabeth I sought to eliminate from her realm. He served courageously in the English mission for six years until 1592 when he was betrayed by the daughter of a man whom he was visiting in prison. Robert suffered tortures for three years before being hanged, drawn and quartered in 1595. In prison he composed numerous poems and prose treatises, one of which to his fellow Catholic inmates follows:

> Our life is like the print of a cloud in the air, like a mist dissolved in the sun, like a passing shadow, like a flower that soon fadeth, like a dry leaf carried with every wind, like a vapour that soon vanishes out of sight. St. Chrysostom calleth it a heavy sleep, fed with false and imaginary dreams; again he calls it a comedy, or rather, in our days, a tragedy, full of transitory shows and disguised passions. St. Gregory Nazianzen calleth it a child's game, who buildeth houses of sand on the shore, which the returning wave washeth away; yea, as Pindar saith, it is no more than the shadow of a shade. It passeth away like the wind; it rideth past like a ship in the sea that leaveth no print of passage; like a bird on the air, of whose way there remaineth no remembrance; like an arrow that flieth to the mark, whose track the air suddenly closeth up. Whatsoever we do, sit we, stand we, sleep we, or wake

we, our ship, saith St. Basil, is always sailing towards our last home. Every day we die, and hourly lose some part of our life; and even while we grow we decrease. We have lost our infancy, our childhood, our youth and all, till this present day; and this very day death by minutes is secretly purloining from us. This St. Gregory well expresseth, saying, "our living is a passing through life, for our life, with her increase, diminisheth. Future things are always beginning, present things always ending, and things past quite dead and gone. No armour resisteth, no threatening prevaileth, no entreaty profiteth against the assault of death." If all other perils and chances spare our life, yet time and age will, in the end, consume it. Better it is, since death is nature's necessary voluntary, which must needs be of necessity; and let us offer to God as a present, what, of due and debt, we are bound to render. What marvel if, when the wind bloweth, the leaf fall; if, when the day appeareth, the night end? — "Our life," saith the same saint, "was a shadow, and it passed; it was a smoke, and it vanished; it was a bubble, and it was dissolved; it was a spider's web, and it was shaken asunder."[12]

3. ISAAC JOGUES AND COMPANIONS

The North American Martyrs include eight Jesuit priests and lay missionaries who suffered martyrdom between the years 1642-49. The Mohawks killed two of them and the Iroquois killed the remainder. The first martyr was René Goupil (1606-42), a lay surgeon. His priest companion, Isaac Jogues (1607-46), was captured with Goupil but escaped after one year's torture and mutilation. He returned to France but less than two years later volunteered again for the mission in North America. For two years he served safely. Then he and Jean Lalande (d. 1646), another lay volunteer, were captured, tortured and tomahawked to death by Mohawks near Albany, New York. Jesuit Anthony Daniel (1601-48) began his missionary work in 1632 by opening a school for Native American boys. He was martyred sixteen years later near Hillsdale, Ontario. John de Brebeuf (1593-1649), who had served in the North American mission for twenty-four years, and Gabriel Lalement (1610-49) were working in a Huron village when an attack by enemy Iroquois occurred. All in the village were killed immediately except the two priests, who were tortured and tomahawked to death the next day. Later the same year two more Jesuits were killed by the Iroquois: Charles Garnier (c. 1605-49) and Noel Chabanel (1613-49) in the village of Saint Jean. The gripping accounts of the Jesuits' heroic physical suffering and spiritual courage can be read in the historic *Jesuit Relations and Allied Documents*.

A stirring excerpt from the letters of Isaac Jogues describes the attack which René Goupil and he suffered:

> They suddenly surround us. In terror, the Hurons abandon the canoes and many take to the dense woods. We were left alone, four Frenchmen and a few others. Christians and catechumens, to the number of twelve or fourteen. Commending themselves to God, they stand on the defensive. But they were quickly outnumbered, and when a Frenchman, René Goupil, who was in the forefront of the fight, was taken with some Hurons, they no longer put up any resistance. Barefoot as I was, I could not and would not escape. Moreover I refused to abandon a Frenchman and the Hurons, since some of those captured were unbaptized, and those who were free ran the risk of falling into the hands of the enemy who were combing the woods for them. I stood alone therefore, and voluntarily surrendered to the prisoners' guard, choosing to be companion in their peril as I had been on their journey. The guard was amazed at my action, and not without fear came up and placed me among them. I immediately heard the Frenchman's confession, instructed the Hurons in the faith, and baptized them;

and as prisoners kept coming in, my work of instruction and baptism increased in proportion.

And now the executioners' first feeling of admiration for me yielded to ferocity. They turned on me with their fists and knotted sticks, left me half-dead on the ground, and a little later tore away my nails in the same way, and bit off my two forefingers which caused me incredible agony. They did likewise to René Goupil. . . .

René and I had been warned of danger, and went towards a hill to say our prayers. We made an offering of our lives to God and began the Rosary. We had reached the fourth decade when we met two young men who ordered us to return to the village. "This encounter does not promise well, especially in the circumstances," I said to René. "Let us commend ourselves to God and our Lady." At the gate of the village, one of the two men draws a hatchet which he has kept hidden, and aims a blow at René's head. He fell half-dead, but remembered according to our pact to call upon the most holy Name of Jesus. Expecting a like blow, I bare my neck and fall on my knees, but after a time the barbarian bids me get up; he has no permission, he says, to kill me. I rise, and give the last absolution to my dear companion who was still breathing, and the barbarian finally put an end to his life with two further blows. He was not more than thirty-five years of age, a man of extraordinary simplicity and innocence of life, of invincible patience and perfect conformity to the will of God. Next day, at peril of my own life, I searched for his body to lay it in the earth. They had tied a rope around his neck, dragged him naked through the whole village, and then thrown him into the river at some distance away. I found him by the river bank, half-eaten by dogs. There, in the bed of a dry torrent, I cover him with stones, deciding to go back the following day with a pick-axe to make the burial more secure. I return to the spot with tools — but they have taken my brother away. I look for him everywhere. I wade waist-high into the river, groping with hands and feet for his body, but they assure me that the flood has carried it away. I hold funeral obsequies for him, singing the psalms and prayers appointed by the Church. Groaning and sighing, I mingle my tears with the torrent.[13]

4. THE FOUR CHURCHWOMEN OF EL SALVADOR

In 1980 tragedy occurred in the back fields of El Salvador as army officers brutally beat, raped and killed four churchwomen. These women represent the sufferings of the 75,000 persons, including Archbishop Oscar Romero, who have died during the twelve-year civil war at the hands of either the right-wing military and death squads or left-wing rebels.

On that sad December 2, Maryknoll Sisters Ita Ford and Maura Clarke flew back to San Salvador airport, where Ursuline Sister Dorothy Kazel and lay missioner Jean Donovan waited. The four never returned home. Their burned-out minibus was discovered the next day twenty-five miles southeast of the airport. Inquiries uncovered that local peasants had been forced by soldiers to bury the bodies of the women. The United States ambassador personally led the search for the bodies. All four women were found, shot in the head, and apparently raped.

The United Nations investigated these and other deaths. The UN published in March, 1993 the report of its Truth Commission, who interviewed over 2,000 witnesses to alleged war crimes. The Commission concluded: "The detention and execution of the churchwomen was planned prior to their arrival at the airport. Sub-sergeant Luis Antonio Colindres Aleman was following orders from superiors when he executed the women."[14] The report reveals that a cover-up was then put in motion, with the knowledge and cooperation of the minister of defense, the director of the national guard and other leading military officers. Some lesser officers remain, at this writing, in prison even though a general amnesty has been decreed for those who committed war atrocities. The Salvadoran government continues to treat the murder of the church-women as a criminal rather than a political act.

A few months before she died, Sr. Ita wrote a letter to her niece on the occasion of her sixteenth birthday. Ita reveals the combination of realism and idealism which guided her own life and which she offers as a gift to her niece:

August 16, 1980

Dear Jennifer:

The odds that this note will arrive for your birthday are poor — but know I'm with you in spirit as you celebrate sixteen big ones. I hope it's a special day for you.

I want to say something to you — and I wish I were there to talk to you — because sometimes letters don't get across all the meaning and feeling. But I'll give it a try anyway.

First of all, I love you and care about you and how you are. I'm sure you know that — and that holds whether you're a genius or a jerk, an angel or a goof-off. A lot of that is up to you and what you decide to do with your life.

What I want to say, some of it isn't too jolly birthday talk, but it's real. Yesterday I stood looking down at a sixteen year old who had been killed a few hours earlier. I know of a lot of kids even younger who are dead. This is a terrible time in El Salvador for youth. A lot of idealism and commitment are getting snuffed out here now.

The reasons why so many people are being killed are quite complicated — yet there are a few simple strands. One is that many people have found a meaning to live, sacrifice, and even die for. And, whether their life-span is sixteen years, sixty, or ninety, for them their life has had a purpose. In many ways, they are fortunate people.

Brooklyn is not passing through the drama of El Salvador but some things hold true wherever one is — and at whatever age. What I'm saying is I hope you come to find that which gives life a deep meaning for you. Something worth living for, maybe even worth dying for — something that energizes you, enthuses you and enables you to keep moving ahead.

I can't tell you what it might be, that's for you to find, to choose, to love. I can just encourage you to start looking and support you in the search.

Maybe this sounds weird and off the wall — and maybe no one else will talk to you like this — but, then, too, I'm seeing and living things that others around you aren't. All I know is that I want to say to you — Don't waste the gifts and opportunities you have to make yourself and others happy.

I hope this doesn't sound like a sermon — because I don't mean it that way. Rather, it's something that you learn here and I want to share it with you. In fact, it's my birthday present to you. If it doesn't make sense right at this moment, keep this letter and read it some time from now. Maybe it will be clearer. Or ask me about it — OK?

A very happy birthday to you and much, much love.

Ita[15]

General Observations

Christians have suffered martyrdom throughout the Church's 2,000 years of history. The Church defines a martyr as "one who has given or exposed his life in testimony to the truth or relevance of the Christian faith."[16]

Waves of persecutions for a decade or more swept across the Roman Empire, Spain, England, Japan, the New World, France, Vietnam, Korea and the Communist world. Isolated anti-Christian persecutions have occurred in virtually every century and on every continent except Australia.

Persecutions were usually directed against the leaders of the faith and occasionally against the masses of the believers. In the former situation the leaders were customarily imprisoned for some months which allowed them time to reconsider their positions. These attacks were directed against the clergy, religious and lay leaders. Their numbers mounted to the hundreds. The latter kind of persecution was aimed against the masses as well as the leaders. Imprisonments were brief, with the temporary reprieve being determined by the whim of those doing the killing. The number of these martyrs mounted each time into the thousands and tens of thousands. In both situations trials were usually held whereby the persecuted faced trumped-up charges and the opportunity to recant. Individuals rarely recanted. When groups of persons were being persecuted, trials were held more summarily. In both kinds of persecution heinous cruelty characterized the tortures and deaths.

Persecutions against the masses include those of Rome, Japan, Vietnam and Korea. The Roman persecutions were conducted on and off by ten individual emperors over a period of more than 300 years. Ironically, the most amoral and self-indulgent emperors did not lead the persecutions. Instead the most professional administrators who hoped to revive the Empire led the persecutions. The total number of Christians martyred by the Roman emperors is estimated at a minimum of 10,000 and maximum of 100,000.[17] Three Japanese persecutions were led by two shoguns between 1597 and 1632. In the first two persecutions many hundreds of laity were martyred, and in the last persecution many hundreds of clergy and religious were killed. In Vietnam incredibly barbarous persecutions extended intermittently from 1625 to 1886. The number of martyrs is estimated at 130,000. In Korea, six separate waves of persecution swept across the country between 1791 and 1866. This slaughter resulted in the deaths of 10,000 Catholics.

Persecutions restricted to the clergy, religious and lay leaders include those of England, France, and the New World. King Henry VIII initiated a century-and-a-half long (1535-1680) Protestant persecution of Catholics in England. Six different governments, that is, four kings, one queen and the commonwealth government, accounted for 312 martyrs of whom approximately 250 were priests. An interim government led by the Catholic Mary Tudor slew hundreds of Protestants. In France, the 1789 revolution introduced a decade of anti-religious activities including two periods of extensive persecutions. In 1792 four Parisian prisons were raided by the masses and 1400 prisoners were killed; approximately 400 of the political prisoners were priests. Official documents identify by name 191 of these September Martyrs. Two years later another surge of anti-religious passion swelled in various parts of the countryside. Within ten months six convents were raided and over sixty nuns were killed for being "pious counter-revolutionaries." In the New World three Jesuits were killed in Paraguay in 1628 because of their assistance to Indians whom the Spanish authorities wished to enslave. In North America, six Jesuits and two lay missionaries were killed by Iroquois and Mohawk Indians between 1642-49, as the missionaries conducted the evangelization and education of the Huron Indians.

The vast majority of canonized martyrs are people who served in positions of leadership. Clergy and religious, plus economically and politically powerful lay persons, predominate among the named martyrs. Many other per-

sons, tens of thousands of others in fact, suffered martyrdom and oftentimes are not named individually. These
were the masses of people.

Many martyrs were killed in isolated incidents rather
than as part of a wave of anti-religious persecution. A
Celtic princess fled from the incestuous advances of her
widowed father. Her confessor and two friends accompanied her to Antwerp, where her father eventually tracked
her and killed all four persons. In Uganda twenty-one
young pages refused to participate in the pediophiliac
activities of the king and suffered martyrdom because of
their faith-based refusal. In Moorish Spain, some forty-
eight individuals took the initiative to present themselves
to the caliph and denounce Muhammed; they suffered the
expected consequences.

The list of martyrs includes a large number of children. In no other category of saints are so many children
included. Individual youthful martyrs are readily remembered in the persons of Agnes, Agatha and Maria Goretti.
Many other youthful martyrs are found among the Christians of the Roman Empire, Moorish Spain and the Pacific
Rim.

According to the Catholic Church, three conditions
must be met in order for someone to be declared a martyr.
The person (1) must suffer death, (2) at the hands of an
attacker who is motivated by a hatred for the faith, and (3)
death must be freely accepted in defense either of truth or
virtue.[18] When persons would not offer sacrifice to Roman
gods or sign the English Oath of Supremacy or the French
Civil Constitution, clearly the issue was defense of Christian or Catholic doctrinal truth. When persons would not
perform immoral sexual acts or cease from aiding their
Indian neighbors, clearly the issue was Christian virtue.

Interestingly almost all persecutors operated from an
admixture of political and religious motivation. The Roman administrators sought to unite the realm politically by

organizing people religiously. When the Christians refused to offer sacrifice to pagan gods, the emperors eliminated these politico-religious opponents. The English kings, queen and commonwealth wished to assert authority against the pope. When Catholics supported Rome and not England, the political authority would not tolerate this perceived insubordination. The French revolutionaries fought for political change and viewed Church persons as obstructionists. The rebels effectively eliminated religious leaders who were political opponents. In Vietnam, Japan and Korea, opponents of foreign cultural influence slaughtered not only foreigners but even native persons who adopted the Western religion. Only in a few instances, such as in Moorish Spain, were persecutors motivated apparently by purely religious reasons.

Tertullian's observation that "the blood of the martyrs is the seed of Christians" was verified time and again in Church history.[19] Martyrs' deaths profoundly manifested their faith in action. Their convictions of the truth about God, Jesus and the Church, as well as the martyrs' willingness to die for that truth astounded and confounded unbelieving observers. Many of these onlookers were so challenged that they themselves investigated and converted to Christianity.

No relationship mattered more for the martyrs than eternal life with God. "Love for life did not deter them from death" (Rv 12:11). The noblewoman Perpetua withstood the tears and pleadings of her father, the cries of her newborn son for her breast and courageously gave herself instead to the beasts of the Roman games.[20] Thomas More forsook his career and his family in Reformation England rather than admit that "a temporal lord could or ought to be head of the spiritual."[21] As Thomas ascended the scaffolding for his beheading, he explained his position that he was "the king's good servant but God's first."[22] The young Frenchman, Bl. Theophanes Venard, revealed the same priority just before his martyrdom in Vietnam in the last century:

My darling sister,

How I cried when I read your letter! Yes, I knew well the sorrow I was going to bring upon my family, and especially upon you, my dear little sister. But don't you think it cost me tears of blood, too, to take such a step, and give you all such pain? Whoever cared more for home and a home life than I? All my happiness here below was centered there. But God, who had united us all in links of the tenderest affection, wished to wean me from it.[23]

The Church in the twentieth century continues to suffer persecution. Right-wing fascists and left-wing secularists have confiscated Church property, closed Church institutions and confined, if not killed, clergy and laity. Many of these victims are popularly believed, although not officially declared, to be saints.

Application Of The Theme:

Common Vision: Martyrs preferred Christ more than all else, even more than life itself. Their faith, hope and love of Christ gave them promise of eternal life. They believed that human life does not end but only changes. They believed that death could not separate them from the love of God that comes to them in Jesus Christ.

Common Way: Martyrdom was the passageway to life's goal: union with Jesus Christ in eternal life. Martyrdom brought the martyrs home. Most martyrs were given opportunities to avoid martyrdom. Martyrs willingly chose instead to die for Christ.

Common Bond With Each Other: The martyrs stood united. The martyrs fell united. Just as they found strength in ministry from prayer and community, so too they found strength in martyrdom from prayer and community. They sang hymns and prayed for each other and their persecutors.

Common Bond With God: "To live is Christ; to die is gain" (Ph 1:21). This was the motivation and mission of the co-martyrs. They proclaimed unequivocally by their deaths what they had proclaimed all during their lives. Their final witness was the confirmation of their lives. They longed to see the face of God. No one was able to dissuade them; they were going home!

APPENDIX: CO-MARTYR SAINTS

ROMAN EMPIRE

Roman persecutions numbered ten. Able administrative emperors zealously pursued anti-Christian persecutions because they hoped to revive the Empire by enforcing submission to the Roman gods, who were believed to protect the Empire. The persecutors of greatest infamy included Nero, who initiated the first great persecution in 64; Domitian, who ruled during 88-96; Marcus Aurelius, who ruled between 165-77; Decius, who was emperor between 249-51; and, finally, Diocletian and Galerius, who successively led the last and worst of the persecutions from 303-12. Galerius' successor was Constantine. He issued the Edict of Milan, which officially tolerated Christianity. In the East, persecutions continued for a few more years especially during the short-lived reigns of Licinius in 320-21 and Christian-raised Julian the Apostate during 361-63. Much scholarly research and debate has taken place over the actual number of Roman martyrs; estimates have ranged between 10,000 and 100,000.[24]

The martyrdom of **Ignatius of Antioch** (d. 105) and

his companions, **Rufus** (d. 105) and **Zosimus** (d. 105), is described in this chapter.

Justin Martyr (100-165) converted to Christianity at about thirty years of age "by reading the Scriptures and witnessing the heroism of the martyrs."[25] This well-educated Greek from Palestine opened a school of philosophy at Rome. An opponent whom he defeated in a debate denounced him to the pagan authorities. Justin and six companions, namely, **Charita**, **Chariton**, **Eulepistus**, **Hierax**, **Liberanius** and **Paeon**, refused to offer sacrifice to the gods and were beheaded. "Justin is the first Christian apologist, and a layman, to have written on Christianity at any length, and in his writings he sought to reconcile the claims of faith and reason."[26]

The married women **Perpetua** (d. 203) and **Felicity** (d. 203), along with three other catechumens and their instructor **Saturus** (d. 203), were martyred in Carthage, North Africa. Perpetua kept a diary, to which Saturus added. An eye-witness, perhaps Tertullian, completed the diary. Perpetua was an aristocrat, Felicity was her slave. Both women were young mothers. Perpetua was nursing her new-born son and handed him over to her pagan father when she entered the dungeon to await her sentence. Felicity was pregnant when arrested and gave birth in prison, where her child was taken from her. All six adults were mauled by wild beasts before being beheaded. The aristocratic demeanor of Perpetua so disconcerted the sword-wielding executioner that she guided his trembling blade to her neck. The two women are named in the First Eucharistic Prayer.

Pope **Pontian** (d. c. 236) and anti-pope **Hippolytus** (d. c. 235) died of ill-treatment at the salt mines in Sardinia, where both had been exiled at the beginning of the persecution of Emperor Maximinus. Hippolytus, a major theological writer, had been elected anti-pope by a small group of followers when he challenged the Christological teachings of one of Pontian's predecessors. In exile, Pontian reconciled Hippolytus to the Church.

Denis (d. c. 258), a missionary from Rome who

became the first bishop of Paris, **Rusticius** (d. c. 258), a priest, and **Eleutherius** (d. c. 258), a deacon, had been very successful in winning converts. They suffered decapitation during the persecution of Decius. Their bodies were retrieved from the Seine River and a chapel was built over their grave site. This chapel became the Benedictine Abbey of St. Denis and the burial place for the kings of France.

In Upper Egypt near Antinoe **Timothy** (d. c. 286) and his wife of twenty days, **Maura** (d. c. 286), were nailed to a wall where they remained hanging for nine days before expiring. He was a lector, who refused to hand over the sacred books during the Diocletian persecution. She was called to persuade him. Instead she encouraged him to remain steadfast.

The following year, it is reported, virtually an entire legion (6000 men) of Roman soldiers suffered death rather than offer sacrifice to the gods. These soldiers, who had been recruited from Upper Egypt, were on march from Rome, and across the Alps to suppress a revolt in Gaul. While the army was passing through Switzerland, the emperor prepared the public pagan sacrifice. This **Theban Legion** refused to attend. Twice their ranks were decimated. Then they were slaughtered en masse. Their Christian leader was **Maurice**. Numerous historical records give evidence to this story. "The story can therefore be accepted as substantially true, but it is almost unbelievable that the whole legion was Christian and that the whole of it was put to death. Probably a very large number of soldiers were put to death and that gave rise to the story as now told."[27]

Another soldier who died for the faith was **Marcellus** (d. 298), who was killed in Tangiers. This centurion refused at the emperor's birthday celebration to offer incense in his honor. Marcellus "threw away his arms and insignia and declared himself a Christian."[28] An attending notary, **Cassian** (d. c. 298), refused to write the official report of the case. He too was killed.

Palatias (d. 302) and her maidservant **Laurentia** (d.

302) died at Fermo near Palatias' native Ancona during the reign of Diocletian. They refused to offer sacrifice to the pagan gods.

Marcellinus (d. 304), a priest, and **Peter** (d. 304), an exorcist, were arrested and martyred during the persecution of Decius. In prison they converted many persons including the jailer, his wife and their daughter. These two are named in the First Eucharistic Prayer. Constantine constructed a basilica over their grave site.

Orentius (d. 304) and his six brothers died for the faith after he single-handedly defeated at Antioch a representative opponent of an enemy army, but he refused to pay homage to the Roman gods. His brothers stood with him in torture and death.

Bishop **Januarius** of Naples (d. c. 305) suffered martyrdom after he and his deacon **Festus** (d. c. 305) visited in prison two other deacons, **Sossus** (d. c. 305) and **Proclus** (d. c. 305), and two laymen, **Euticius** (d. c. 305) and **Acutius** (d. c. 305). "Januarius' relics ended up in Naples, and for the past four centuries a vial containing a solid red substance reputed to be his blood liquefies and often bubbles and boils when exposed in the cathedral there."[29] This phenomenon has occurred on the saint's feast day and related days every year since 1631, without fail and without scientific explanation.

Two brothers of Nice, **Vincent** (d. 305) and **Orontius** (d. 305), were killed along with their friend **Victor** (d. 305) in the province of Gerona while the three were preaching the Gospel to the people of the Spanish Pyrenees. Their bodies were retrieved and returned to Embrun, France.

A popular, though not entirely verified, account focuses on the **Four Crowned Ones** (d. 306). Two stories have merged into one. The first account relates that four sculptors, and later a fifth sculptor, were martyred by Diocletian because they refused to offer sacrifice to the gods. These five craftsmen were beaten with leaden scourges and then drowned in the river in Pannonia. The second account states that in the following year Diocletian again martyred a group of five men but this time the incident occurred in Rome and the recalcitrants were soldiers. Allegedly, Diocletian had these men scourged and then drowned in the local sewer. The stories seem to be Roman and Pannonian versions of the one event.

Celtic Martyrs

Dymphna (d. c. 650) fled from Ireland to Belgium to escape the incestuous advances of her recently widowed chieftain father. Her chaplain **Gerebern** (d. c. 650) and two other persons accompanied her. After arriving at Antwerp, they settled at Gheel. They lived as recluses until Dymphna's father arrived. The chief killed his daughter's three companions, and after she refused to return with him, the father beheaded her. When the relics of Dymphna and Gerebern were discovered in the thirteenth century, many cures of the mentally ill occurred there.

Martyrs of Moorish Spain

Cordoba, Spain witnessed the martyrdom of forty-eight Christians by Moslem rulers between the years 850 and 859. The ironic aspect of the martyrdom was that it occurred despite the generally peaceful coexistence which Moslems and Christians enjoyed. The Islamic government did not actively search for non-believers. "As the sources unambiguously demonstrate, the majority of the victims deliberately invoked capital punishment by publicly blaspheming Muhammad and disparaging Islam."[30] Some Cordoban Christians hailed the dead as martyrs, while others viewed these dead as self-immolators, who initiated their own deaths.

Two young women, **Flora** (d. 851) and **Maria** (d. 851), were among the forty-eight martyrs of Moorish Spain. Flora was secretly raised a Christian by her Christian mother. She was betrayed to the authorities by her brother. She was scourged and was returned to his custody so that he could attempt to have her apostatize. She escaped to a church. While praying there, she met Maria, the sister of a deacon who had recently been martyred. They both decided to give themselves up to the Moorish municipal authorities. They were sent to a brothel for punishment. They yielded in neither faith nor virtue. Their final punishment was decapitation.

Martyrs of Reformation England

England experienced nearly a century and half (1535-1680) of persecution against Catholics. King Henry VIII began the rupture between the government and the Church. This erstwhile "Defender of the Faith" became disgruntled when Rome refused to approve his divorce. He pursued a decade-long persecution, in which he created forty-nine martyrs, all but seven of whom were priests. John Cardinal Fisher, Sir Thomas More and Bl. Margaret Pole were famous among his martyrs. Henry's successor, Edward VI, made no martyrs. Catholic "Bloody" Mary Tudor, however, "brought harsh persecutions of Protestants, hundreds of whom perished."[31] In 1558 Queen Elizabeth I began her forty-five year reign during which she killed 188 persons for the faith, two-thirds of whom were priests. Edmund Campion and Bl. Margaret Clitherow were among her famous victims. James I killed another twenty-five in his fourteen years as king. Charles I ascended the throne and killed twenty-four persons between 1628 and 1646. During the commonwealth years only two persons, both priests, were martyred. Charles II renewed the persecutions by martyring twenty-five persons during his twenty-five years as king. Most of these were priests.

John Fisher (1469-1535) and **Thomas More** (1478-1535) were beheaded two weeks apart in the Tower of London. They dared to oppose Henry VIII's Act of Succession and Act of Supremacy, which attempted to legitimize the king's second marriage and his role as supreme head of the Church in England.

Fisher suffered imprisonment for ten months before his decapitation. He achieved renown in his thirty-year dual position as chancellor of Cambridge University and bishop of Rochester. He served also as administrator of the chairs of divinity at Oxford and Cambridge, as chaplain to the mother of Henry VIII and as erudite defender of the faith against the Protestants. Fisher was close friends with Thomas More, and these two were close friends with the humanist, Erasmus. Fisher owned "one of the finest libraries in Europe."[32] While imprisoned, Fisher was named a cardinal of the Church by the pope. This ecclesiastical promotion exacerbated Henry's anger towards Rome and Fisher. Fisher literally stood alone among the bishops in his public opposition to the king.

Thomas More won acclaim as a lawyer and author. King Henry VIII appointed him diplomat to France and Flanders, member of the Royal Council, knight of the king, speaker of the House of Commons, High Steward of Cambridge University, and finally Lord Chancellor of England. More refused, however, to support the king's aggressive measures against the Church's property, doctrine and moral teachings, especially refusing to recognize as royal heirs the offspring of Henry's second marriage. More was imprisoned. After fifteen months in the Tower he was beheaded. His last words were that he was "the king's good servant but God's first."[33]

Four years later **Bl. John Beche** (d. 1539), a friend of John Fisher and Thomas More, suffered their same fate. Beche, as head of the Benedictine abbey at Colchester, signed the Oath of Supremacy even though he generally opposed the king's ecclesiastical policies. He saw no great danger in signing just a document. When the king dissolved the abbey in 1538, however, Beche "openly denied the king's right to do this."[34] Beche was arrested, charged with treason, and executed the following year.

Bl. Margaret Pole (1471-1541) was the only woman martyred by King Henry VIII. She was Henry's aunt, niece to two previous kings of England, and governess of Henry's first daughter. The king had remarked that she was "the holiest woman in England."[35] Margaret was also the mother of Reginald Pole, who was the cousin and critic of Henry. Reginald became a lay cardinal twenty years before being ordained archbishop of Canterbury. While living in Rome, he wrote privately and later publicly in opposition to Henry's second marriage and claims of supremacy of the Church of England. Henry vowed to destroy the famous family. He arrested in 1538 a brother and the mother of Reginald and executed the brother. Three years later he beheaded the mother. Reginald could not safely return to England until Henry died and the Catholic Queen Mary Tudor came into power. In 1553 he was appointed papal legate to England where he ministered zealously until he died in 1557.

The **Forty English and Welsh Martyrs** died in the reign of Queen Elizabeth I. "Without question it was Elizabeth I's intention to supplant the old religion with the new in a bloodless manner. It is significant that there were no martyrs in the first twelve years of her reign, and only five in the years 1570 to 1577."[36] The numbers soon mounted, however, and the long-reigning queen is responsible for the deaths of 188 martyrs. **Robert Southwell** (c. 1561-95), whose letter to his companion prisoners is presented in this chapter, died during her reign. So too did **Edmund Campion** (c. 1540-81) who "was raised a Catholic, given a scholarship to St. John's College, Oxford, when fifteen, and became a fellow when only seventeen."[37] He signed the Oath of Supremacy and became an Anglican deacon in 1564. Doubts about Protestantism, however, arose within him. In 1569 he traveled to Ireland, where his Catholic faith was restored. He went to Douai, where he studied and joined the Jesuits. After some years as an administrator at Rome and having taught for one year at a college in Prague, he and another Jesuit were chosen to be missionaries to England. "His extraordinary success caused him to be hunted down relentlessly."[38] He was "the object of one of the most intensive manhunts in English history."[39] Within the year he was betrayed and was offered rich inducements to apostatize. When he refused, he was hanged, drawn and quartered at Tyburn Prison.

MARTYRS OF IRELAND

The Irish suffered terrible persecution at the hands of the English, from the time of Henry VIII in 1535 up to the Irish Emancipation in 1829. Queen Elizabeth had decreed: "Every Romish priest found in the island is deemed guilty of rebellion. He shall be hanged until half-dead, then his head taken off, his bowels drawn out and burned and his head fixed in some public place."[40] During these almost 300 years many thousands died for the faith. The laity died mostly in isolated massacres, while the clergy were continuously victimized. Between 1647 and 1649, in three massacres 2,000 Catholics at Cashel, 2,000 at Wexford and 3,000 at Drogheda were put to death. The names of 259 victims were identified and were submitted to Rome in 1915 for consideration for beatification. This list includes thirty-seven lay men, three lay women and the rest are clerics. The manner of death was particularly sacrilegious and brutal: some priests were shot while saying Mass or hearing confessions; other victims were drowned or burned at the stake; others were hanged, drawn and quartered; some suffered decapitation or other kinds of dismemberment.[41]

One particularly insidious incident was the Popish Plot, which was fabricated by Englishman Titus Oates in 1678 and continued until 1681. Oates alleged that Catholics had conspired to massacre Protestants, burn London and kill the king. Oates himself was an unsuccessful student, three times unsuccessful Anglican minister, and a convicted perjurer. Still, the allegations were credited and many Catholics died. "More than twenty-five Catholics were executed in England, many more died in prison, and many hundreds were imprisoned."[42] The last of these martyrs was **Oliver Plunkett** (1629-81). Irish-born, he studied in Rome, taught there for fifteen years before being appointed archbishop of Armagh and then Primate of Ireland. Although many clergy fled Ireland during the Popish Plot turmoil, Plunkett remained to minister to the people. He was discovered, and was accused of propagating the Catholic religion and of conspiring to kill the king. He was imprisoned in solitary confinement for nine months before becoming the last Catholic martyred at Tyburn Prison.

MARTYRS OF INDIA

On the coast of India, near Goa and north of Bombay, five Jesuits and some Indian laity were martyred by Hindus in 1583. **Rudolph Aquaviva** (1550-83), one of those martyred, was the nephew of the fifth general of the Society. He and other Jesuits had been sent to evangelize the people. The Hindus, however, violently opposed the missionaries. When the Christians attempted to build a church in the locale, the opposition ambushed and killed them.

MARTYRS OF JAPAN

Japan witnessed three periods of persecution: 1597, 1622, and 1617-32.

The first occurred less than fifty years after the arrival of Francis Xavier in 1549. His three-year ministry made great impact. "It is said that by 1587 there were in Japan over two hundred thousand Christians."[43] The first persecution claimed the Japanese Jesuit **Paul Miki** (1562-97) and his companions, whose story is told in the chapter on Benefits of Saintly Companions.

The second persecution took place in 1622 in accordance with the command of the new shogun who mandated that all Christian teachers be banished from Japan and that no Japanese citizen was to have the slightest contact with priests. Those who persisted in teaching the faith or assisting its promotion were liable to death. Although hundreds of

Catholics died for the faith in this year, only twenty-seven persons are named in the official rolls of martyrdom.[44] Most notable among these martyrs were the Dominican priest **Bl. Alphonsus Navarette** (d. 1617) and the Augustinian friar **Bl. Ferdinand Ayala** (d. 1617), who were beheaded at Omura after courageously publicly ministering to persecuted Japanese Catholics.

The third period overlapped the second. The persecution began in 1617 and lasted fifteen years. Officially named are 205 persons: many Franciscans and their tertiaries, Dominicans, Jesuits and lay persons. The religious came principally from Japan, Spain and Italy. The lay persons included many Japanese and some Korean married couples and their children.[45] Outstanding among them was the Franciscan priest **Bl. Apollinaris Franco** (d. 1622), who traveled from Nagasaki to priestless Omura, where he was imprisoned for five years before being burned alive.

Martyrs of the New World

The Jesuit **Martyrs of Paraguay** are the first beatified martyrs of the New World, although they are not America's first martyrs.[46] **Bl. Roque Gonzalez** (1576-1628), **Bl. Alonso Rodriquez** (d. 1628) and **Bl. Juan de Castillo** (d. 1628) devoted themselves to the improvement of the lot of the Indians. Paraguayan-born Roque worked for twenty years in the formation of the Indian settlements. These three priests opposed Spanish imperialism, the Spanish Inquisition and the enslavement of the Indians. The Spanish leaders detested the priests and their stance. The local medicine men too opposed the priests. One medicine man allegedly instigated the raid against the priests. Gonzalez and Rodriquez were tomahawked, and de Castillo was stoned to death.

The eight Jesuit **North American Martyrs** (1644-49), who included six priests and two lay volunteers, are described in this chapter.

MARTYRS OF VIETNAM

Christianization in Vietnam began in the fifteenth century and was so fruitful that by 1659 two vicariates had been formed. Opposition, however, arose too. Between 1625 and 1886 political leaders issued a total of fifty-three anti-Christian edicts and murdered over 130,000 believers.[47] The cruelty was barbaric. Martyrs were branded on the face with letters indicating "false religion." They lived in cages so small that they could neither stand up nor stretch out. They were ill-fed and ill-clothed. The majority died by strangulation or decapitation. While almost all of these martyrs remain anonymous, attempts have succeeded recently to identify and then beatify 117 of them.[48] Their names are listed under the Martyrs of Indo-China. Those named include bishops, priests, a seminarian, lay catechists, Dominican tertiaries and a lay woman. The mistreatment of these Christians equals only the cruelty inflicted under Roman emperors. Most well known are **Andrew Dung-Lac**, **Tommaso Thien** and **Emanuele Phung**.

MARTYRS OF THE FRENCH REVOLUTION AND ITS AFTERMATH

During the French Revolution of 1789 and its ten-year chaotic consequences, hundreds of Catholics, especially clergy and religious, died for the faith.

The Church hierarchy had identified itself and the institution with the Old Regime. Many higher clergy were indifferent to the sufferings of ordinary people, and many of the lower clergy were ignorant of the teachings and liturgical practices of the Church. In 1790, when the Constituent Assembly passed the Civil Constitution of the Clergy and Religious, the hierarchy overwhelmingly rejected it. A significant number of the lower clergy and religious signed it, although many of them soon recanted. One year later, the pope condemned the Civil Constitution. The total rejection of the Civil Constitution by the Church confirmed the revolutionaries' view that the Church was their symbolic and real enemy.

When the European war was going badly for the revolutionaries in 1792, their leaders easily incited the rebels against the royalists and clergy. Marauding bands vented their fury against the Church. In Paris alone 1400 people were killed in a few weeks; the vast majority were civil criminals but at least 400 were priests being held as political prisoners.[49] Among the victims, 191 persons, all clergy except for one lay brother and five laymen, have been officially named and recognized as the **Martyrs of Paris**.[50] All the martyrs were men: ninety-five died at a Carmelite convent, seventy-two at a Vincentian seminary, twenty-one in an abbey, and three in a city jail.

In 1794 a new wave of persecutions engulfed the Church. In January the nineteen **Martyrs of Laval** were executed; they included fifteen priests, three nuns and the blood sister of one nun. In June, four Sisters of Charity of St. Vincent de Paul died as the **Martyrs of Arras** on charges of being "pious counter-revolutionaries."[51] During the next month thirty-two members of two convents, the Ursuline Sisters and the Perpetual Adorers of the Blessed Sacrament, were killed and counted as the **Martyrs of Orange**.[52] In that same month another sixteen nuns became known as the Carmelite **Martyrs of Compiegne**.[53] In October eleven more sisters died as the Ursuline **Martyrs of Valenciennes**; "[they] were brought up for trial, and on their stating openly that they had come back to Valenciennes to teach the Catholic faith they were sentenced to death."[54]

The **Martyrs of Arras** included the superioress **Bl. Madeleine Fontaine**, seventy-one years of age, and her three community members, who were all in their forties. Evidence of alleged anti-revolutionary activities was planted in the convent. The nuns were arrested and imprisoned. Four months later they were called to the home of a notorious apostate priest. The sisters would not consent to taking the Constitutional Oath. The priest sent them on that same day to the tribunal at Cambrai. There Madeleine was condemned as a "pious counterrevolutionary" and the other three as her accomplices. They were led straightaway to the guillotine. Madeleine was the last to be called forward. As she drew near to the instrument of death, she turned to the crowd and shouted, "Listen, Christians! We are the last victims. The persecution is going to stop; the gallows will be destroyed; the altars of Jesus will rise again gloriously."[55] Her prophecy came true. By the end of the year, violent outcries against the executions forced all executions to end. Six weeks after the nuns' deaths, however, one more execution took place, that of the apostate priest who had condemned the sisters.

MARTYRS OF KOREA

The Church in Korea claims an extraordinary number of martyrs. Korea is "unique in the history of the Church by reason of the fact that it was founded entirely by lay people."[56] The scholar Yi Sung-hun discovered books about the Catholic religion. He and other Korean scholars sought to learn more. In 1784 Yi went to Peking to inquire about the faith. There he studied the Christian religion and was baptized. Back in Korea he and others propagated the faith. For their work of evangelization they met rejection from their families and neighbors and persecution from the government. Eventually two Chinese priests were missioned to Korea where the faith had taken root and had prospered without any priest. Their mission was short-lived. Forty more years passed before the Paris Foreign Mission Society undertook its ministry in 1836. Until that time, the Christian community consisted only of lay people. Wave after wave of persecution slaughtered the members of this rapidly growing faith community. At the 1984 canonization of 103 Korean Martyrs, Pope John Paul II preached: "Thus, in less than a century, it [Korea] could already boast of some ten thousand martyrs. The years 1791, 1801, 1827, 1839, 1846 and 1866 are forever signed with the holy blood of [your] martyrs and engraved in [your] hearts."[57] Some of the popularly recognized names include **Andrew Kim Tae-gon**, the first Korean priest; **Paul Chong Ha-sang**, **Augustine Yu Chin-gil** and **Charles Cho Shin-chol**, the emissaries to China in search of missionary priests; and seventeen-year-old **Agatha Yi**, who along with her younger brother remained steadfast in the faith even though she had been falsely informed that her parents had betrayed the faith. Agatha responded to the false report: "Whether my parents betrayed or not is their affair. As for us, we cannot betray the Lord of heaven whom we have always served."[58] Upon witnessing the faith of this adolescent, six adult Christians voluntarily presented themselves to the magistrate for reception of the fate of all martyrs.

MARTYRS OF UGANDA

Charles Lwanga (d. 1886) **and his twenty-one companions** refused to acquiesce to the homosexual and pedophiliac desires of the local king. They became known as the Martyrs of Uganda. They continued the tradition of African martyrs such as Cyprian, Felicity and Perpetua. Pope Paul VI's homily delivered at their canonization also mentions the Ugandan members of the Anglican Church, who died for the name of Christ.

MARTYRS OF THE TWENTIETH CENTURY

Throughout Eastern Europe and China, countless thousands of Christians suffered death because of their opposition to communism's atheistic ideology.

Throughout Central and South America, countless thousands of Christians have suffered and many thousands have died in defense of human, civil and religious rights. Not a few among these modern martyrs are church leaders: religious and lay, men and women.[59] Described in this chapter are **The Four Churchwomen of El Salvador** (d. 1980).

The question of how broadly or narrowly to define

martyrdom remains a question. Popular martyrs include Archbishop **Vladimir** (d. 1918) and the twice married, divorced, separated and evenual nun **Marie Skobtsova** (d. 1945) in Russia; priests **Maximilian Kolbe** (d. 1941) and **Jerzy Popieluszko** (d. 1984) in Poland, Bishop **Vilmos Apor** (d. 1945) in Hungary, Maryknoll Bishop **Francis X. Ford** (d. 1952) in China; priests **Miguel Pro** (d. 1927) in Mexico, **Hector Gallego** (d. 1971) and the Vincentian **Nicolas Van Kleef** (d. 1989) in Panama, the Polish Franciscans **Zbigniew Strzalkowski** and **Michal Tomaszek** in Peru (1991); the French religious sisters **Alice Domon** and **Leonie Duquet** (1977) in Argentina; and three Jesuit priests: **John Conway, Martin Thomas** and **Christopher Shepherd-Smith** in Rhodesia (d. 1977). Thousands, if not millions, of others have died with them.[60]

Hundreds of thousands have suffered persecution with them, most notably Jozsef Cardinal Mindszenty (d. 1981) in Hungary, Archbishop Alojzije Stepinac (d. 1960) of Yugoslavia, Primate Stefan Wyszynski (d. 1981) of Poland and Josyf Cardinal Slipyi of the Ukraine (d. 1984). Many others, non-Catholics and non-Christians as mentioned in the introduction to this chapter, have suffered persecution and death for the sake of human, civil and religious rights.

Notes for Chapter 11

[1]   *Dictionary of Quotations*, p. 437.10.

[2]   Actually the use of the Greek word "martyr" meaning one who dies for the sake of one's faith originated in the second century. "Never in the OT and only rarely in the NT does the term extend beyond its basic, often juridical, meaning of witness, to embrace what later centuries have commonly understood by the word martyr, namely, one who voluntarily suffers death for his beliefs," as quoted by Dicharry, "Martyr (In The Bible)," p. 314.

[3]   "Mt 23:29-37; 21:35; 22:6; 5:12; Lk 13:33f; 6:23; 11:47f+. These are based on Jewish traditions rather than on the text of the OT which has little information of this type." John L. McKenzie, *Dictionary of the Bible*, pp. 698-99.

4   Murphy, "Martyr," p. 314.

5   C. Bernard Ruffin, *The Twelve*, pp. 185-86.

6   McKenzie, p. 650.

7   *Celebrating the Eucharist*, p. 132.

8   Murphy, p. 312.

9   Tertullian, *Apologeticus*, XXXIX, i.

10 *Dictionary of Quotations*, p. 604.10.

11 From a letter to the Romans by Saint Ignatius, as found in *The Liturgy of the Hours*, vol. IV, pp. 1490-91.

12 *Letters from the Saints* (1964), pp. 176-77.

13 Letter of Isaac Jogues to his Jesuit Provincial, as found in *Letters from the Saints* (1964), pp. 37, 38 and 41.

14 Janice McLaughlin, "Full Story Finally Told," p. 40.

15 Letter of Sr. Ita Ford, Maryknoll Sister, to her niece, Jennifer Sullivan, as provided by William Ford, Esq.

16 Murphy, p. 312.

17 Ibid., p. 314.

18 T. Gilby, "Martyrdom, Theology Of," p. 314.

19 Tertullian, *Apologeticus*, XXXIX, i.

20 *Butler's Lives of the Saints*, vol. I, pp. 493-98.

21 Butler, vol. III, p. 54.

22 Delaney, *Dictionary of Saints*, p. 414.

23 Butler, vol. IV, p. 282.

24 Gilby, p. 314.

25 *The Book of Saints*, p. 328.

26 Delaney, p. 335.

27 *The Book of Saints*, p. 532.

28 Ibid., p. 336.

29 Delaney, p. 310.

30 Wolf, *Christian Martyrs in Muslim Spain*, p. 1.

31 Kirchner, *Western Civilization since 1500*, p. 58.

32 Delaney, p. 229.

33 Ibid., p. 414.

34 *The Book of Saints*, p. 316.

35 Delaney, p. 474.

36 Caraman, "Martyrs of England and Wales," p. 323.

37 Delaney, p. 130.

38 *The Book of Saints*, p. 175.

39 Delaney, p. 130.

40 D'Arcy, *The Saints of Ireland*, p. 190.

41 Ibid., pp. 200-09.

42 T.A. Birrell, "Oates Plot," p. 590.

43 Butler, vol. I, p. 259.

44 Butler, vol. III, pp. 533-34.

45 Butler, vol. II, pp. 445-51.

46 Albert J. Nevins, *American Martyrs From 1542*, pp. 9-13, lists 146 American martyrs of whom 27 died before 1628.

47 Booklet for *Canonizzazione Dei Beati Andrea Dung-Lac, Presbitero; Tommaso Thien E Emanuele Phung, Laici; Girolamo Hermosilla Valentino Berrio-Ochoa, O.P. E Altri 6 Vescovi Teofano Venard, Presbitero E 105 Compagni Martiri*, Rome, 1988; p. 7.

48 Ibid.

49 Norwood, *Strangers and Exiles*, vol. 2, p. 187.

50 Butler, vol. III, pp. 472-74.

51 Butler, vol. II, p. 655.

52 Butler, vol. III, p. 59.

53 Ibid., pp. 132-34.

54 Butler, vol. IV, pp. 141-42.

55 Butler, vol. II, p. 665.

56 *Osservatore Romano*, May 14, 1984; p. 5.

57 Ibid., p. 20.

58 Ibid., p. 5.

59 Many books have been published about these martyrs; cf. William J. O'Malley, *The Voice of Blood*.

60 Bruno Chenu, *The Book of Christian Martyrs*, p. 163.

THE IMAGES OF SAINTS

Rarely are the saints pictured with their friends. Many times the saints are portrayed alone with their eyes raised to God. Other times they are depicted with their arms extended in service to others. Nonetheless the saints often experienced satisfying relationships. These relationships helped to sustain them in their service of God and God's people. With their saintly companions they shared life-goals, lifestyle, friendship with each other and friendship with the Lord.

What is wrong with the popular image of the saints as solitary persons? The image is neither accurate nor attractive. In real life the saints grew up in family settings. They learned from and instructed others. They prayed with others. They shared ministry with others. The saints loved people and people loved being with the saints. Even hermits and pillar-sitting stylites regularly interacted with many people. Even monks lived in community.

What are the consequences of an inaccurate and unattractive image of the saints? The consequences are considerable. The saints, second only to Jesus and Mary, model the Christian life. If the model is inaccurate, then people will pursue a means which is incapable of achieving its goal. If the model is unattractive, then few people will seek to be saints. The image portrayed must come from real life if the image is to be realizable. The image portrayed must be attractive if it is to arouse a response. Any-

311

thing less will frustrate people in their efforts to find and follow a path that leads to holiness.

The saints took seriously the gospel mandate to live Christian community. They shared their prayer and material goods. They went forth two by two or more to preach the Word. They expressed their love for God by their love for one another, and especially for the poor. After all, they were only doing what the Lord himself had observed and commanded: "Whatsoever you do to the least of my brethren, you do unto me" (Mt 25:40), and "Love one another as I have loved you" (Jn 15:12). No saint gets to heaven alone. The Christian vocation calls people to go beyond introspection to involvement. The saints, by the grace of God, reflected the trinitarian image of God by involving themselves with others and for others.

This communitarian aspect of the saints' lives did not take away their individuality and independence. They remained strong individuals, but they looked beyond individualism to see themselves as individuals-in-community. They asserted their independence, but they did so in a way that affirmed all people's interdependence.

We revere the saints precisely because they emulated Christ. Christ's life presents the paramount example of experiencing significant and supportive relationships. Successive scenes from his life bear this out: his birth at Bethlehem, the flight into Egypt, his growing up in the carpenter's shop at Nazareth, his adolescent discussion with the elders in the Temple, his call of the disciples, his and their early ministry in Galilee, their journey together through Samaria, his and their ministry in Judea and its culmination at Jerusalem. Jesus was the quintessential man for others and with others. He lived in the world to reveal God's love. He called his listeners to follow him in this world and to join him in the next. Jesus sought and found the companionship of family, friends and disciples.

The life of Mary, the first and perfect disciple of her son

Jesus, similarly reveals the role of significant relationships: her engagement to Joseph, her visit to Elizabeth, the nativity at Bethlehem, the flight into Egypt, the home life at Nazareth, the loss and then discovery of her son during Passover in Jerusalem, her and her friends' discipleship with Jesus and their presence at the crucifixion, Jesus' last words in which he urged his mother and his beloved disciple to take care of each other. Mary constantly shared the company of others for the purposes of support and service.

Virtually all the saints entwined their lives in the lives of others. They found companions in the ten kinds of relationships presented in this book. Many times, but by no means all times, their companions too became saints. The love that the saints experienced in relationships with God and with friends enabled the saints to possess and express that love for other people. At times the saints separated themselves from others for the purpose of experiencing the private quiet time that all persons need in the delicate balance of prayer and action, of taking care of others and oneself. The saints sought solitude but they were not solitary figures. The saints were social people.

We in the West at the end of the twentieth century place much emphasis on human relationships. We desire to be close to people. Our spirituality focuses more on horizontal than vertical relationships. Our path to a relationship with God takes us through our relationships with other people. Some few mystics may encounter God directly but most contemporary Christians experience God indirectly through other people. Something, however, is often missing in our relationships. As Mother Teresa of Calcutta notes, "The greatest poverty in the Western world is that of loneliness."

Why not then portray the saints in their relationships? The saints model for us relationships which are both happy and holy. The quality of their friendships would encourage us in our friendships. The relationships of the saints with one another were a good in themselves but they were not an end in themselves. They provided enjoyment and assistance towards the absolute end, that is, relationship with God and with each other in eternal life.

Artists play a public role in presenting the images of saints. Religious statuary and stained glass windows in churches and chapels impact on congregations for generations. What images of the saints' relationships do they portray? The members of the Holy Family are rarely pictured as a family unit. In many churches Mary and Joseph are pictured on opposite sides of the nave, with Mary holding the infant Jesus and Joseph holding a carpenter's tool. Why are the three not pictured together? Why are they not embracing each other? Patron saints of our parishes fare no better. Most are pictured alone, unless they are serving needy persons. A priest friend was startled to discover in proofreading this text that St. Henry, who is the patron of his home parish, was married and that Henry's wife was also a saint. In the parish church Henry is pictured wearing his emperor's crown and holding the cross of Christ, but he is not pictured with his wife, St. Cunegund. A local parish of St. Margaret of Scotland pictures her wearing the queen's crown and cradling in her arm a miniature model of a church. She is pictured neither with her husband nor any of her eight children, not even with her son, St. David. My home parish of St. John the Evangelist shows him standing tall with the crucifix in one raised hand and his gospel text in the other. John is pictured alone. He is standing neither with Jesus whose "beloved disciple" he was, nor with Jesus' mother, whose care Jesus entrusted to John. What image is communicated by these stalwart solitary figures?

Preachers proclaim that the saints embodied in exemplary fashion a response to God's will. Saints heard the Word and the cries of the poor. They responded generously and practically to real needs. Preachers exhort their congregations to do the same for their salvation and the sake of human and Christian community. Preachers rarely speak, however, of the saints' experience of community. Before saints established Christian communities, they built solid interpersonal relationships. All along the course of their lives parents, relatives, teachers and friends accompanied, influenced and helped to form them into the saints they were to become. Sometimes these companions became publicly proclaimed saints themselves. Most of the saints came from Christian communities. They were heroes within the community. They were not the "rugged individuals" praised in secular society. What message is delivered when preachers speak of saints but not of their families, friends and local community which raised and supported them on their way to sanctity?

Teachers do their best to instruct and inspire their students in the ways of Jesus and the saints. Meanwhile students are susceptible to peer pressure to resist these inspirations. The saints, however, confronted negative peer pressure with positive example. They attracted their peers and won them over. They were lovers of life which they joyfully lived to the full. They found the mysterious meaning of life for which most people search their whole lives. They invited and challenged their peers to become their best selves. Because they were charismatic persons, they drew people to themselves by the hundreds and thousands. They possessed a radiance which attracted their contemporaries, an aura which artists for centuries have rendered by a halo. Today's students want to belong to some group somewhere. They often search with integrity for what is simultaneously ideal and real. Teachers can encourage students, as did the saints in this book, to create "a peer group for good."

Parents possess a role of inestimable importance regarding the nature and nurturing of their children. Parents are co-creators with God in bringing their children to life. They provide a home which is described in Church documents as "a little church," "the first school of love" and "the first school of faith." Parents are often assisted by grandparents, aunts, uncles and family friends in both practical and profound ways. Wise parents encourage their children to choose their friends carefully, pointing out to them the saints who chose friends with whom they became saints. People are not born saints. They become saints. Companions affect the decisions they make along the way. Parental influence decreases and friends' influence increases with each successive year. That's why the relationships we have with others are so important.

Readers recognize by now that all relationships matter. All have the potential for great good or evil. May we all learn from and follow the example of the saints in choosing our friends, and for our sake may they be, by the grace of God, truly saintly companions.

BIBLIOGRAPHY

Acta Sanctorum. (67 volumes). Joannes Bollandus and
        Godfried Henschenius, eds. Paris: V. Palme,
        1863-1931.

Aelred of Rievaulx. *Spiritual Friendship.* Mary Eugenia
        Laker, S.S.N.D., tr. Kalamazoo, MI: Cistercian
        Publications, 1977.

Albert the Great, St. and St. Thomas Aquinas. *Albert and
        Thomas.* Simon Tugwell, ed. and tr. Mahwah,
        NJ: Paulist Press, 1988.

Altaner, Berthold. *Patrology.* Hilda C. Graef, tr. New York:
        Herder and Herder, 1961.

Ambrose, St. See *Funeral Orations.*

Ashley, Benedict M. *The Dominicans.* Collegeville, MN: A
        Michael Glazier Book, 1990.

Athanasius, St. *The Life of Saint Antony.* Robert T. Meyer,
        tr. Ancient Christian Writers, vol. 10. New
        York: Newman Press, 1950.

Attwater, Donald. *Saints of the East.* New York: P.J.
        Kenedy, 1963.

Augustine, St. *Augustine of Hippo: Selected Writings.* Mary
        T. Clark, tr. New York: Paulist Press, 1984.

Avallone, Paul. *Don Bosco and His Preventive Technique
        in Education.* Paterson, NJ: Salesiana Publish-
        ers, n.d.

Ball, Ann. *Modern Saints.* Rockford, IL: Tan Books and
        Publishers, Inc. 1983.

Bibliotheca Sanctorum. (13 volumes). Roma: Instituto Giovanni XXIII Nella Pontificia Università Lateranense, 1961.

Birrell, T.A. "Oates Plot." *New Catholic Encyclopedia*. Washington, DC: The Catholic University of America, 1967. Vol. 10. Pp. 590-94.

The Book of Saints. Benedictine Monks of Ramsgate Abbey, eds. Wilton, CT: Morehouse Publishing, 1989.

"Brothers and Sisters." New York: *Christopher News Notes*, July, 1991.

Bruce, F.F. *The Pauline Circle*. Grand Rapids, MI: Wm. B. Eerdmans Publishing Co., 1985.

Burghardt, Walter. *Saints and Society*. Englewood Cliffs, NJ: Prentice-Hall, 1965.

Bushnell, O.A. and Hanley, Mary Laurence. *Song of Pilgrimage in Exile*. Chicago: Franciscan Herald Press, 1980.

Butkovich, Anthony. *Revelations*. Los Angeles: Ecumenical Foundation of America, 1972.

Butler's Lives of the Saints (Four volumes). Herbert Thurston, S.J. and Donald Attwater, eds. Westminster, MD: Christian Classics, 1990.

Callan, Louise. *Philippine Duchesne*. Westminster, MD: Newman Press, 1965.

Caltagirone, Carmen L. *Friendship as Sacrament*. Staten Island, NY: Alba House, 1988.

Caraman, Philip. "Martyrs of England and Wales." *New Catholic Encyclopedia*. Vol. 9. Pp. 319-32.

Carson, Robert E. "Damien, Father (Joseph De Veuster)." *New Catholic Encyclopedia*. Vol. 4. Pp. 626-27.

Catherine of Siena, St. *Catherine of Siena: Selected Spiritual Writings*. Mary O'Driscoll, ed. New Rochelle, NY: New City Press, 1993.

_____. *Catherine of Siena as Seen in Her Letters*. Vida D. Scudder, tr. and ed. New York: E.P. Dutton, 1905.

Celebrating the Eucharist. Collegeville, MN: Liturgical Press.

Chenu, Bruno and others. *The Book of Christian Martyrs*. New York: Crossroad Publishing Company, 1990.

Clare of Assisi, St. *Clare of Assisi: Early Documents*. Regis J. Armstrong, ed. and tr. New York: Paulist Press, 1988.

Clark, Elizabeth A. *Women in the Early Church*. Thomas Halton, ed. Wilmington, DE: Michael Glazier, Inc., 1983.

Clissold, Stephen. *The Saints of South America*. Charles Knight & Co., Ltd., 1972.

Cluny, Roland. *Holiness in Action*. D.A. Askew, tr. New York: Hawthorne Books, 1963.

Cole, Basil. "Mary and Joseph: Their love for each other." *Homiletic and Pastoral Review*. October, 1981.

Congregation of the Mission. *The Liturgy of the Hours: Proper of the Congregation of the Mission*. New York: Catholic Book Publishing Co., 1978.

Costelloe, Laurence. *Saint Bonaventure: Seraphic Doctor, Minister General of the Franciscan Order*. New York: Longmans and Green, 1911.

Cullen, Paul. "The new American saints?" *Our Sunday Visitor*. July 13, 1989. Pp. 10-11.

Cunningham, Lawrence S. *The Meaning of Saints*. San Francisco: Harper & Row Publishers, 1980.

D'Arcy, Mary Ryan. *The Saints of Ireland*. St. Paul, MN: Irish American Cultural Institute, 1985.

Davitt, Thomas, C.M. *Justin de Jacobis, CM*. Dublin, Ireland: Vincentian Fathers, 1975.

Deanesly, Margaret. *Augustine of Canterbury*. London: Thomas Nelson & Sons, Ltd., 1964.

De Broglie, Emmanuel. *The Life of Blessed Louise de Marillac, Co-foundress of the Sisters of Charity of St. Vincent de Paul*. Joseph Leonard, tr. London: Burnes & Oates, 1933.

De Foucauld, Charles. *Lettres a Mme de Bondy*. Paris: Desclee de Brouwer, 1966.

Delaney, John J. *Dictionary of Saints*. Garden City, NY: Doubleday & Company, Inc., 1980.

Delaney, John J. and Tobin, James Edward. *Dictionary of Catholic Biography*. Garden City, NY: Doubleday & Company, Inc., 1961.

Delany, Selden Peabody. *Married Saints*. New York: Longmans, Green and Co., 1935.

Delehaye, Hippolyte, S.J. *The Legends of the Saints*. V.M. Crawford, tr. South Bend, IN: University of Notre Dame Press, 1961.

Dicharry, Warren F. "Martyr (In The Bible)." *New Catholic Encyclopedia*. Vol. 9. P. 314.

Dictionary of Quotations. Bergen Evans, ed. New York: Delacorte Press, 1968.

Dietzen, John. "Canonizing a Married Couple." *The Catholic Standard and Times*. June 11, 1992. P. 30.

The Documents of Vatican II. Walter M. Abbott, ed. Joseph Gallagher, tr. New York: Guild Press, 1966.

Doig, Desmond. *Mother Teresa: Her People and Her Work*. New York: Harper & Row, Publishers, 1976.

Dolan, Albert H. *The Little Flower's Mother*. Chicago: The Carmelite Press, 1927.

Dolan, Gilbert. *St. Gertrude the Great*. London: Sands & Company, 1913.

Dubay, Thomas, S.M. *Fire Within*. San Francisco, CA: Ignatius Press, 1989.

Duckett, Eleanor Shipley. *The Wandering Saints of the Early Middle Ages*. New York: Norton, 1959.

Duquoc, Christian and Floristan, Casiano. *Models of Holiness*. New York: The Seabury Press, 1979.

Early Christian Biographies. Roy Joseph Deferrari, ed. Fathers of the Church, vol. 15. Washington, D.C.: Catholic University of America Press, 1952.

Early Dominicans: Selected Writings. Simon Tugwell, ed. New York: Paulist Press, 1982.

The Encyclopedia of Catholic Saints. Wilkes-Barre, PA: Dimension Books, 1966.

Englebert, Omer. *The Lives of the Saints*. Christopher and Anne Fremantle, tr. New York: D. McKay Co., 1951.

Fathers Talking: An Anthology. Aelred Squire, ed. Kalamazoo, MI: Cistercian Publications, 1986.

Ferder, Fran. *Words Made Flesh*. Notre Dame, IN: Ave Maria Press, 1988.

Fitz, Raymond L. and Cada, Lawrence J. "The Recovery of Religious Life," *Review for Religious*. Vol. 34. Pp. 690-718.

Foley, Barbara. *Zelie Martin*. Boston: Daughters of St. Paul, 1960.

Fox, John. *Fox's Book of Martyrs: A History of the Lives, Sufferings and Triumphant Deaths of the Early Christian and the Protestant Martyrs*. William Byron Forbush, ed. Grand Rapids, MI: Zondervan Publishing House, 1967.

Francis de Sales, St. *Francis de Sales, Jane de Chantal: Letters of Spiritual Direction*. Peronne M. Thibert, tr. New York: Paulist Press, 1988.

Frend, W.H.C. *Martyrdom and Persecution in the Early Church*. Oxford: Basil Blackwell, 1965.

Funeral Orations by Saint Gregory Nazianzen and Saint

Ambrose. Leo P. McCauley, S.J., ed. New York: Fathers of the Church, Inc., 1953.

Galloway, Paul. "Heaven Can Wait." *Chicago Tribune*. August 27, 1989. Section 5, page 10.

Gannon, John Mark. *The Martyrs of the United States of America and Related Essays*. Easton, PA: Mack Printing Co., 1957.

Garvey, John. *Saints for Confused Times*. Chicago: Thomas More Press, 1976.

Gentili, Antonio. *The Barnabites: A Historical Profile*. Santa Zanchettin, tr. Youngstown, NY: The North American Voice of Fatima, n.d.

Gilby, Thomas. "Martyrdom, Theology Of." *New Catholic Encyclopedia*. Vol. 9. Pp. 314-15.

Gillis, James M. *The Paulists*. New York: The Macmillan Company, 1932.

Gregory Nazianzen, St. See *Funeral Orations*.

Gregory of Nyssa, St. *Ascetical Works*. Virginia Woods Callahan, tr. Fathers of the Church, vol. 58. Washington, D.C.: Catholic University of America Press, 1967.

Gregory the Great, St. *St. Gregory the Great: Dialogues*. Odo Zimmerman, tr. Fathers of the Church, vol. 39. New York: Fathers of the Church, Inc., 1959.

Habig, Marion A. *The Franciscan Book of Saints*. Chicago: Franciscan Herald Press, 1979.

Hoever, Hugo Rev., S.O.Cist. *Lives of the Saints*. New York: Catholic Book Publishing Co., 1989.

Hostie, Raymond. *The Life and Death of Religious Orders*. Washington, DC: Center for Applied Research in the Apostolate, 1983.

Husslein, Joseph Casper. *Heroines of Christ*. Milwaukee: Bruce, 1939.

Hutchinson, R.A. *Diocesan Priest Saints*. St. Louis: Herder, 1958.

Iberian Fathers. Claude W. Barlow, tr. Fathers of the Church, vol. 62. Washington, D.C.: Catholic University of America Press, 1969.

Jacks, L.V. *Mother Marianne of Molokai*. New York: Macmillan, 1935.

Jaramilli, Diego. *Los Amigos Del Evangelio*. Mexico: Publicaiones Kerygma, 1985.

Jerome, St. *The Principal Works of St. Jerome*. W.H. Fremantle, ed. and tr. Nicene and Post-Nicene Fathers, Second Series, vol. 6. Grand Rapids, MI: Wm. B. Eerdmans Publishing Company, 1892.

Johnson, Paul. *A History of Christianity*. New York: Atheneum, 1979.

Katrij, Julian J. *A Byzantine Rite Liturgical Year*. Demetrius Wysochansky, tr. Detroit: Basilian Fathers Publication, 1983.

Kelly, Margaret John. "The Relationship of Saint Vincent and Saint Louise From Her Perspective." *Vincentian Heritage*. Vol. 11 (1990). No. 1. Pp. 77-114.

Kevane, Eugene. *Augustine the Educator*. Westminster, MD: Newman Press, 1964.

Kirchner, Walther. *Western Civilization To 1500*. New York: Barnes & Noble Books, 1960.

_____. *Western Civilization Since 1500*. New York: Barnes & Noble Books, 1966.

Leech, Kenneth. *Soul Friend*. San Francisco: Harper & Row, Publishers, 1977.

Leifeld, Wendy. *Mothers of the Saints*. Ann Arbor, MI: Servant Publications, 1991.

Lepp, Ignace. *The Ways of Friendship*. Bernard

Murchland, tr. Riverside, NJ: Macmillan Company, 1966.

Letters from the Saints. Benedictine Monk of Stanbrook Abbey, ed. New York: Hawthorne Books, Inc., 1964.

Letters from the Saints. Claude Williamson, ed. London: Rockliff Books, 1958.

The Liturgy of the Hours. Vols. I - IV. New York: Catholic Book Publishing Co., 1976.

The Lives of the Dominican Saints. Providence, RI: The Dominican Fathers, 1940.

Lodi, Enzo. *Saints of the Roman Calendar*. Staten Island, NY: Alba House, 1993.

Lovasik, Rev. Lawrence G., S.V.D. *Best-Loved Saints*. New York: Catholic Book Publishing Co., 1984.

Majchrzak, Colman Jerome. *A Brief History of Bonaventurism*. Washington, DC: Catholic University Press, 1957.

Maloney, Robert. *The Way of Vincent de Paul*. New York: New City Press, 1992.

Marie Louise Trichet: The Folly of Love. Strasbourg, France: Editions du Signe, 1993.

Martindale, C.C., S.J. *What are Saints?* Wilmington, DE: Michael Glazier, Inc., 1982.

Martyrdom Today. Johannes Baptist Metz and Edward Schillebeeckx, eds. Vol. 163 of *Concilium*. New York: The Seabury Press, 1983.

Mary Mazzarello, St. *The Letters of Saint Mary Mazzarello*. Maria Esther Posada, ed. Mary Lineberger, tr. Haledon, NJ: Salesian Sisters, 1981.

McCabe, James Patrick. *Critical Guide to Catholic Reference Books*. Littleton, CO: Libraries Unlimited, 1971.

McGinley, Phyllis. *Saint-Watching*. New York: The Crossroad Publishing Co., 1989.

McKenzie, John L. *Dictionary of the Bible*. Milwaukee: The Bruce Publishing Co., 1965.

McLaughlin, Janice. "Full Story Finally Told." *Maryknoll Magazine*. December, 1993. Pp. 39-43.

Molinari, Paul, S.J. *Saints*. New York, NY: Sheed and Ward, 1965.

Montfort, Louis Marie de. *God Alone: The Collected Writings of St. Louis Marie de Montfort*. Bay Shore, NY: Montfort Publications, 1987.

Murphy, Francis X. "Martyr." *New Catholic Encyclopedia*. Vol. 9. Pp. 312-314.

Neill, Mary, OP and Chervin, Ronda. *Great Saints - Great Friends*. Staten Island, NY: Alba House, 1990.

Nevins, Albert J. *American Martyrs From 1542*. Huntington, IN: Our Sunday Visitor, 1987.

Norwood, Frederick A. *Strangers And Exiles: A History of Religious Refugees*. Nashville: Abingdon Press, 1969.

O'Donnell, Hugh. "The Relationship of Saint Vincent and Saint Louise from His Perspective: A Personal and Theological Inquiry." *Vincentian Heritage*. Vol. 11 (1990). No. 1. Pp. 59-76.

Ohrbach, Barbara Milo. *A Token of Friendship*. New York: Clarkson N. Potter, Inc. Publishers, 1987.

O'Malley, William J. *The Voice of Blood: Five Christian Martyrs of Our Time*. Maryknoll, NY: Orbis Books, 1980.

1000 Years of Irish Poetry. Kathleen Hoagland, ed. New York: The Devin-Adair Company, 1953.

O'Reilly, Myles. *Memorials of Those Who Suffered for the Catholic Faith in Ireland in the 16th, 17th, and 18th Centuries*. New York: The Catholic Publication Society, 1869.

The Oxford Dictionary of Popes. J.N.D. Kelly, ed. Oxford: Oxford University Press, 1986.

The Oxford Dictionary of Saints. David Hugh Farmer, ed. Oxford: Oxford University Press, 1987.

Paulinus of Nola. *The Poems of Paulinus of Nola*. P.G. Walsh, tr. Ancient Christian Writers, vol. 40. New York: Newman Press, 1975.

Poulos, George. *Orthodox Saints*. (Four volumes). Brookline, MA: Holy Cross Orthodox Press, 1991.

Premoli, Orazio M. *Storia dei Barnabiti*. Roma: Desclee & C., 1913.

The Radical Tradition: Revolutionary Saints in the Battle for Justice and Human Rights. Gilbert Markus, ed. New York: Doubleday, 1992.

Ravier, Andre. *Ignatius of Loyola and the Founding of the Society of Jesus*. Maura Daly, et. al., tr. San Francisco: Ignatius Press, 1987.

The Roman Martyrology. Raphael Collins, tr. Westminster, MD: The Newman Bookshop, 1946.

Ruffin, C. Bernard. *The Twelve*. Huntington, IN: Our Sunday Visitor, Inc.; 1984.

Saint of the Day. (Two volumes). Leonard Foley, O.F.M., ed. Cincinnati: St. Anthony Messenger Press, 1974 and 1975.

Sainthood: Its Manifestations in World Religions. Richard Keickhefer and George D. Bond, eds. Berkeley: University of California Press, 1988.

The Saints Always Belong to the Present. R. Stephen Almagno, O.F.M., ed. San Francisco: Ignatius Press, 1985.

Saints and Their Cults: Studies in Religious Sociology, Folklore and History. Stephen Wilson, ed. New York: Cambridge University Press, 1983.

Sarno, Robert J. *Diocesan Inquiries Required by the Legislator in the New Legislation for the Causes of Saints*. Roma: Pontifica Universitas Gregoriana, 1987.

Sellner, Edward C. "St. Augustine's Friendships." *Spirituality Today*. Autumn 1991. Vol. 43. No. 3. Pp. 240-57.

Silent Pilgrimage to God. Jeremy Moiser, tr. Maryknoll, NY: Orbis Books, 1975.

Stebbing, George. *The Redemptorists*. London: Burns, Oates and Washbourne Ltd., 1924.

Stein, Edith. *Life in a Jewish Family: 1891-1916*. L. Gelber and Romaeus Leuven, eds. Josephine Koeppel, tr. Washington, DC: ICS Publications, 1986.

Stella, Pietro. *Don Bosco: Life And Work*. John Drury, tr. New Rochelle, NY: Don Bosco Publications, 1985.

Steven, Clifford. *The One Year Book of Saints*. Huntington, IN: Our Sunday Visitor, Inc., 1989.

The Tablet. Vol 86. No. 34. November 20, 1933.

Therese of Lisieux, St. *The Autobiography of St. Therese of Lisieux. The Story of a Soul*. John Beevers, tr. Garden City, NY: Image Books, 1957.

Thorpe, Osmund. *Mary MacKillop*. Sydney, Australia: Principal Press, 1980.

Tylenda, Joseph N. *Jesuit Saints & Martyrs*. Chicago: Loyola University Press, 1984.

Valentine, Mary Hester. *Saints For Contemporary Women*. Chicago: Thomas More Press, 1987.

Van Zeller, Hubert. *The Benedictine Nuns*. Baltimore: Helicon, 1965.

Vincent de Paul, St. *Conferences of St. Vincent de Paul to the Sisters of Charity*. (Four volumes). Joseph

Leonard, tr. Westminster, MD: Newman Press, 1957.

Wadell, Paul J., C.P. *Friendship and the Moral Life*. Notre Dame, IN: University of Notre Dame Press, 1989.

Ward, Felix. *The Passionists*. New York: Benzinger Brothers, 1923.

Ward, Maisie. *Saints Who Made History: The First Five Centuries*. New York: Sheed and Ward, 1960.

Weinstein, Donald and Bell, Rudolph M. *Saints and Society*. Chicago: University of Chicago Press, 1982.

White, Kristin E. *A Guide to the Saints*. New York: Ballantine Books, 1991.

The Wisdom of the Saints: An Anthology. Jill Haak Adels, ed. New York: Oxford University Press, 1987.

Wolf, Kenneth Baxter. *Christian Martyrs in Muslim Spain*. New York: Cambridge University Press, 1988.

Woodward, Kenneth L. *Making Saints*. New York: Simon and Schuster, 1990.

Workman, Herbert B. *Persecution in the Early Church*. Oxford: Oxford University Press, 1980.

Wright, John J. *The Saints Always Belong to the Present*. San Francisco: Ignatius Press, 1985.

Wright, Wendy M. *Bond of Perfection: Jeanne de Chantal & Francois de Sales*. New York: Paulist Press, 1985.

_____. " 'Hearts Have a Secret Language' - The Spiritual Language of Francis de Sales and Jane de Chantal." *Vincentian Heritage*. Vol. 11. (1990) No. 1. Pp. 45-58.

Wust, Louis and Marjorie. *Louis Martin, An Ideal Father*. Boston: Daughters of St. Paul, 1957.

SAINTS LISTING

	Husband/Wife	Parent/Child	Sibling	Relative	Friend	Teacher/Student	Master/Disciple	Co-Founder	Co-Worker	Co-Martyr
Adalbald (d. 652)	✠	✠								
Adalbero (d. 909)				✠						
Adalbert of Magdeburg (d. 981)						✠				
Adalbert of Prague (956-97)						✠				
Adalhard (753-827)						✠				
Adalsind (d. c. 715)		✠	✠							
Adelaide (931-99)									✠	
Adele (d. c. 734)				✠						
Adeline, Bl. (d. 1125)		✠								
Adrian (d. 710)									✠	
Aelred of Rievaulx (1109-67)									✠	
Agape (d. 304)		✠								
Agapitus I, Pope (535-36)				✠						
Agatha Yi (1846)										✠
Agia (d.c. 714)	✠									
Agnes of Assisi (c. 1197-1253)		✠					✠			
Agnes of Prague, Bl. (1205-82)					✠				✠	
Agricola (c. 497-580)					✠					
Aidan (d. 651)							✠		✠	
Alberic of Citeaux (d. 1109)								✠		
Alberic of Utrecht (d. 784)				✠						
Albert the Great (c. 1206-80)						✠				
Albina (4th century)					✠					
Alcuin, Bl. (c. 735-804)						✠				
Aldegundis (630-84)		✠	✠							
Aldetrudis (d.c. 696)		✠	✠							
Alexander Sauli (1534-92)					✠					
Alexis Falconieri (c. 1200-1310)				✠					✠	

	Husband/Wife	Parent/Child	Sibling	Relative	Friend	Teacher/Student	Master/Disciple	Co-Founder	Co-Worker	Co-Martyr
Alipius (c. 360-430)					❖	❖	❖		❖	
Alix Le Clerq, Bl. (1576-1622)								❖		
Alonso Rodriguez, Bl. (d. 1628)										❖
Aloysius Gonzaga (1568-91)					❖					
Alphege (d. 951)			❖							
Alphonsus de Liguori (1696-1787)							❖			
Alphonsus Navarette, Bl. (d. 1617)										❖
Alphonsus Rodriguez (1533-1617)					❖	❖				
Amadeo Amedei (13th century)								❖		
Amadeus da Silva (1420-82)			❖							
Amandus (d. 7th century)					❖					
Amator (d. 418)	❖									
Amatus (d. c. 630)								❖		
Ambrose of Milan (c. 340-97)			❖		❖	❖				
Ambrose Sansedeni (1220-86)						❖				
Ananias (1st century)							❖			
Andrew Caccioli (d. 1254)							❖			
Andrew Dung-Lac (d. 1839)										❖
Andrew Fournet (1752-1834)								❖		
Andrew Kim Tae-gon (1846)										❖
Andrew of Spello, Bl. (d. 1254)							❖			
Andrew the Apostle (1st century)			❖				❖			
Anna Garcia, Bl. (1549-1626)							❖			
Anna Michela, Bl. (12th century)	❖									
Anne of Nazareth (1st century)	❖			❖						
Anselm (c. 1033-1109)					❖					
Anseric of Soissons (6th century)						❖				
Anthony of Padua (1195-1231)							❖			

	Husband/Wife	Parent/Child	Sibling	Relative	Friend	Teacher/Student	Master/Disciple	Co-Founder	Co-Worker	Co-Martyr
Anthony Pechersky (983-1073)								✙		
Anthony Zaccaria (1502-39)								✙		
Antony of the Desert (251-356)					✙		✙			
Apphia (1st century)	✙						✙			
Aquila (1st century)	✙						✙			
Arnulf of Metz (d. c. 643)		✙		✙						
Arsenius (c. 355-c. 450)							✙			
Asella (d.c. 406)					✙					
Athanasius (c. 297-373)					✙		✙		✙	
Athenodorus (d.c. 269)			✙			✙				
Attalas (d. 627)							✙			
Augustine of Canterbury (d. 604)							✙		✙	
Augustine of Hippo (354-430)		✙			✙	✙	✙		✙	
Augustine Yu Chin-gil (1846)										✙
Authaire (7th century)		✙								
Avitus of Clermont (d.c. 600)					✙					
Balthasar (1st century)							✙			
Barnabas (1st century)			✙				✙			
Bartholomew (1st century)							✙			
Bartholomew Ferrari (1499-1544)								✙		
Bartholomew of Braganza (c. 1200-71)							✙			
Bartholomew of Rossano (d. 1065)							✙	✙		
Bartolomea Capitanio (1807-33)								✙		
Basil the Elder (d. 370)	✙	✙								
Basil the Great (329-79)		✙	✙	✙	✙	✙	✙			
Bathildis (d. 680)					✙				✙	
Beatrice da Silva (1424-90)			✙							
Bede the Venerable (c. 672-735)						✙			✙	

	Husband/Wife	Parent/Child	Sibling	Relative	Friend	Teacher/Student	Master/Disciple	Co-Founder	Co-Worker	Co-Martyr
Begga (d. 693)		❖	❖							
Benedict of Nursia (c. 480-c. 547)			❖							
Benedict of Urbino, Bl. (1560-1625)									❖	
Benedicta (d. 10th century)			❖							
Benen (d. 467)							❖			
Benno of Osnabruck, Bl. (d. 1088)					❖					
Bernard of Clairvaux (1090-1153)			❖		❖		❖		❖	
Bernardino of Siena (1380-1444)						❖				
Bertilia (7th century)	❖	❖								
Bertinus (d. 700)									❖	
Blesilla (363-83)		❖	❖		❖					
Boisil (d. 664)							❖			
Bonaiunta Manetto (13th century)								❖		
Bonaventure (1221-74)					❖	❖				
Bonfiglio Monaldo (13th century)								❖		
Boniface (c. 680-754)				❖	❖	❖			❖	
Bonnadonna, Bl. (d. 1260)	❖						❖			
Boris (d. 1015)		❖	❖							
Brendan the Navigator (c. 484-c. 577)						❖				
Brice (d. 444)							❖			
Bridget of Sweden (1303-73)		❖							❖	
Brigid of Ireland (c. 450-525)					❖					
Bronislava, Bl. (d. 1259)				❖						
Bruno of Cologne (925-65)		❖								
Bruno of Rheims (c. 1030-1101)					❖	❖			❖	
Cadoc (d. c. 575)		❖			❖					
Caesaria (d.c. 529)			❖							
Caesarius of Arles (470-543)			❖							

	Husband/Wife	Parent/Child	Sibling	Relative	Friend	Teacher/Student Master/Disciple	Co-Founder	Co-Worker	Co-Martyr
Caesarius of Nazianzen (c. 329-69)		✠	✠						
Camillus de Lellis (1550-1614)						✠			
Canute of Denmark (d.c. 1086)		✠							
Carina (d. 360)	✠								
Caspar (1st century)						✠			
Cassian of Tangiers (d.c. 298)									✠
Catherine of Siena (1347-80)					✠				
Catherine of Sweden (c. 1331-81)		✠			✠			✠	
Catherine Soiron, Bl. (d. 1794)			✠						
Cecilia (3rd century)	✠								✠
Cecilia (d. 10th century)			✠						
Cedd (d. 664)			✠						
Celestine I, Pope (d. 432)								✠	
Celina (5th century)		✠							
Celsus of Armagh (1079-1129)								✠	
Ceolfrid (642-716)								✠	
Ceslau Bl. (d. 1242)			✠	✠	✠	✠			
Chad (d. 672)			✠					✠	
Charita (d. 165)									✠
Chariton (d. 165)									✠
Charles Borromeo (1538-84)					✠				
Charles Cho Shin-chol (1846)									✠
Charles de Foucald (1858-1916)				✠					
Charles Lwanga (d. 1886)									✠
Charles the Good, Bl. (1081-1127)		✠							
Chionia (d. 304)			✠						
Christopher of Romangnola (1172-1272)						✠			
Chromatius (d.c. 407)					✠				

	Husband/Wife	Parent/Child	Sibling	Relative	Friend	Teacher/Student	Master/Disciple	Co-Founder	Co-Worker	Co-Martyr
Chrysanthos (d. 283)	✤									
Clare of Assisi (1194-1253)			✤		✤		✤	✤	✤	
Clare Xamada, Bl. (d. 1622)	✤									
Claude La Colombiere (1641-82)					✤					
Claudia (1st century)										✤
Cleophas (1st century)	✤	✤								
Clodaldus (d.c. 560)				✤						
Clodulf of Metz (c. 605-c. 696)		✤								
Clotilde, Queen (c. 474-545)				✤						
Clotsind (c. 635-714)		✤	✤							
Colette (1381-1447)									✤	
Colman of Cloyne (530-606)						✤				
Colman of Dromore (6th century)						✤				
Colman of Lann Elo (c. 555-611)				✤						
Columba (c. 521-97)				✤		✤	✤			
Columban (c. 540-615)						✤	✤		✤	
Comgall (c. 517-603)						✤				
Constantine of Yaroslav (d. 1321)		✤								
Constantine the Great (d. 337)		✤								
Cornelius (d. 253)						✤			✤	✤
Cosmas (d. 303)			✤						✤	
Crispus (1st century)						✤				
Cunegund of Germany (d. 1039)	✤			✤	✤					
Cunegund of Poland, Bl. (1224-92)			✤							
Cuthbert (d. 687)					✤					
Cuthbert Mayne (1544-77)										✤
Cuthburga (d.c. 725)			✤							
Cynesburga (7th century)			✤	✤						

	Husband/Wife	Parent/Child	Sibling	Relative	Friend	Teacher/Student	Master/Disciple	Co-Founder	Co-Worker	Co-Martyr
Cyneswide (7th century)			✤	✤						
Cyprian (c. 200-58)									✤	✤
Cyril of Alexandria (c. 376-444)									✤	
Cyril of Jerusalem (c. 315-86)									✤	
Cyril of Moravia (c. 825-69)			✤						✤	
Damaris (1st century)							✤			
Damasus I, Pope (c. 304-84)					✤					
Damian (d. 303)			✤						✤	
Damien the Leper (1840-89)									✤	
Daniel the Stylite (c. 409-93)							✤			
Daria (d. 283)	✤									
David I of Scotland (1084-1153)		✤		✤					✤	
David of Yaroslav (d. 1321)		✤								
Deicolus (c. 530-625)									✤	
Delphine, Bl. (1283-1360)	✤						✤			
Delphinus (d. 404)					✤					
Denis (d.c. 258)										✤
Dentelinus (7th century)		✤	✤							
Diana d'Andalo (c. 1201-36)					✤					
Dichu (5th century)							✤			
Dionysius the Areopagite (1st century)							✤			
Dismas (1st century)							✤			
Dominic Barberi, Bl. (1792-1849)							✤			
Dominic de Guzman (1170-1221)		✤	✤				✤			
Dominic Savio (1842-57)						✤				
Dominic Xamada, Bl. (d. 1622)	✤									
Donatian (d. 289 or 304)			✤							
Drausius of Soissons (6th century)						✤				

	Husband/Wife	Parent/Child	Sibling	Relative	Friend	Teacher/Student	Master/Disciple	Co-Founder	Co-Worker	Co-Martyr
Droctoveus (d.c. 580)						✜				
Dunstan (c. 910-88)				✜						
Dymphna (d.c. 650)										✜
Eata (d. 686)							✜			
Ebba the Elder (d. 683)			✜							
Edith of Polesworth (d.c. 925)				✜						
Edith of Wilton (962-84)		✜		✜						
Edith Stein (1891-1942)			✜							
Edmund Rich (c. 1180-1240)					✜		✜			
Edward the Confessor (1033-66)					✜					
Edwin, King (c. 585-633)	✜			✜						
Egbert (c. 639-729)						✜				
Elfleda (d. 714)					✜	✜				
Eligius (c. 590-660)					✜					
Elizabeth Bichier (1773-1838)								✜		
Elizabeth of Hungary (1207-31)	✜	✜		✜			✜			
Elizabeth of Jerusalem (1st century)	✜	✜		✜						
Elizabeth of Portugal (1271-1336)				✜						
Elzear (1285-1323)	✜						✜			
Emanuele Phung (d. 1839)										✜
Emeric, Bl. (1007-31)	✜			✜		✜				
Emiliana (d.c. 550)				✜						
Emma (d.c. 1045)						✜				
Emmelia (d. 370)	✜	✜								
Enda (d.c. 530)			✜						✜	
Eoban (d. 755)									✜	
Epaphroditus (1st century)							✜			
Ephraem of Syria (c. 306-c. 373)					✜					

	Husband/Wife	Parent/Child	Sibling	Relative	Friend	Teacher/Student	Master/Disciple	Co-Founder	Co-Worker	Co-Martyr
Epiphanius of Pavia (439-96)			✥		✥					
Erastus (1st century)						✥				
Ercongota (d.c. 660)		✥	✥							
Erconwald (d.c. 686)			✥							
Ermenburga (d.c. 700)		✥								
Ermengilda (d.c. 700)		✥	✥							
Ethelbert (616-560)		✥				✥			✥	
Ethelburga of Barking (d.c. 678)			✥							
Ethelburga of Gaul (d.c. 664)						✥				
Ethelburga of Kent (d.c. 674)	✥	✥								
Etheldreda (d. 679)			✥							
Euelpistus (d. 165)										✥
Eugene of Glendalough (d.c. 618)									✥	
Eugene III, Bl. (d. 1153)						✥			✥	
Eugene of Toledo (d. 657)				✥						
Eusebia (d.c. 680)		✥		✥						
Eusebius of Cremona (d.c. 423)						✥				
Eusebius of Vercelli (c. 283-371)						✥				
Eustochium Julia (d.c .419)		✥	✥	✥	✥					
Euthymius (d. 1028)		✥						✥		
Eutropius (d. 404)						✥				
Fabiola (d. 399)					✥					
Fanchea (d.c. 530)			✥							
Felix (d. 304)		✥								
Felix (d.c. 750)			✥							
Felix II, Pope (d. 492)				✥						
Felix of Valois (1126-1212)								✥		
Finnian of Clonard (c. 470-c. 549)						✥				

	Husband/Wife	Parent/Child	Sibling	Relative	Friend	Teacher/Student	Master/Disciple	Co-Founder	Co-Worker	Co-Martyr
Finnian of Strangford (d.c. 579)						❖				
Flavian (d. 449)									❖	
Flora (d. 851)										❖
Florentina (d.c. 636)		❖								
Foillan (d.c. 655)		❖								
Frances Bizzocca, Bl. (d. 1626)	❖									
Francis Borgia (1510-72)					❖		❖			
Francis de Sales (1567-1622)					❖			❖		
Francis of Assisi (c. 1181-1226)					❖		❖	❖		
Francis Solano (1549-1610)									❖	
Francis Xavier (1506-52)						❖	❖			
Fulgentius (468-533)		❖								
Fursey (d.c. 648)		❖								
Gabriel Lalement (1610-49)										❖
Gaius (1st century)							❖			
Gall of Clermont (c. 489-554)			❖							
Gall of Switzerland (d.c. 635)									❖	
Gaudentius (d.c. 410)					❖					
Genevieve (c. 422-500)							❖			
Gerard, Bl. (d. 1138)		❖					❖		❖	
Gerard Majella (1726-55)							❖			
Gerard of Clairvaux (d. 1138)		❖					❖			
Gerard Sagredo (d. 1046)					❖					
Germanus of Autun (c. 496-576)					❖					
Germanus of Auxerre (c. 378-448)							❖		❖	
Gertrude of Altenberg, Bl. (1227-97)	❖									
Gertrude of Hamage (d. 649)			❖							
Gertrude of Helfta (c. 1256-1302)					❖		❖		❖	

	Husband/Wife	Parent/Child	Sibling	Relative	Friend	Teacher/Student	Master/Disciple	Co-Founder	Co-Worker	Co-Martyr
Gertrude of Nivelles (626-59)		✛	✛							
Gertrude of Remiremont (d. 690)				✛						
Gervinus (d. 1075)					✛					
Getulius (d.c. 120)	✛									
Ghebre Michael (1791-1855)							✛			
Gibrian (d.c. 515)			✛							
Gildas (c. 500-70)						✛				
Giles of Assisi, Bl. (d. 1262)							✛			
Giles of Sannur, Bl. (d. 1266)					✛					
Gisella, Bl. (d. 1095)	✛	✛								
Gleb (d. 1015)		✛	✛							
Goban (d. 7th century)			✛							
Godehard (962-1038)									✛	
Godric (d. 1170)					✛					
Goercius (d. 647)				✛						
Gorgonia (d.c. 372)		✛	✛							
Gregory I the Great (c. 540-604)		✛		✛				✛	✛	
Gregory II (d. 731)									✛	
Gregory Nazianzen the Elder (c. 276-374)	✛	✛								
Gregory Nazianzen the Younger (c. 329-89)		✛	✛		✛	✛				
Gregory of Nyssa (c. 330-c. 395)		✛	✛	✛		✛			✛	
Gregory of Tours (540-94)				✛	✛	✛				
Gregory of Utrecht (c. 703-76)				✛		✛				
Gregory Thaumaturgus (c. 213-68)			✛			✛				
Gregory VII (c. 1021-85)					✛					
Guala Romanoni, Bl. (c. 1177-1244)							✛			
Gundeleus (6th century)	✛	✛								

	Husband/Wife	Parent/Child	Sibling	Relative	Friend	Teacher/Student	Master/Disciple	Co-Founder	Co-Worker	Co-Martyr
Gundelindis (d.c. 750)				✧						
Guy, Bl. (d. 12th century)		✧						✧	✧	
Guy Vignotelli, Bl. (c. 1185-1245)							✧			
Gwladys (6th century)	✧	✧								
Hedwig (c. 1174-1243)				✧	✧		✧			
Helen Enselmini, Bl. (1200-42)							✧			
Helen of Constantinople (c. 250-328)		✧							✧	
Heliodorus (c. 332-90)				✧	✧					
Henry II (972-1024)	✧			✧	✧				✧	
Heraclas (c. 180-247)			✧		✧					
Herman the Cripple, Bl. (1013-54)					✧					
Hidulphus (d.c. 707)	✧									
Hierax (d. 165)										✧
Hilarion (d. 304)		✧					✧			
Hilary of Arles (c. 400-49)				✧						
Hilary of Poitiers (d.c. 368)							✧			
Hilda (614-80)				✧		✧				
Hildegard of France, Bl. (d. 783)					✧					
Hildegard of Germany (1098-1179)						✧				
Hippolytus (d.c. 235)										✧
Honorata (d.c. 500)		✧								
Honoratus of Arles (c. 350-429)		✧	✧							
Honoratus of Vercelli (c. 330-415)							✧			
Honorius (d. 653)						✧				
Hormisdas (d. 523)		✧								
Hugh of Cluny (1024-1109)					✧					
Hugh of Grenoble (1052-1132)					✧				✧	
Humbeline, Bl. (1092-1135)		✧					✧		✧	

	Husband/Wife	Parent/Child	Sibling	Relative	Friend	Teacher/Student	Master/Disciple	Co-Founder	Co-Worker	Co-Martyr
Hyacinth (1185-1227)			❖	❖			❖			
Ida of Boulogne, Bl. (1040-1113)					❖					
Ignatius Loyola (1491-1556)					❖					
Ignatius of Antioch (d.c. 107)							❖			❖
Ildephonsus (607-67)				❖		❖				
Illtud (450-535)						❖				
Irenaeus (c. 125-c. 203)							❖			
Irene (d. 304)			❖							
Isaac Jogues (1607-46)										❖
Isaac the Great (d. 439)		❖								
Isabel of France, Bl. (d. 1270)			❖		❖					
Isidore of Madrid (1070-1130)	❖									
Isidore of Seville (c. 560-636)			❖			❖				
Ismael (d. 362)			❖							
Isnardo, Bl. (d. 1244)							❖			
Ita (d.c. 570)						❖				
Itta, Bl. (7th century)	❖	❖								
James Duckett (d. 1602)				❖						
James Morigia (1497-1546)								❖		
James of Nisibis (d. 338)						❖				
James the Elder (d. 42)		❖	❖				❖			
James the Younger (d. 62)		❖	❖	❖			❖			
Jane de Chantal (1572-1641)					❖			❖		
Jason (1st century)							❖			
Jerome (c. 342-420)					❖	❖			❖	
Jesus (4. B.C.-30 A.D.)		❖		❖	❖		❖			
Joachim (1st century)	❖			❖						
Joan of Aza, Bl. (d.c. 1190)		❖								

	Husband/Wife	Parent/Child	Sibling	Relative	Friend	Teacher/Student	Master/Disciple	Co-Founder	Co-Worker	Co-Martyr
Joanna (1st century)							✠			
John Bosco (1815-88)					✠	✠	✠	✠		
John Cassian (c. 360-c. 433)							✠		✠	
John Chrysostom (c. 347-407)					✠		✠			
John de Brébeuf (1593-1649)										✠
John de Lalande (d. 1646)										✠
John Duckett, Bl. (1613-44)				✠						
John Fisher (1469-1535)										✠
John Henry Newman (1801-90)							✠			
John Leonardi (c. 1550-1609)					✠		✠			
John Massias (1585-1645)					✠	✠				
John Merlini (1795-1873)									✠	
John Naisen, Bl. (d. 1626)	✠	✠								
John of Avila (1499-1569)					✠					
John of Beverley (d. 721)						✠				
John of Bithynia (d.c. 1002)		✠						✠		
John of Capistrano (1386-1456)						✠			✠	
John of Chinon (6th century)					✠					
John of God (1495-1550)					✠					
John of Matha (1160-1213)								✠		
John of Perugia, Bl. (d. 1231)							✠			
John of Rieti (d. 1350)			✠							
John of the Cross (1542-91)					✠					
John of the Marches (1394-1476)						✠				
John of York (8th century)							✠			
John Stylites (6th century)							✠			
John the Baptist (1st century)		✠		✠						
John the Beloved Disciple (6-104)		✠	✠		✠		✠			

	Husband/Wife	Parent/Child	Sibling	Relative	Friend	Teacher/Student	Master/Disciple	Co-Founder	Co-Worker	Co-Martyr
John the Dwarf (5th century)							✤			
Jolenta, Bl. (d. 1299)		✤								
Jordan of Saxony, Bl. (d. 1237)					✤		✤			
Joseph Cafasso (1811-60)					✤					
Joseph Calasanz (1556-1648)							✤			
Joseph of Arimathea (1st century)							✤			
Joseph of Bethlehem (1st century)	✤	✤		✤						
Juan de Castillo, Bl. (d. 1628)										✤
Jude Thaddeus (1st century)			✤	✤			✤			
Juliana Falconieri (1270-1341)				✤				✤		
Justine de Jacobis (1800-60)							✤			
Justin Martyr (c. 100-65)										✤
Justinian, Emperor (482-565)	✤									
Justus of Alcala (d. 304)			✤							
Justus of Canterbury (d.c. 627)									✤	
Jutta, Bl. (d. 1136)					✤					
Juvenal, Bl. (1545-1604)					✤					
Kevin (d.c. 618)									✤	
Kieran of Clonmacnois (d.c. 556)									✤	
Lambert of Maestricht (c. 635-c. 705)					✤					
Landericus (7th century)		✤	✤							
Laserian (d. 639)			✤							
Laurentia (d. 302)										✤
Lawrence of Brindisi (1559-1619)									✤	
Lawrence of Canterbury (d. 619)									✤	
Lawrence of Rome (d. 258)									✤	✤
Lazarus of Bethany (1st century)			✤		✤					
Lea (d. 384)					✤					

	Husband/Wife	Parent/Child	Sibling	Relative	Friend	Teacher/Student	Master/Disciple	Co-Founder	Co-Worker	Co-Martyr
Leander (c. 534-c. 600)			❖							
Leo Bizzoccca, Bl. (d. 1626)	❖									
Leo the Great (d. 461)									❖	
Leonorius (d.c. 570)						❖				
Liberanius (d. 165)										❖
Liberius, Pope (d. 355)					❖					
Linus (d.c. 76)							❖			
Lioba (d. 700)				❖	❖				❖	
Loman (d.c. 450)			❖							
Louis de Montfort (1673-1716)								❖		
Louis Guanella, Bl. (1842-1915)					❖	❖				
Louis IX, King of France (1214-70)			❖		❖					
Louis Martin (1823-94)	❖	❖								
Louis Naisen (1619-26)		❖								
Louis of Thuringia, Bl. (1200-27)	❖									
Louis Orioni, Bl. (1872-1940)						❖				
Louise de Marillac (1591-1660)					❖			❖	❖	
Luchesio of Pongibossi, Bl. (d. 1260)	❖						❖			
Lucy of Amelia, Bl. (d. 1350)			❖							
Ludger (d. 809)						❖				
Ludmilla (c. 860-921)				❖						
Luke (1st century)							❖			
Luke Belludi, Bl. (1200-c. 1285)							❖			
Lull (d. 786)				❖		❖			❖	
Lupicinus (d. 480)			❖							
Lupus of Troyes (c. 383-478)			❖	❖					❖	
Lydia Purpuria (1st century)							❖			
Macarius (d.c. 335)									❖	

	Husband/Wife	Parent/Child	Sibling	Relative	Friend	Teacher/Student	Master/Disciple	Co-Founder	Co-Worker	Co-Martyr
Macrina the Elder (c. 270-340)		✤		✤		✤				
Macrina the Younger (c. 330-79)		✤	✤	✤		✤				
Madelberta (7th century)		✤	✤							
Madeleine Fontaine, Bl. (1723-94)										✤
Madeleine Sophie Barat (1779-1865)									✤	
Mafalda, Bl. (1204-52)			✤							
Majolus (c. 906-94)									✤	
Malachy (1095-1148)					✤				✤	
Manetto Antellese (13th century)								✤		
Mannes, Bl. (d.c. 1230)		✤	✤			✤				
Manuel (d. 362)			✤							
Marcella (d. 410)					✤					
Marcellina (d.c. 398)			✤							
Marcellinus (d. 413)										✤
Margaret Clitherow, Bl. (c. 1555-86)										✤
Margaret Mary Alacoque (1647-90)					✤					
Margaret of Scotland (1045-93)		✤		✤						
Maria de la Cabeza (12th century)	✤									
Marianne Cope (1838-1918)									✤	
Marie Louise Trichet, Bl. (1684-1759)								✤		
Mark (d.c. 74)		✤		✤			✤			
Maro (d. 433)					✤	✤				
Martha of Amator (5th century)	✤									
Martha of Bethany (1st century)			✤		✤					
Martin de Porres (1579-1639)					✤	✤				
Martin of Tours (c. 316-97)					✤		✤			
Martinian (d. 458)			✤							
Mary Cleophas (1st century)	✤	✤			✤		✤			

	Husband/Wife	Parent/Child	Sibling	Relative	Friend	Teacher/Student	Master/Disciple	Co-Founder	Co-Worker	Co-Martyr
Mary de Matthias (1805-66)								✧		
Mary Magdalene (1st century)					✧		✧			
Mary, Mother of Mark (1st century)		✧								
Mary, Mother of God (1st century)	✧	✧		✧	✧		✧			
Mary of Abitina (d. 304)		✧								
Mary of Bethany (1st century)			✧		✧					
Mary Salome (1st century)		✧			✧		✧			
Matilda (896-968)		✧								
Matthew (1st century)							✧			
Matthias (1st century)							✧			
Maura (d.c. 286)	✧									✧
Maurice (d.c. 287)										✧
Mauront (d. 701)		✧	✧							
Maximinus (d.c. 347)							✧		✧	
Mechtilde of Helfta (1241-98)						✧			✧	
Mel (d.c. 488)				✧						
Melania the Elder (c. 342-410)				✧	✧		✧			
Melania the Younger (383-439)	✧			✧	✧				✧	
Melasippus (d. 360)	✧									
Melchior (1st century)							✧			
Mellitus (d. 624)									✧	
Methodius (c. 826-84)			✧						✧	
Michael Cozaki, Bl. (d. 1597)		✧								
Michael Rua, Bl. (1837-1910)						✧	✧			
Milburga (d. 715)		✧	✧							
Mildgytha (d.c. 676)		✧	✧							
Mildred (d.c. 700)		✧	✧							
Mobhi (d.c. 545)						✧	✧			

	Husband/Wife	Parent/Child	Sibling	Relative	Friend	Teacher/Student	Master/Disciple	Co-Founder	Co-Worker	Co-Martyr
Mochae (6th century)					✦					
Mochta (c. 445-c. 535)						✦				
Monica Naisen, Bl. (d. 1626)	✦	✦								
Monica of Tagaste (c. 331-87)		✦								
Nepotian (d. 395)				✦						
Nerses I the Great (d.c. 373)		✦								
Nicetas (c. 335-c. 414)					✦					
Nicholas Giustiniani, Bl. (d.c. 1180)	✦									
Nicholas Palea, Bl. (1197-1255)						✦				
Nicodemus (1st century)						✦				
Nilus of Rome (c. 910-1004)						✦	✦			
Nilus the Elder (d.c. 430)						✦				
Nivard, Bl. (c. 1100-58)			✦			✦			✦	
Nonna (d. 374)	✦	✦								
Nothelm (d.c. 740)									✦	
Odilo (962-1049)									✦	
Olga (c. 879-969)				✦						
Oliver Plunkett (1629-81)										✦
Olympias (c. 361-408)					✦	✦				
Onesimus (1st century)						✦				
Orentius (d.c. 304)			✦							✦
Oswald of Northumbria (c. 604-42)			✦	✦					✦	
Ottilia (d.c. 720)				✦						
Ouen (c. 610-84)		✦								
Paeon (d. 165)										✦
Palladius (d. 432)						✦			✦	
Pambo (d.c. 390)						✦				
Pammachius (d. 410)					✦					

	Husband/Wife	Parent/Child	Sibling	Relative	Friend	Teacher/Student	Master/Disciple	Co-Founder	Co-Worker	Co-Martyr
Paphserios (d. 3rd century)			❖							
Pastor (d. 304)			❖							
Patrick of Ireland (c. 389-c. 461)			❖	❖	❖		❖		❖	
Paul Miki (1562-97)										❖
Paul of Constantinople (d.c. 350)									❖	
Paul of Tarsus (d.c. 65)							❖			
Paul of the Suez (d. 3rd century)			❖							
Paul the Hermit (c. 229-342)					❖					
Paul the Simple (d.c. 339)							❖			
Paula (347-404)		❖			❖				❖	
Paulinus of Nola (c. 354-431)						❖				
Paulinus of Trier (d. 358)							❖		❖	
Paulinus of York (c. 584-644)									❖	
Pepin of Landen, Bl. (d. c. 639)	❖	❖								
Peregrine, Bl. (d. 1240)						❖	❖			
Perpetua (d. 203)										❖
Peter Canisius (1521-97)							❖			
Peter Chrysologus (406-c. 450)									❖	
Peter Claver (1580-1654)					❖					
Peter Favre, Bl. (1506-46)					❖	❖	❖		❖	
Peter Fourier (1565-1640)								❖		
Peter Nolasco (c. 1189-1258)					❖		❖	❖		
Peter of Alcántara (1499-1562)					❖					
Peter of Canterbury (d. 606)									❖	
Peter of Sebastea (c. 340-91)		❖	❖			❖				
Peter of Tarantaise (1225-76)							❖			
Peter of Verona (1205-52)					❖		❖			
Peter the Apostle (d.c. 64)			❖				❖		❖	

	Husband/Wife	Parent/Child	Sibling	Relative	Friend	Teacher/Student	Master/Disciple	Co-Founder	Co-Worker	Co-Martyr
Philastrius (d. 387)						✧				
Philemon (1st century)	✧						✧			
Philip Benizi (1233-85)									✧	
Philip Neri (1515-95)					✧		✧			
Philip the Apostle (1st century)							✧			
Philippine Duchesne, Bl. (1769-1852)									✧	
Phoebe (1st century)							✧			
Pinian (d. 432)	✧				✧				✧	
Pius X, Pope (1835-1914)					✧					
Plato of Bithynia (d. 813)				✧						
Plutarch (d.c. 202)			✧			✧				
Polycarp (c. 69-c. 155)							✧			
Priscilla of Corinth (1st century)	✧						✧			
Priscilla of Rome (d.c. 98)		✧					✧			
Prosper of Aquitaine (c. 390-c. 465)									✧	
Pudens (1st century)		✧					✧			
Quenburga (d. 8th century)			✧							
Quodvultdeus (d.c. 450)						✧				
Radegund, Queen (518-87)					✧					
Raymond Nonnatus (c. 1204-40)							✧			
Raymond of Capua, Bl. (1330-99)					✧					
Raymond of Peñafort (1175-1275)					✧			✧		
Reginald of St. Gilles (1183-1220)							✧			
Remigius (c. 437-530)		✧								
Richard de Wyche (c. 1197-1253)					✧		✧			
Richard of Lucca (d. 720)		✧								
Rictrudis (c. 612-88)	✧	✧			✧					
Rizzerio, Bl. (d. 1236)						✧	✧			

	Husband/Wife	Parent/Child	Sibling	Relative	Friend	Teacher/Student	Master/Disciple	Co-Founder	Co-Worker	Co-Martyr
Robert Bellarmine (1542-1621)					❖					
Robert of Molesmes (c. 1024-1110)					❖			❖		
Robert of Newminster (1100-59)					❖				❖	
Robert Southwell (c. 1561-95)										❖
Rogatian (d. 289-or 304)		❖								
Romanus (d.c. 460)		❖								
Romaricus (d. 653)			❖					❖		
Roque Gonzalez, Bl. (1576-1628)										❖
Rose of Lima (d. 1586)					❖	❖				
Rufus (d.c. 107)										❖
Sabel (d. 362)		❖								
Salberga (7th century)								❖		
Samson (c. 485-565)						❖				
Sanchia, Bl. (1182-1229)		❖								
Saturian (d. 458)		❖								
Saturninus the Father (d. 304)	❖									
Saturninus the Son (d. 304)	❖									
Saturus (d. 203)										❖
Scholastica (d. 543)		❖								
Sexburga (d.c. 699)	❖	❖								
Silas (1st century)							❖			
Silverius, Pope (d.c. 537)	❖									
Simeon (d.c. 107)				❖						
Simeon Stylites (c. 517-92)							❖		❖	
Simon the Zealot (1st century)				❖			❖			
Sixtus II, Pope (d. 258)									❖	
Sosteneo Sostenei (13th century)								❖		
Stephen Harding (d. 1134)								❖		

	Husband/Wife	Parent/Child	Sibling	Relative	Friend	Teacher/Student	Master/Disciple	Co-Founder	Co-Worker	Co-Martyr
Stephen of Hungary (975-1038)	✣	✣		✣						
Sturmi (d. 779)									✣	
Sylvia (6th century)		✣								
Symeon of Edessa (d. 570)					✣					
Symphorosa (d.c. 135)	✣									
Tarsilla (d.c. 581)				✣						
Tathai (6th century)						✣				
Teresa of Avila (1515-82)					✣		✣			
Teresa of Portugal, Bl. (d. 1250)			✣							
Teresa Soiron, Bl. (d. 1794)			✣							
Tetta (d.c. 772)									✣	
Thecla (d.c. 790)				✣					✣	
Theodard of Maestricht (d.c. 668)						✣				
Theodora, Empress (6th century)	✣									
Theodore of Canterbury (602-90)									✣	
Theodore of Yaroslav (d. 1299)		✣								
Theodore Studites (759-826)				✣						
Theodosius Pechersky (d. 1074)								✣		
Theodotion (d. 3rd century)			✣							
Therese of Lisieux (1873-97)		✣								
Thomas Aquinas (c. 1225-74)					✣	✣				
Thomas Cozaki, Bl. (d. 1597)		✣								
Thomas More (1478-1535)										✣
Thomas the Apostle (1st century)							✣			
Tibba (7th century)				✣						
Tigris (5th century)			✣							
Tigrius (d. 406)							✣			
Timothy (d.c. 286)	✣									✣

	Husband/Wife	Parent/Child	Sibling	Relative	Friend	Teacher/Student	Master/Disciple	Co-Founder	Co-Worker	Co-Martyr
Timothy (d.c. 97)						✤				
Titus (1st century)						✤				
Trophimus (1st century)						✤				
Turibius de Mogrobejo (1538-1605)					✤				✤	
Turibius of Spain (d.c. 450)									✤	
Uggiccione Uggiccioni (13th century)								✤		
Ulric (c. 890-973)				✤						
Urban II, Bl. (c. 1042-99)					✤					
Utlan (d. 686)			✤							
Valerian (d. 389)					✤					
Venantius (d.c. 400)			✤							
Victor (d. 305)										✤
Vincent de Paul (c. 1580-1660)					✤			✤	✤	
Vincent Madelgarius (c. 615-77)	✤	✤								
Vincent of Lerins (d.c. 445)			✤							
Vincentia Gerosa (1784-1847)								✤		
Vitalian (d. 672)									✤	
Vitalis (1063-1122)			✤							
Vladimir I of Kiev (c. 975-1015)		✤		✤						
Votus (d.c. 750)			✤							
Walbert (d.c. 678)	✤	✤								
Walburga (d. 779)		✤	✤						✤	
Waldebert (d.c. 665)								✤		
Waldetrudis (d.c. 688)	✤	✤	✤							
Wenceslaus (c. 903-29)				✤						
Wigbert (d.c. 738)					✤				✤	
Wilfrid of Northumbria (634-709)						✤				
Wilfrid of York (d.c. 744)						✤	✤			

	Husband/Wife	Parent/Child	Sibling	Relative	Friend	Teacher/Student	Master/Disciple	Co-Founder	Co-Worker	Co-Martyr
Wilfrida, Queen (d.c. 988)		✦								
Willibald (c. 700-86)		✦	✦						✦	
Willibrod (c. 658-739)					✦				✦	
Winebald (d. 761)		✦	✦						✦	
Withburga (d.c. 743)			✦							
Wolfgang of Wurzburg (c. 930-94)					✦					
Zachary, Pope (d. 752)									✦	
Zebinus (5th century)							✦			
Zechariah (1st century)	✦	✦								
Zelie Martin (1831-77)	✦	✦								
Zosimus (d. 105)										✦